"I BELIEVE,
THAT I MAY UNDERSTAND."

These words give fitting expression to the God-centered thought of St. Augustine— thought in which all the resources of consciousness are turned toward the reality of God and its demands on the human soul. In Augustine, the Golden Age of the great Fathers of the Church reached its highest point.

Vernon J. Bourke has spent a lifetime translating, analyzing, and teaching the wisdom of Augustine. In this Mentor-Omega volume Professor Bourke presents the living center of Augustine's thought. He has selected the writings included here from the vast bulk of Augustine's work. He has also included a biographical introduction, brief introductions to each chapter, and bibliography to make this Mentor-Omega edition a volume of St. Augustine's writings that will be read with pleasure, studied with profit.

MENTOR-OMEGA BOOKS
of Special Interest

The Confessions of St. Augustine

The classic autobiography of the man who journeyed from sin to sainthood. Newly translated by Rex Warner. (#MT490—75¢)

The Essential Erasmus

The first single volume in English to show the full range of thought of one of the great Catholic minds of the Renaissance. Selected and newly translated with introduction and commentary by John P. Dolan. (#MT571—75¢)

The Essential Newman *Vincent Ferrer Blehl, ed.*

The central writings of the master of English prose who infused new vigor into the nineteenth-century Catholic Church. Selected and edited by an eminent Newman scholar. (#MT488—75¢)

Elements of Christian Philosophy *by Etienne Gilson*

The noted French philosopher illuminates the key ideas of the theology of St. Thomas Aquinas. (#MT489—75¢)

THE
ESSENTIAL
AUGUSTINE

SELECTED AND WITH
COMMENTARY BY
VERNON J. BOURKE

A MENTOR·OMEGA BOOK

PUBLISHED BY THE NEW AMERICAN LIBRARY

From twenty centuries of literature and scholarship, Mentor-Omega Books present a treasury of Catholic thought for the modern reader.

FIRST PRINTING, NOVEMBER, 1964

ACKNOWLEDGMENTS

We hereby acknowledge permission of the following to reprint selections from the translations specified; identification by series symbol and volume number is made at the beginning of each selection from the first two series.
The Catholic University of America Press, for selections from the following Augustine volumes in the Fathers of the Church Series: FOC 1, copyright 1948; FOC 6, copyright 1950; FOC 5, copyright 1953 by The Catholic University of America Press.
Rev. J. Quasten, Director, Ancient Christian Writers Series, published by The Newman Press, for selections from the following volumes:
ACW 2, copyright 1946; ACW 29, copyright © 1960; ACW 30, copyright © 1961 by The Newman Press.
The University Press of Virginia for selections from C. M. Sparrow, *St. Augustine's De libero arbitrio voluntatis*. Copyright 1947 by The University of Virginia Press.

Library of Congress Catalog Card Number 64-8194

MENTOR TRADEMARK REG. U.S. PAT. OFF. AND FOREIGN COUNTRIES
REGISTERED TRADEMARK—MARCA REGISTRADA
HECHO EN CHICAGO, U.S.A.

MENTOR-OMEGA BOOKS are published *in the United States* by The New American Library of World Literature, Inc., 501 Madison Avenue, New York, New York 10022, *in Canada* by The New American Library of Canada Limited, 156 Front Street West, Toronto 1, Ontario, *in the United Kingdom* by The New English Library Limited, Barnard's Inn, Holborn, London, E.C. 1, England

PRINTED IN THE UNITED STATES OF AMERICA

Note on Translation Sources

A footnote at the beginning of each selection indicates the source of the translation. The following abbreviations are used:

ACW: *Ancient Christian Writers,* ed. J. Quasten et al., Westminster, Md.: Newman Press, 1946-1961.

FOC: *Fathers of the Church,* ed. R. J. Deferrari et al., Washington: Catholic University of America Press, 1948-1962.

Sparrow, C. M., *St. Augustine's De libero arbitrio voluntatis,* Charlottesville: University of Virginia Studies, 1947.

Dods: *The Works of Aurelius Augustinus,* ed. Marcus Dods, 15 vols., Edinburgh: T. & T. Clark Co., 1871-1876.

Nicene: *A Select Library of the Nicene and Post-Nicene Fathers,* 8 vols., ed. Philip Schaff, New York: The Christian Literature Co., 1887-1892.

One selection from the *Confessions,* in Chapter VI, is taken from the noted version by E. B. Pusey in *Library of the Fathers of the Holy Catholic Church,* Oxford, 1838.

Several selections from St. Louis University dissertations and theses are used with the kind permission of the respective translators: Rev. J. H. Taylor, S.J., *De Genesi ad litteram, XII* (1948); Rev. T. P. Maher, S.J., *De Musica, VI* (1939); and the Rev. Carl A. Hangartner, S.J., Gerald R. Sheahan, S.J., and William G. Renn, S.J., *De vera religione* (1945, 1946, 1947).

The translations marked V. J. B. are made for this volume by the editor.

For further reference, an exhaustive list of the writings of St. Augustine is in Appendix III.

CONTENTS

I. THE MAN
AND HIS WRITINGS

Saint Augustine of Hippo has exerted an incredibly great influence on the mentality, culture, and religious attitudes of Western man. His works are still read at least as much as in any previous Christian century. A recent bibliography (van Bavel) lists more than five thousand studies of his life and thought published during the decade 1950 to 1960! His profound insights strike a responsive chord in the hearts of readers representing a great variety of backgrounds.

Born in 354, at Tagaste in the Roman Province of Numidia, North Africa, Augustine was the son of Patricius and Monica. His father remained a pagan until shortly before his death (A.D. 370) but Monica was a zealous Christian and has long been recognized as a saint. Augustine was not baptized as a child but was simply registered as a catechumen (a stage preceding full membership) in the Catholic Church.

While he learned some Punic from his nurse, Augustine grew up speaking Latin, the language in which he received all his formal education. Elementary studies were done in the school at Tagaste. For four or five years (365-369) he studied classical literature at a nearby town, Madaura, a place noted for its good schools. His sixteenth year was spent in idleness at home, a period much regretted in the *Confessions* because of his youthful sins. With the help of a wealthy benefactor, Romanianus of Tagaste, Augustine was next sent to the large African City of Carthage, for advanced studies in rhetoric. He was to prepare for a career in law or government. Except for one year spent at home teaching grammar, Augustine studied and taught in Carthage from 370 to 383. He became an accomplished scholar in what we would call today the speech and communication arts.

During his twenties Augustine was still not a baptized Christian and he visited at church services only occasionally.

He established a home in Carthage and fathered a boy named Adeodatus ("God's Gift"). Carthage was a cosmopolitan seaport, a haven for many religious sects. Augustine became interested in Manicheism, a religion founded by the Persian prophet Mani two centuries earlier. The Manichees spoke of Christ as a great prophet; they claimed, however, that Mani had brought a later message to the effect that there are two supreme gods. One was the good divinity and the source of all light; the other was the god of evil and darkness. Fascinated with the dramatic possibilities of an eternal struggle between two such deities, Augustine eagerly sought more knowledge of Manicheism. He became an auditor in the sect and was told to await the coming of Faustus, a Manichee bishop, who would explain the finer points. When Faustus eventually came to Carthage, Augustine found him an engaging speaker but possessed of no great wisdom.

In 383, somewhat discouraged with his teaching career and suspicious of the pretensions of Manicheism, Augustine took ship for Rome. Partly, his move was inspired by ambition for greater success at the heart of the Empire; partly, he desired to break his Carthaginian associations and make a fresh start in life. After a few months in Rome, he abandoned his ties with Manicheism and briefly fell into a skeptical frame of mind. The following year saw him engaged as a municipal teacher of rhetoric in Milan, the north Italian city which was not only the residence of the Roman emperors but also the episcopal see of the famous St. Ambrose. It was in Milan that Augustine learned something of Neoplatonic philosophy and turned his thoughts to spiritual concerns. From Ambrose, and more especially from the priest Simplicianus, he discovered that Christianity had resources previously unknown to him. Eventually he made his critical decision to become a full member in the Church of his mother. The story of his famous conversion is the high point of his *Confessions.* Augustine was baptized by Bishop Ambrose, on the eve of Easter, April 25, 387.

Returning to Africa in the following year, Augustine set up a sort of monastery for himself and some other lay Christians in Tagaste. His mother had died at Rome, before the return to Africa; in 389 Adeodatus died. By 391 Augustine had been ordained a priest for the church at Hippo, a seacoast town not far from Tagaste. Soon Augustine was the most active and influential churchman that Africa has ever had. Consecrated bishop in 395, he built up the diocese of Hippo, engaged in numerous religious controversies (against Donatists, Pelagians, and Arians), participated actively in yearly councils of the African bishops, and traveled back and forth across North Africa in zealous defense of his faith. For thirty-five years he was the pillar of Christianity, not simply in Hippo or Numidia but throughout the civilized world.

Lasting fame, however, came from his tremendous literary production. From the time of his conversion in 386 until his death in 430, he wrote about one thousand books. These "books" are roughly the equivalent of a chapter in a modern publication. Another way of suggesting the extent of his writings would be to say that they are about equal to fifteen volumes in a standard encyclopedia. Several of Augustine's works are well known among the "great books" of Western literature. The *Confessions* is one of the most widely read autobiographies. Its first nine books tell the story of his life up to the return to Africa. In the *City of God* we have a stirring defense of the role of Christianity in the history of the Empire and a vast reinterpretation of the social and political structuring of mankind. Its twenty-two books took more than a dozen years (412-426) in the writing. Among other things that grew out of the *City of God* was the Holy Roman Empire, which Charlemagne mistakenly felt to be the realization of Augustine's plan of a holy society. The effects of this development in political Augustinianism are still evident in continental Europe. Still another masterpiece is the treatise *On the Trinity*; fifteen books in this work develop the central theme in patristic theology. Among Augustine's Biblical studies, there are several attempts to explain the opening verses of the Book of Genesis, the *Literal Commentary on Genesis* being the longest and the best. However, Augustine's longest work was none of these: it is a massive exposition of the Psalms, labeled the *Enarrations on the Psalms* by the Renaissance editor, Erasmus. Each day during his priestly life, Augustine spent some time in meditation on the Psalms. He took care to jot down his thoughts and often used them as sermon notes. The result is a huge collection in which are discernible most of the themes and insights that crop up elsewhere in Augustine's better-known treatises.

Toward the end of his life, in 426, Augustine had the foresight to write a review of his books, excluding the sermons and letters. The *Retractations* (from *retractare,* to treat again, not from *retrahere,* to retract) provide information about the chronology, authenticity, and occasions of the many writings of Augustine. We have little difficulty in determining the canon of his literary output.

The remainder of this first chapter offers some samples of Augustine's autobiographical writings other than the well-known *Confessions,* and a portion of his own introduction to his writings, from the beginning of the *Retractations.* At the back of the book will be found an alphabetical list of the English titles of Augustine's works, together with Latin titles, dates, and information on the chief editions and English versions of each item. There is no complete set of St. Augustine's works in English. It is hoped that the information here supplied will be of assistance to those who wish to read more in the greatest of the Fathers of the Latin Church.

HOW AUGUSTINE CAME TO THE EPISCOPACY*

2.   Now, I do not propose to keep you very long, especially in view of the fact that I am sitting as I speak while you are suffering on your feet. All, or nearly all of you, are aware that we live in the house that is called the Bishop's House, and that we follow the example, as much as we can, of those holy men who are mentioned in the Acts of the Apostles: "not one of them said that anything he possessed was his own, but they had all things in common." [Acts 4:32] Since some of you, perhaps, are not sufficiently careful observers of our way of life to know this as I would like you to know it, I am saying what it is like, and briefly, as I have said.

I, whom by God's favor you observe as your bishop, came as a young man to this City [Hippo], as many of you know. I was looking for a place to establish a monastery and to live together with my brethren. Of course, I had abandoned my worldly ambition and refused to be what I might have been; in fact, I did not seek to become what I am now. "I have chosen to be an abject in the house of my God, rather than to dwell in the tabernacles of sinners." [Ps. 83:11] I dissociated myself from those who love the world, and made no effort to be on the level of those who rule the people. Nor did I choose a higher place at my Lord's table but a lower one, much removed. And it pleased Him to say to me: Go up higher. At that point, I was so much afraid of the office of bishop that, since my reputation had begun to be of some importance among God's servants, I would not visit any

* *Sermon 355;* 2, trans. V.J.B.

place that I knew to be without a bishop. I took this precaution and did as much as I could to achieve salvation in a low position, lest I run into danger in a high one. As I have said, however, the servant should not contradict his master.

I came to this City to see a friend whom I thought I might win over for God and have him with us in the monastery: I felt safe, because this place had a bishop. I was caught and made a priest; then, through this step, I reached the episcopate. I brought nothing: I came to this church with nothing more than the clothes that I wore at the time. Since I had this intention to live in a monastery with my brethren, the venerable [Bishop] Valerius of happy memory, who knew my plan and desire, gave me this garden in which the monastery is now located. I started to assemble brethren who were well-disposed as my colleagues, men who possessed nothing, as I had nothing, and who followed my example. Thus, as I sold my meager little estate and gave it to the poor, so also did those who wished to live with me; our purpose was to live in common: indeed, what was common to us was that great and most rewarding prize, God Himself.

I reached the episcopate and saw that it is necessary for a bishop to provide continuous hospitality for various visitors and travelers, and if I did not do this as a bishop, I would have been deemed discourteous. However, if this sort of behavior were permitted in a monastery, it would have been unfitting. Consequently, I decided to maintain a community of priests with me in this episcopal house.

Notice how we live. In our community, no one is permitted to own anything, though possibly some do. It is permitted to no one: if some do own property, they do so without permission. However, I think well of my own brethren, and since I always maintain this good opinion, I have omitted any inquiry into this matter, for to ask would have given the impression that I suspected some evil. In fact, I know, and all who live with me know, what our objective is and what is the rule of our life.

AUGUSTINE CHOOSES ERACLIUS AS HIS SUCCESSOR*

1. Since God willed it, I came to this City [Hippo] when I was in the prime of life; although I was young then, I am now old. I know how churches

* *Letter 213*, 1, 5 and 6; trans. V.J.B.

are usually disturbed after the death of their bishops by ambitious and quarrelsome men. Because I have frequently observed this and been saddened by it, I must insofar as I can make arrangements in advance so that it may not happen in this City.... So, lest anyone complain about me, I bring to the attention of all of you my wishes, which I also believe to be the will of God: I wish the priest Eraclius to be my successor....

5. He will remain a priest as he is, until God wills him to be your bishop. But I shall, with the merciful help of Christ, start now to do what I have not done up to the present. You all know what I have wanted to do for several years and what you did not allow me to do. It was agreed between you and me that no one would bother me for five days of the week, in view of the Scriptural studies which my brethren and fellow bishops at the two Councils of Numidia and Carthage saw fit to impose on me. The arrangements were recorded, the agreement was made, you shouted your approval. Your agreement and your shouts of approval were repeated orally. For a short time, the agreement in regard to me was observed, and then it was rudely broken: I am not allowed time to do what I wish. I am involved in men's problems both before and after noon. I beseech you and adjure you through Christ to allow me to shift the burden of my regular affairs to this young man, the priest Eraclius, whom today in the name of Christ I designate as my successor....

6. For your charity and benevolence, I give thanks before the Lord, our God; or rather, I thank God for them. And so, brethren, whatever matters you are accustomed to bring before me, present them to him. When he needs my advice, I shall not refuse my help: far be it from me to withdraw completely. Nevertheless, whatever problem you used to set before me, bring it to him. Let him consult me, if by chance he cannot discern what ought to be done; or he may seek me out as a helper, when he had previously known me as a father. In this way, you will not be deprived of anything, and I will for a while (however much more time God grants me in this life) devote myself not to idleness or retirement but to Holy Scripture as He permits and endows me. This may work to His advantage and also, through Him, to yours. Let no one envy me my retirement, since my retirement involves a great deal of work.

AUGUSTINE ON HIS OWN WRITINGS*

1. For some time, I have been thinking over and considering the task which I am now beginning with the help of God. . . . For I do not feel that I should put off reviewing with judicial severity my works, whether in the form of books, letters or treatises, and noting like a censor anything that displeases me. For, except for an imprudent person, no one will dare to criticize me because I am criticizing my own errors. However, if he says that I should not have uttered things that would later displease me, he is right and in agreement with me. In fact, he is criticizing the same things that I do, for I would not have to criticize them, if I had written what I ought.

2. However, let each person interpret what I am doing, as he wills. For myself, the Apostle's view of this matter merits attention, where he says, "If we judged ourselves, we might not be judged by God." [I Cor. 11:31] There is also the text, "In the multitude of words, you will not escape sin." [Prov. 10:19] which frightens me a good deal. Not because I have written much, or because many things that I have said have been copied down even though I did not dictate them (far be it from me to regard as verbosity what has to be said, even though the result is a large and prolix quantity of words), yet I cringe from this text of Scripture because there is no doubt that from many of my discussions a good many things could be gathered which, if not false, might definitely appear, or even might be proved, unnecessary. What one of the faithful did not Christ frighten, when He said, "For every idle word that men shall speak, they shall render an account on the day of judgment." [Matt. 12:36] Hence, on this point the Apostle James said, "Let every man be swift to hear but slow to speak"; [Jas. 1:19] and elsewhere he said, "Be ye not many masters, my brethren, knowing that you receive the greater judgment. All of us offend in many things. If any man offend not in word, the same is a perfect man." [Jas. 3:1ff] As for myself, I do not now lay claim to such perfection, even now that I am elderly; how much less, when I began as a young man to write or speak to the

* *Retractions,* Prologue, I, 1-3; trans. V.J.B.

people. So much notoriety was then accorded me that, wherever I found myself, I had to speak to the people; rarely could I keep silent and listen to others and be "quick to hear but slow to speak." As a result, I judge myself before the one Master Whose judgment of my offenses I desire to avoid. I think there can be many teachers when there are plural views that are diversified and mutually opposed. But when all say the same thing and speak the truth, they do not depart from the teaching of one true Teacher. They sin, on the other hand, not when they say a good deal in agreement with Him but when they add their own notions. This is how they fall from much speaking into false speaking.

3.   Now I was glad to write this work, so that I might put it in the hands of those men from whom I could not recall and correct the books that I had already produced. Nor, indeed, do I pass over those things that I wrote while still a catechumen, when I had abandoned the earthly expectations that I had formerly held but was still filled with the literary affectations of this world. In fact, these writings did come to the attention of copyists and readers, and they can be read with some profit, provided one is prepared to ignore their several faults, or if one cannot ignore the mistakes at least one can pay no attention to them. So, let all those who will read this work imitate me not in my errors but in my progress toward the better. For, whoever will read my little works in the order in which they were written, will perhaps discover how much progress I made in writing. To enable the reader to do this, I shall take care in this work to inform him as to this order, as much as I can.

II. FAITH AND REASON

Augustine's position on the relation of faith and reason influences all the rest of his thinking; it could be argued that Augustinianism is essentially a certain way of looking at these key notions. Reason (*ratio*) does not mean discursive thinking, as in Aristotelian logic; instead, the Augustinian reason is (in the psychological usage) the gaze of the mind (*aspectus mentis*). The culmination of such "gazing" is a vision, a clear seeing of the object of knowledge. We shall read more about such visions, at the end of Chapter IV.

Faith, on the other hand, is an acceptance of, or assent to, something that is not clearly seen. There is a basis for belief in the testimony of others but what is required in the believer is an effort of will. At the beginning of Chapter X, a passage is quoted which describes three kinds of objects of belief: (i) the "facts" of history, which no historian can witness for himself; (ii) the conclusions of mathematics and other such studies, which are understood as soon as they are believed; and (iii) the truths about God, which are believed by many but understood by few men in this life. This illustrates the scope that Augustine assigns to faith.

Actually the source of Augustine's views on faith and reason is a text from Isaias (7:9, Septuagint), which simply says: "Unless you will have believed, you will not understand" (*nisi credideritis non intelligetis*). The reading has been corrected in later texts ("if you will not believe, you shall not continue"), but this is a case of a fortunate error, more influential than the truth. From this misreading there developed a whole program of Christian intellectualism among the Latin Fathers of the Church and the theologians of the middle ages. It was not by chance that the *Proslogion* of St. Anselm of Canterbury was subtitled *Faith Seeking Understanding* (*fides quaerens intellectum*). Augustine did not say that a person had to be highly educated, or a sophisticated thinker, in order to get to Heaven; simple religious faith is enough for salvation. However, he did insist that those who have an opportunity to develop an understanding of what they believe are duty bound to make the best possible use of their talents.

If simple faith and a developed understanding are twin roads to knowledge, this does not mean that Augustine equated them with what would today be called theology and philosophy. In his own usage, *theologia* mostly designates pagan efforts (Varro and Porphyry) to build a system of polytheistic religious teachings. Augustine does not refer to himself as a theologian. *Philosophia* is usually taken by Augustine in its etymological sense ("the love of wisdom") and is equated with the finest use of the human mind. As he approvingly reports of Plato: "he did not doubt that to philosophize is to love God" [*City of God*, VIII, 8]. Even prescinding from the peculiarities of early Latin usage and thinking only of the present meanings of the words, we would have to say that Augustine distinguishes faith from both philosophy and theology, because both the philosophy and the theologian work in the area of understanding. Augustine sometimes (*On Christian Doctrine*, 5, 8) refers to Christian doctrine as the true *philosophia*.

After his disillusionment with Manicheism, Augustine was momentarily attracted to the sophisticated skepticism of the later Platonic Academy. During his first residence in Rome he felt that it might be better to withhold judgment on all important matters. However, Augustine was too sincere a thinker to remain long in this uncommitted position; he soon decided that the pose of the skeptic is untenable. His first published writing (*Against the Academics*) is a blunt rejection of academic skepticism. He returns to the problem in later treatises (*City of God* and *The Trinity*) and argues that the immediate presentations of consciousness are bases for unassailable judgments. The most striking of these arguments is the *si fallor sum* ("if I make a mistake in thinking, I exist") of the third from last selection in this chapter. Many scholars have discussed the resemblance of this insight to Descartes' *cogito ergo sum*. When Father Arnauld (who knew Augustine's works well) first drew Descartes' attention to the similarity of thought and expression, the French thinker merely said that he was happy to have so great a thinker for his patron.

The distinction between knowledge (*scientia*) and wisdom (*sapientia*) is also fundamental in Augustinianism. We shall see in Chapter III how Augustine places the human soul on a level between God and bodies, where it is able to look upward (*ratio superior*) to consult the divine truths, or downward (*ratio inferior*) to consider bodily thing and events. The disposition, or habit, which enables the human mind to judge in accord with the divine truths is *wisdom,* while the habit that perfects the lower reason is *knowledge.* Both are useful, but knowledge depends on wisdom and not the reverse.

In a confrontation theory of knowledge such as Augustine's, where the mind sees knowable things when the two are compresent, there is no possibility of error on the highest level of vision. One either sees that seven plus three equals ten, or one does not and is ignorant. Yet Augustine admits that erroneous judgments are made by men. Error consists in taking one thing for another, by virtue of willing to do so; error becomes a volitional fault. "Bodies themselves are in no way present within the mind but only their images; and so, when we assent to the latter in place of the former, we err; thus error consists in assenting to one item in place of another" (*The Trinity,* IX, 11, 16). As a result of this stress on the function of willing, Augustine's explanation of error usually approximates the notion of a moral fault.

These are some of the points to look for in the selections that follow.

BELIEF IS VOLITIONAL CONSENT*

21.54.
Consider now whether anybody believes, if he be unwilling; or whether he believes not, if he shall have willed it. Such a position, indeed, is absurd (for what is believing but consenting to the truth of what is said? and this consent is certainly voluntary): faith, therefore, is in our own power. But, as the Apostle says: "There is no power but comes from God," [Rom. 13:1] what reason then is there why it may not be said to us even of this: "What hast thou which thou hast not received?" [I Cor. 4:7] —for it is God who gave us even to believe. Nowhere, however, in Holy Scripture do we find such an assertion as, There is no volition but comes from God. And rightly is it not so written, because it is not true: otherwise God would be the author even of sins (which Heaven forbid!), if there were no volition except what comes from Him; inasmuch as an evil volition alone is already a sin, even if the effect be wanting. . . .

* *On the Spirit and the Letter,* 21.54; 34.60; trans. Dods.

Let this discussion suffice, if it satisfactorily meets *34.60.* the question we had to solve. It may be, however, objected in reply, that we must take heed lest someone should suppose that the sin would have to be imputed to God which is committed by free will, if in the passage where it is asked, "What hast thou which thou didst not receive?" the very will by which we believe is reckoned as a gift of God, because it arises out of the free will which we received at our creation. Let the objector, however, attentively observe that this will is to be ascribed to the divine gift, not merely because it arises from our free will, which was created naturally with us; but also because God acts upon us by the incentives of our perceptions, to will and to believe, either externally by evangelical exhortations, where even the commands of the law also do something, if they so far admonish a man of his infirmity that he betakes himself to the grace that justifies by believing; or internally, where no man has in his own control what shall enter into his thoughts, although it appertains to his own will to consent or to dissent.

TO BELIEVE IS TO THINK WITH ASSENT*

And therefore, commending that grace which is not *5.* given according to any merits but is the cause of all good merits, he says, "Not that we are sufficient to think anything as of ourselves, but our sufficiency is of God." [2 Cor. 3:5] Let them give attention to this, and well weigh these words, who think that the beginning of faith is of ourselves, and the supplement of faith is of God. For who cannot see that that thinking is prior to believing? For no one believes anything unless he has first thought that it is to be believed. For however suddenly, however rapidly, some thoughts fly before the will to believe, and this presently follows in such wise as to attend them, as it were, in closest conjunction, it is yet necessary that everything which is believed should be believed after thought has preceded; although even belief itself is nothing else than to think with assent. For it is not every one who thinks that believes, since many think in order that they may not believe; but everybody who believes, thinks—both thinks in believing, and believes in thinking.

* *Predestination of the Saints,* 5; trans. Dods.

BELIEVING IS ONE THING, UNDERSTANDING ANOTHER*

E. I grant now that God gave it. But does it not
4. seem to you, I ask, that if it has been given for doing
right, we should not be able to pervert it to a sinful
use? Like justice, which too is given to man for right living—
for could anyone live evilly by his own justice? So no one
would be able to sin by his will, if that will had been given
him to do right.

A. God will grant, I hope, that I shall be able to answer
you; or rather that you yourself will find the answer from
that greatest teacher of all, the truth within your own heart.
But I would have you tell me briefly if you have sure
knowledge of what I asked you, that God gave us free will;
whether or not we conclude that God should not have given
that which we acknowledge that He gave. For if it is not
certain that He did give it, we may rightly ask whether it was
well given, so that when we find that it was well given, we
will also find that it was given by Him who gave all goods
to men: if on the other hand we find it not well given, we
shall know that it was not given by Him whom to blame
were impious. But if it is certain that He himself gave it,
however it was given we must acknowledge that it neither
should not have been given, nor given otherwise than as it
was given. For He gave it whose act can nowise be rightly
censured.

E. Though I hold these things with unshaken faith,
5. yet since I do not hold them by knowledge, let us
inquire into them as if all were uncertain. For I see
that as it is uncertain whether free will was given us for
doing right, since we can also sin by it, that other question
becomes also uncertain, whether it should have been given.
But if it is uncertain that it was given for doing right, and
also uncertain whether it should have been given, it is not
certain that it was given by Him whom it were impious to
believe had given anything He should not have given.

A. At least you are certain that God exists?

* On Free Choice, II, 2, 4-6; trans. Carroll Mason Sparrow,
St. Augustine on Free Will (Charlottesville: University of Virginia Studies, 1947), pp. 35-37. Used with permission.

E. Even that I do not hold by reason, but by steadfast faith.
A. If then one of those fools of whom it is written: *The fool hath said in his heart, There is no God,* [Ps. 13:1] should say this to you, and not be willing to believe what you believe, but want to know whether you were believing the truth; would you leave the man, or would you think that in some way he should be persuaded of what you so firmly believe; especially if he had the will not to oppose it obstinately, but wished eagerly to know?
E. What you said last advises me well enough as to how I should answer him. For however unreasonable he might be, he would admit that nothing whatever, and least of all so great a matter, should be argued about insincerely or with obstinacy. This granted, he would first try to convince me that he was asking in good faith, and that he had no hidden guile or obstinacy about the matter.

Then I should show (as I think anyone could easily do) that since he himself was demanding that matters hidden in his own mind be believed by another who did not know them, that it would be only reasonable for him to believe that God exists, from the books of those great men who have left written testimony that they lived with the Son of God, and who have written also of things seen by them which could not possibly be if there were no God: and he would be a simple fellow indeed to criticize me for believing those men when he wanted me to believe him. But that which he could not rightly object to he could in no wise make an excuse for his unwillingness to imitate.
A. If then, as to whether God exists, it is enough for you that it should not seem unreasonable to believe those great men, why, pray, do you not think we should likewise take on the authority of those same men all those other things which we subjected to inquiry as if they were unsure and not clearly known? We should then have to trouble no further to examine them.
E. But that which we believe, we desire also to know and understand.

6. *A.* You remember rightly; we cannot go back on the position we took at the beginning of our former discussion. For believing is one thing, and understanding another; and we must first believe whatever great and divine matter we desire to understand. Else would the Prophet have said in error, *Except ye believe, ye shall not understand.* [Isa. 7:9, Septuagint] Then too our Lord himself, both by

His words and His acts, exhorted those whom He called to salvation to first believe. But afterward, when He spoke of the gift itself that was to be given to believers, He did not say, "This moreover is eternal life, that ye believe," but *This is life eternal, that they might know thee the only true God, and Jesus Christ, whom thou hast sent.* [John 17:3] Again, He says to believers, *Seek and ye shall find.* [Matt. 7:7] But one cannot speak of that being found which is believed without knowledge, nor does anyone become prepared to find God who does not first believe that which he is afterward to know. Wherefore, following our Lord's precepts, let us seek earnestly. For what He himself encourages us to seek, that same shall we find by His showing, so far as such things may be found in this life, and by such as we. For it is to be believed that these things are seen more clearly and known more perfectly by those better than we, even while they live on earth, and certainly by the good and pious after this life. And so we must hope it will be with us, and despising things earthly and mortal must love and desire these things in every way.

AUTHORITY AND REASON*

20.43. ... And now—that you may grasp my whole meaning in a few words—whatever may be the nature of human wisdom, I see that I have not yet understood it. Nevertheless, although I am now in the thirty-third year of my life, I do not think that I ought to despair of understanding it some day, for I have resolved to disregard all the other things which mortals consider good, and to devote myself to an investigation of it. And, whereas the reasonings of the Academics used to deter me greatly from such an undertaking, I believe that through this disputation I am now sufficiently protected against those reasonings. Certainly, no one doubts that we are impelled toward knowledge by a twofold force: the force of authority and the force of reason. And I am resolved never to deviate in the least from the authority of Christ, for I find none more powerful. But, as to what is attainable by acute and accurate reasoning, such is my state of mind that I am impatient to grasp what truth is —to grasp it not only by belief, but also by comprehension.

* *Against the Academics,* III, 20.43; trans. FOC 1 (1948) 220.

Meanwhile, I am confident that I shall find among the Platonists what is not in opposition to our Sacred Scriptures.

TWO WAYS TO KNOWLEDGE*

9.26. It remains for me to declare how instruction is to be imparted to the studious youths who have resolved to live after the manner described above. Likewise, with regard to the acquiring of knowledge, we are of necessity led in a twofold manner: by authority and by reason. In point of time, authority is first; in the order of reality, reason is prior. What takes precedence in operation is one thing; what is more highly prized as an object of desire is something else. Consequently, although the authority of upright men seems to be the safer guide for the uninstructed multitude, reason is better adapted for the educated. Furthermore, since no one becomes learned except by ceasing to be unlearned, and since no unlearned person knows in what quality he ought to present himself to instructors or by what manner of life he may become docile, it happens that for those who seek to learn great and hidden truths authority alone opens the door. But, after one has entered, then without any hesitation he begins to follow the precepts of the perfect life. When he has become docile through these precepts, then at length he will come to know: (a) how much wisdom is embodied in those very precepts that he has been observing before understanding; (b) what reason itself is, which he—now strong and capable after the cradle of authority—follows and comprehends; (c) what intellect is, in which all things are, or rather, which is itself the sum total of all things; (d) and what, beyond all things, is the source of all things. To this knowledge, few are able to arrive in this life; even after this life, no one can exceed it.

As to those who are content to follow authority alone and who apply themselves constantly to right living and holy desires, while they make no account of the liberal and fine arts, or are incapable of being instructed in them—I know not how I could call them happy as long as they live among men. Nevertheless, I firmly believe that, upon leaving the body, they will be liberated with greater facility or difficulty according as they have lived the more virtuously or otherwise.

* *On Order*, II, 9.26-27; trans. FOC 1 (1948) 303-305.

27. Authority is, indeed, partly divine and partly human, but the true, solid and sovereign authority is that which is called divine. In this matter there is to be feared the wonderful deception of invisible beings that, by certain divinations and numerous powers of things pertaining to the senses, are accustomed to deceive with the utmost ease those souls that are engrossed with perishable possessions, or eagerly desirous of transitory power, or overawed by meaningless prodigies.

We must, therefore, accept as divine that Authority which not only exceeds human power in its outward manifestations, but also, in the very act of leading a man onward, shows him to what extent It has debased Itself for his sake, and bids him not to be confined to the senses, to which indeed those things seem wondrous, but to soar upward to the intellect. At the same time It shows him what great things It is able to do, and why It does them, and how little importance It attaches to them. For, it is fitting that by deeds It show Its power; by humility, Its clemency; by commandment, Its nature. And all this is being delivered to us so distinctly and steadily by the sacred rites into which we are now being initiated: therein the life of good men is most easily purified, not indeed by the circumlocution of disputation, but by the authority of the mysteries.

But human authority is very often deceiving. Yet it rightly seems to show itself at its best in those men who propose various proofs for their teachings, insofar as the mind of the unlearned can grasp them, and who do not live otherwise than how they prescribe that one ought to live. If certain goods of fortune accrue to these men, they reveal themselves great men in the use of those things, but still greater in their contempt of them; and then it is most difficult to lay blame on anyone who puts trust in those men when they enunciate principles of right living.

REASON AND AUTHORITY IN MANICHEISM*

1. If, Honoratus, a heretic, and a man trusting heretics seemed to me one and the same, I should judge it my duty to remain silent both in tongue and pen in this matter. But now, whereas there is a very great difference

* *The Value of Believing*, 1-4; trans. Dods.

between these two: forasmuch as he, in my opinion, is a heretic, who, for the sake of some temporal advantage, and chiefly for the sake of his own glory and preeminence, either gives birth to, or follows, false and new opinions, but he who trusts men of this kind is a man deceived by a certain imagination of truth and piety. This being the case, I have not thought it my duty to be silent towards you, as to my opinions on he finding and retaining of truth: with great love of which, as you know, we have burned from our very earliest youth: but it is a thing far removed from the minds of vain men, who, having too far advanced and fallen into these corporeal things, think that there is nothing else than what they perceive by those five well-known reporters of the body; and what impressions and images they have received from these, they carry over with themselves, even when they essay to withdraw from the senses; and by the deadly and most deceitful rule of these think that they measure most rightly the unspeakable recesses of truth. Nothing is more easy, my dearest friend, than for one not only to say, but also to think, that he has found out the truth; but how difficult it is in reality, you will perceive, I trust, from this letter of mine. And that this may profit you, or at any rate may in no way harm you, and also all into whose hands it shall chance to come, I have both prayed, and do pray, unto God; and I hope that it will be so, forasmuch as I am fully conscious that I have undertaken to write it, in a pious and friendly spirit, not as aiming at vain reputation, or trifling display.

2.　　　It is then my purpose to prove to you, if I can, that the Manichees profanely and rashly inveigh against those who, following the authority of the Catholic Faith, before they are able to gaze upon that Truth, which the pure mind beholds, are by believing forearmed, and prepared for God Who is about to give them light. For you know, Honoratus, that for no other reason we fell in with such men, than because they used to say that, apart from all terror of authority, by pure and simple reason, they would lead within to God, and set free from all error those who were willing to be in their hearers. For what else constrained me, during nearly nine years, spurning the religion which had been set in me from a child by my parents, to be a follower and diligent hearer of those men, save that they said that we are alarmed by superstition, and are commanded to have faith before reason, but that they urge no one to have faith without having first discussed and made clear the truth? Who would not be enticed by such promises, especially the mind of a young man desirous of the truth, and further a proud and talkative mind by discussions of certain learned men in the school? such as they then found me, disdainful forsooth as of old wives' fables, and desirous to grasp and drink in, what they promised, the open and pure Truth? But that reason, on the other hand, recalled me, not to be altogether joined to them, so that I continued in that rank which they call of Hearers, so that I resigned not the hope and business of this world; save that I noticed that they also are rather eloquent and full in refutation of others, than abide firm and sure in proof of what is their own. But of myself what shall I say, who was already a Catholic Christian? Teats which now, after very long thirst, I almost exhausted and dry, I have returned to with all greediness, and with deeper weeping and groaning have shaken together and wrung them out more deeply, that so there might flow what might be enough to refresh me, affected as I was, and to bring back hope of life and safety. What then shall I say of myself? You, not yet a Christian, who, through encouragement from me, execrating them greatly as you did, were hardly led to believe that you ought to listen to them and make trial of them, by what else, I pray you, were you delighted, call to mind, I entreat you, save by a certain great presumption and promise of reasons? But because they disputed long and much with very great copiousness and vehemence concerning the errors of unlearned men, a thing which I learned too late at length to be most easy for any moderately educated man; if even of their own they implanted in us anything, we thought that we were obliged to retain it, insomuch as there fell not in our way other things wherein to acquiesce. So they did in our case what crafty fowlers are wont to do, who set branches smeared with bird-lime beside water to deceive thirsty birds. For they fill up and cover anyhow the other waters which are around, or fright them from them by alarming devices, that they may fall into their snares, not through choice, but want.

3.   But why do I not make answer to myself, that these fair and clever similes, and charges of this nature may be poured forth against all who are teachers of any thing by any adversary, with abundance of wit and sarcasm? But I thought that I ought to insert something of this kind in my letter, in order to admonish them to give over such pro-

ceedings; so that, as he [Cicero] says, apart from trifles of commonplaces, matter may contend with matter, cause with cause, reason with reason. Wherefore let them give over that saying, which they have in their mouths as though of necessity, when anyone who has been for some long time a hearer has left them: "The Light hath made a passage through him." For you see, you who are my chief care (for I am not overanxious about them), how empty this is, and most easy for anyone to find fault with. Therefore I leave this for your own wisdom to consider. For I have no fear that you will think me possessed by indwelling Light, when I was entangled in the life of this world, having a darkened hope, of beauty of wife, of pomp of riches, of emptiness of honors, and of all other hurtful and deadly pleasures. For all these, as is not unknown to you, I ceased not to desire and hope for, at the time when I was their attentive hearer. And I do not lay this to the charge of their teaching; for I also confess that they also carefully advise to shun these. But now to say that I am deserted by light, when I have turned myself from all these shadows of things, and have determined to be content with that diet merely which is necessary for health of body; but that I was enlightened and shining, at a time when I loved these things, and was wrapped up in them, is the part of a man, to use the mildest expression, wanting in a keen insight into matters, on which he loves to speak at length. But, if you please, let us come to the cause in hand.

4. For you well know that the Manichees move the unlearned by finding fault with the Catholic Faith, and chiefly by rending in pieces and tearing the Old Testament: and they are utterly ignorant, how far these things are to be taken, and how drawn out they descend with profit into the veins and marrows of souls as yet as it were but able to cry. And because there are in them certain things which are some slight offense to minds ignorant and careless of themselves (and there are very many such) they admit of being accused in a popular way: but defended in a popular way they cannot be by any great number of persons, by reason of the mysteries that are contained in them. But the few who know how to do this do not love public and much talked of controversies and disputes: and on this account are very little known, save to such as are most earnest in seeking them out. Concerning then this rashness of the Manichees, whereby they find fault with the Old Testament and the Catholic Faith, listen, I entreat you, to the considerations which move me. But I desire and hope that you will receive them in the same spirit in which I say them. For God, unto Whom are known the secrets of my conscience, knows, that in this discourse I am doing nothing of evil craft; but, as I think it should be received, for the sake of proving the truth, for which one thing we have now long ago determined to live; and with incredible anxiety, lest it may have been most easy for me to err with you, but most difficult, to use no harder term, to hold the right way with you.

THE RELATION OF AUTHORITY TO REASON*

24.45. And so even the very medicine of the soul, which Divine Providence and ineffable Goodness administers, is perfectly beautiful in degree and distinction. For it is divided between authority and reason. Authority demands faith, and prepares man for reason. Reason leads him on to knowledge and understanding. But reason is not entirely useless to authority; it helps in considering what authority is to be accepted. Certainly the greatest authority is that of the known and clearly evident Truth Itself. But since we dwell among the temporal and are drawn by love of them from things that are eternal, some temporal medicine which calls not the learned but the believers to salvation is of primary importance, not in the order of nature or excellence, but in the order of time. For wherever you fall, there you must strive to rise. Therefore, we must strive by use of the very material forms which hold us down, in order to understand those which the body does not report. I call those forms material which our bodies can perceive, that is, those which our eyes, ears, and other bodily senses perceive. To cling eagerly to material, bodily forms of cognition is a necessity for children, a near necessity for the adolescent, but no necessity at all for adults.

25.46. Divine Providence, then, not only counsels individual men in private, but also counsels the entire human race in common. Therefore, what goes on in the individual soul, God, who gives the inspiration, and the souls He inspires, are aware. But what God advises all men, He has

*The True Religion, 24.45-25.47; trans. Gerald R. Sheahan, S.J., De vera religione (Chapters 18-38) (St. Louis University Master's Thesis, 1946), pp. 27-35. Used with permission.

preferred to impart through historical data and through prophecies. Now, faith in temporal matters, whether they be past or future, thrives more on belief than on knowledge. But we must here consider what men and what books we should believe to ensure the proper worship of God, our only means of salvation. In this matter our first consideration is whether we should believe those who call us to the worship of many gods or those who call us to worship one God. Who would doubt that he should certainly believe those who call him to worship one God, since even the worshipers of many gods agree upon one Supreme God and Ruler of all things. And certainly, enumeration begins with the number one. Primarily, then, we should believe those who hold that there is but one God, that He is supreme, the only, the true God, and that He alone is worthy of adoration. Only if the truth does not shine forth among these must we look elsewhere. Just as in nature itself the wider influence lies with the one that reduces all things to unity, and just as among men in general no large group has any strength without mutual consent—that is, unity of belief; so in religion we should yield more completely and with deeper trust to the influence of those who call us to the worship of one God.

47.   Our second consideration has to do with the dissension among men about the worship of the one God. We are told that our forefathers, showing that degree of Faith by which one mounts from the temporal to the eternal, were led along by visible miracles (of course, miracles cannot be otherwise). Through their experience miracles were made unnecessary for the following generations. For the Catholic Church has scattered its foundations throughout the whole world. Therefore, firstly, those miracles are not permitted to continue into our own day, for fear that our souls should be constantly in search of visible things, and that mankind would grow cold through familiarity with the very things whose novelty warmed it. Secondly, we should no longer doubt that we are to believe the men who, in spite of the fact that they were preaching a doctrine followed by a minority, could nevertheless persuade nations to follow them. For at present the question is whom we should believe; later it will be proper to start reasoning about the divine and the invisible. Of course, the reasoning faculty of a purer soul, one that has attained to the lucid truth, is in no way subordinate to human authority; but this stage is reached only with the absence of all pride.

If this were not the case there would be no heretics, no schismatics, no circumcised in the flesh, no creature- and icon-worshipers. And if these did not exist before the promised perfecting of men, there would be much less effort expended in seeking the truth.

IF I AM DECEIVED, I EXIST*

26.
For we both *are,* and *know* that we are, and *take delight* in our being and knowing. Moreover, in these three things no true-seeming illusion disturbs us; for we do not come into contact with these by some bodily sense, as we perceive the things outside us—colors, e.g., by seeing, sounds by hearing, smells by smelling, tastes by tasting, hard and soft objects by touching—of all which sensible objects it is the images resembling them, but not themselves, that we perceive in the mind and hold in the memory, and which excite us to desire the objects. However, without any delusive representation of images or phantasms, I am most certain that I am, that I know, and that I delight in this, On none of these points do I fear the arguments of the skeptics of the Academy who say: what if you are deceived? For if I am deceived, I am. For he who does not exist cannot be deceived; and if I am deceived, by this same token I am. And since I am if I am deceived, how am I deceived in believing that I am? For it is certain that I am, if I am deceived. Since therefore I, the person deceived, should be, even if I were deceived, certainly I am not deceived in this knowledge that I am. Consequently, neither am I deceived in knowing that I know. For, as I know that I am, so I know this also, that I know. And when I love these two [being and knowing], I add to them a third, that is, my love, which is of equal importance. For neither am I deceived in this, that I love, since in those things which I love I am not deceived; even if these were false, it would still be true that I loved false things. For how could I justly be blamed and prohibited from loving false things, if it were false that I loved them? Since these facts are true and real, who doubts that, when these things are loved, the love of them is itself true and real?

* *City of God,* XI, 26; trans. Dods, revised by V.J.B.

I KNOW THAT I AM ALIVE*

21. First, of what sort and how great is the very knowledge itself that a man can attain, be he ever so skillful and learned, by which our thought is formed with truth, when we speak what we know? For to pass by those things that come into the mind from the bodily senses, among which so many are otherwise than they seem to be, that he who is overmuch pressed down by their resemblance to truth, seems sane to himself, but really is not sane—whence it is that the Academic philosophy has so prevailed as to be still more wretchedly insane by doubting all things—passing by, then, those things that come into the mind by the bodily senses, how large a proportion is left of things which we know in such manner as we know that we live? In this, indeed, we are absolutely without any fear lest perchance we are being deceived by some resemblance of the truth; since it is certain that he too who is deceived, yet lives. And this again is not reckoned among those objects of sight that are presented from without, so that the eye may be deceived in it; in such way as it is when an oar in the water looks bent, and towers seem to move as you sail past them, and a thousand other things that are otherwise than they seem to be: for this is not a thing that is discerned by the eye of the flesh. The knowledge by which we know that we live is the most inward of all knowledge, of which even the Academic cannot insinuate. Perhaps you are asleep, and do not know it, and you see things in your sleep. For who does not know that what people see in dreams is precisely like what they see when awake? But he who is certain of the knowledge of his own life does not therein say "I know I am awake" but "I know I am alive"; therefore, whether he be asleep or awake, he is alive. Nor can he be deceived in that knowledge by dreams; since it belongs to a living man both to sleep and to see in sleep. Nor can the Academic again say, in confutation of this knowledge, "Perhaps you are mad, and do not know it": for what madmen see is precisely like what they also see who are sane; but he who is mad is alive. Nor does he answer the Academic by saying "I know I am not mad" but "I know I am alive." Therefore he who says he knows he is alive, can neither be deceived nor lie. Let a

*On the Trinity, XV, 12.21-22; trans. Dods.

thousand kinds then of deceitful objects of sight be presented to him who says "I know I am alive"; yet he will fear none of them, for he who is deceived yet is alive. But if such things alone pertain to human knowledge, they are very few indeed; unless that they can be so multiplied in each kind, as not only not to be few, but to reach in the result to infinity. For he who says "I know I am alive" says that he knows one single thing. Further, if he says "I know that I know I am alive," now there are two; but that he knows these two is a third thing to know. And so he can add a fourth and a fifth, and innumerable others, if he holds out. But since he cannot either comprehend an innumerable number by additions of units, or say a thing innumerable times, he comprehends this at least, and with perfect certainty, viz. that this is both true, and so innumerable that he cannot truly comprehend and say its infinite number. This same thing may be noticed also in the case of a will that is certain. For it would be an impudent answer to make to any one who should say "I will to be happy" that perhaps you are deceived. And if he should say, "I know that I will this, and I know that I know it," he can add yet a third to these two, viz. that he knows these two; and a fourth, that he knows that he knows these two; and so on *ad infinitum*. Likewise, if any one were to say, "I will not to be mistaken," will it not be true, whether he is mistaken or whether he is not, that nevertheless he does will not to be mistaken? Would it not be most impudent to say to him "Perhaps you are deceived?" when beyond doubt, whereinsoever he may be deceived, he is nevertheless not deceived in thinking that he wills not to be deceived. And if he says he knows this, he adds any number he chooses of things known, and perceives that number to be infinite. For he who says, "I will not to be deceived, and I know that I will not to be so, and I know that I know it," is able now to set forth an infinite number here also, however awkward may be the expression of it. And other things too are to be found capable of refuting the Academics, who contend that man can know nothing. But we must restrict ourselves, especially as this is not the subject we have undertaken in the present work. There are three books of ours on that subject [*Against the Academics*], written in the early time of our conversion, which he who can and will read, and who understands them, will doubtless not be much moved by any of the many arguments which they have found out against the discovery of truth. For whereas there are two kinds of knowable things—one, of those things which the mind perceives by the bodily senses; the other, of those which it perceives by itself—these philosophers have babbled much against the bodily senses, but have never been able to throw doubt upon those most certain perceptions of things true which the mind knows by itself, such as is that which I have mentioned, "I know that I am alive." But far be it from us to doubt the truth of what we have learned by the bodily senses; since by them we have learned to know the heaven and the earth, and those things in them which are known to us, so far as He who created both us and them has willed them to be within our knowledge. Far be it from us too to deny that we know what we have learned by the testimony of others: otherwise we know not that there is an ocean; we know not that the lands and cities exist which most copious report commends to us; we know not that those men were, and their works, which we have learned by reading history; we know not the news that is daily brought us from this quarter or that, and confirmed by consistent and conspiring evidence; lastly, we know not at what place or from whom we have been born: since in all these things we have believed the testimony of others. And if it is most absurd to say this, then we must confess, that not only our own senses, but those of other persons also, have added very much indeed to our knowledge.

22. All these things, then, both those which the human mind knows by itself, and those which it knows by the bodily senses, and those which it has received and knows by the testimony of others, are laid up and retained in the storehouse of the memory; and from these is begotten a word that is true, when we speak what we know, but a word that is before all sound, before all thought of a sound. For the word is then most like to the thing known, from which also its image is begotten, since the sight of thinking arises from the sight of knowledge, when it is a word belonging to no tongue, but is a true word concerning a true thing, having nothing of its own, but wholly derived from that knowledge from which it is born. Nor does it signify when he learned it, who speaks what he knows; for sometimes he says it immediately upon learning it; provided only that the word is true, i.e. sprung from things that are known.

KNOWLEDGE AND WISDOM*

14.21. For knowledge also has its own good measure, if that in it which puffs up, or is wont to puff up, is conquered by love of eternal things, which does not puff up but, as we know, edifieth. [I Cor. 8:1] Certainly without knowledge the virtues themselves, by which one lives rightly, cannot be possessed, by which this miserable life may be so governed that we may attain to that eternal life which is truly blessed.

14.22. Yet action, by which we use temporal things well, differs from contemplation of eternal things; and the latter is reckoned to wisdom, the former to knowledge. For although that which is wisdom can also be called knowledge, as the apostle too speaks, where he says, "Now I know in part, but then shall I know even as also I am known"; [I Cor. 13:12] when doubtless he meant his words to be understood of the knowledge of the contemplation of God, which will be the highest reward of the saints; yet where he says, "For to one is given by the Spirit the word of wisdom, to another the word of knowledge by the same Spirit," [I Cor. 12:8] certainly he distinguishes without doubt these two things, although he does not there explain the difference, nor in what way one may be discerned from the other. But having examined a great number of passages from the Holy Scriptures, I find it written in the Book of Job that holy man being the speaker, "Behold, piety, that is wisdom; but to depart from evil is knowledge." [Job 28:8] In thus distinguishing, it must be understood that wisdom belongs to contemplation, knowledge to action. For in this place he meant by piety the worship of God, which in Greek is called theosebeia. For the sentence in the Greek MSS. has that word. And what is there in eternal things more excellent than God, of whom alone the nature is unchangeable? And what is the worship of Him except the love of Him, by which we now desire to see Him, and we believe and hope that we shall see Him; and in proportion as we make progress, see now through a glass in an enigma, but then in clearness? For this is what the Apostle Paul means by "face to face." [I Cor. 13:12] This is also what John says,

* On the Trinity, XII, 14.21-15.25; trans. Dods.

"Beloved, now we are the sons of God, and it doth not yet appear what we shall be; but we know that, when He shall appear, we shall be like Him; for we shall see Him as He is." [I John 3:2] Discourse about these and the like subjects seems to me to be the discourse itself of wisdom. But to depart from evil, which Job says is knowledge, is without doubt of temporal things, since it is according to time that we are in evil, from which we ought to abstain, that we may come to those good eternal things. And therefore, whatsoever we do prudently, boldly, temperately, and justly, belongs to that knowledge or discipline wherewith our action is conversant in avoiding evil and desiring good; and so also whatsoever we gather by the knowledge that comes from inquiry, in the way of examples either to be guarded against or to be imitated, and in the way of necessary proofs respecting any subject, accommodated to our use.

23.   When a discourse then relates to these things, I hold it to be a discourse belonging to knowledge, and to be distinguished from a discourse belonging to wisdom, to which those things belong which neither have been, nor shall be, but are; and on account of that eternity in which they are, are said to have been, and to be, and to be about to be, without any changeableness of times. For neither have they been in such way as that they should cease to be, nor are they about to be in such way as if they were not now; but they have always had and always will have that very absolute being. And they abide, but not as if fixed in some place as are bodies; but as intelligible things in incorporeal nature, they are so at hand to the glance of the mind, as things visible or tangible in place are to the sense of the body. And not only in the case of sensible things posited in place there abide also intelligible and incorporeal reasons of them apart from local space; but also of motions that pass by in successive times, apart from any transit in time, there stand also like reasons, themselves certainly intelligible, and not sensible. And to attain to these with the eye of the mind is the lot of few; and when they are attained as much as they can be, he himself who attains to them does not abide in them, but is as it were repelled by the rebounding of the eye itself of the mind, and so there comes to be a transitory thought of a thing not transitory. And yet this transient thought is committed to the memory through the instructions by which the mind is taught; that the mind which is compelled to pass from thence may

be able to return thither again; although, if the thought should not return to the memory and find there what it had committed to it, it would be led thereto like an uninstructed person, as it had been led before, and would find it where it had first found it, that is to say, in that incorporeal truth, whence yet once more it may be as it were written down and fixed in the mind. For the thought of man, for example, does not so abide in that incorporeal and unchangeable reason of a square body, as that reason itself abides: if, to be sure, it could attain to it at all without the fantasy of local space. Or if one were to apprehend the rhythm of any artificial or musical sound, passing through certain intervals of time, as it rested without time in some secret and deep silence, it could at least be thought as long as that song could be heard; yet what the glance of the mind, transient though it was, caught from thence, and absorbing as it were into the belly, so laid up in the memory, over this it will be able to ruminate in some measure by recollection, and to transfer what it has thus learned into systematic knowledge. But if this has been blotted out by absolute forgetfulness, yet once again, under the guidance of teaching, one will come to that which had altogether dropped away, and it will be found such as it was.

15.24. And hence that noble philosopher Plato endeavored to persuade us that the souls of men lived here even before they bore these bodies; and that hence those things which are learnt are rather remembered as having been known already, than taken into knowledge as things new. For he has told us that a boy, when questioned I know not what respecting geometry, replied as if he were perfectly skilled in that branch of learning. For being questioned step by step and skillfully, he saw what was to be seen, and said that which he saw. But if this had been a recollecting of things previously known, then certainly everyone, or almost everyone, would not have been able so to answer when questioned. For not everyone was a geometrician in the former life, since geometricians are so few among men that scarcely one can be found anywhere. But we ought rather to believe that the intellectual mind is so formed in its nature as to see those things which by the disposition of the Creator are subjoined to things intelligible in a natural order, by a sort of incorporeal light of an unique kind; as the eye of the flesh sees things adjacent to itself in this bodily light, of which light it is made to be receptive, and adapted to it. For none the more does this fleshly eye, too, distinguish black things from white without a teacher, because it had already known them before it was created in this flesh. Why, lastly, is it possible only in intelligible things that anyone proplerly questioned should answer according to any branch of learning, although ignorant of it? Why can no one do this with things sensible, except those which he has seen in this his present body, or has believed the information of others who knew them, whether somebody's writings or words? For we must not acquiesce in their story who assert that the Samian Pythagoras recollected some things of this kind, which he had experienced when he was previously here in another body; and others tell yet of others, that they experienced something of the same sort in their minds: but it may be conjectured that these were untrue recollections, such as we commonly experience in sleep, when we fancy we remember, as though we had done or seen it, what we never did or saw at all; and that the minds of these persons, even though awake, were affected in this way at the suggestion of malignant and deceitful spirits, whose care it is to confirm or to sow some false belief concerning the changes of souls, in order to deceive men. This, I say, may be conjectured from this, that if they truly remembered those things which they had seen here before, while occupying other bodies, the same thing would happen to many, nay to almost all; since they suppose that, as the dead from the living, so, without cessation and continually, the living are coming into existence from the dead; as sleepers from those that are awake, and those that are awake from them that sleep.

25.   If therefore this is the right distinction between wisdom and knowledge, that the intellectual cognizance of eternal things belongs to wisdom, but the rational cognizance of temporal things to knowledge, it is not difficult to judge which is to be preferred or postponed to which. But if we must employ some other distinction by which to know these two apart, which without doubt the apostle teaches us are different, saying, "To one is given by the Spirit the word of wisdom; to another the word of knowledge, by the same Spirit"; still the difference between those two which we have laid down is a most evident one, in that the intellectual cognizance of eternal things is one thing, the rational cognizance of temporal things another, and no one doubts but that the former is to be preferred to the latter.

ERROR AND IGNORANCE*

17. For although we ought with the greatest possible care to avoid error, not only in great but even in little things, and although we cannot err except through ignorance, it does not follow that, if a man is ignorant of a thing, he must forthwith fall into error. That is rather the fate of the man who thinks he knows what he does not know. For he accepts what is false as if it were true, and that is the essence of error. But it is a point of very great importance what the subject is in regard to which a man makes a mistake. For on one and the same subject we rightly prefer an instructed man to an ignorant one, and a man who is not in error to one who is. In the case of different subjects, however—that is, when one man knows one thing, and another a different thing, and when what the former knows is useful, and what the latter knows is not so useful, or is actually hurtful—who would not, in regard to the things the latter knows, prefer the ignorance of the former to the knowledge of the latter? For there are points on which ignorance is better than knowledge. And in the same way, it has sometimes been an advantage to depart from the right way—in traveling, however, not in morals. It has happened to myself to take the wrong road where two ways met, so that I did not pass by the place where an armed band of Donatists lay in wait for me. Yet I arrived at the place whither I was bent, though by a roundabout route; and when I heard of the ambush, I congratulated myself on my mistake, and gave thanks to God for it. Now, who would not rather be the traveler who made a mistake like this, than the highwayman who made no mistake? And hence, perhaps, it is that the prince of poets puts these words into the mouth of a lover in misery: [Virgil, *Eclog.* 8.41] "How I am undone, how I have been carried away by an evil error!" for there is an error which is good, as it not merely does no harm, but produces some actual advantage. But when we look more closely into the nature of truth, and consider that to err is just to take the false for the true, and the true for the false, or to hold what is certain as uncertain, and what is uncertain as certain, and that error in the soul is hideous and repulsive just in proportion as it appears fair and plausible

* *Enchiridion,* 17; trans. Dods.

when we utter it, or assent to it, saying, "Yea, yea; Nay, nay"—surely this life that we live is wretched indeed, if only on this account, that sometimes, in order to preserve it, it is necessary to fall into error. God forbid that such should be that other life, where truth itself is the life of the soul, where no one deceives, and no one is deceived. But here men deceive and are deceived, and they are more to be pitied when they lead others astray than when they are themselves led astray by putting trust in liars. Yet so much does a rational soul shrink from what is false, and so earnestly does it struggle against error, that even those who love to deceive are most unwilling to be deceived. For the liar does not think that he errs, but that he leads another who trusts him into error. And certainly he does not err in regard to the matter about which he lies, if he himself knows the truth; but he is deceived in this, that he thinks his lie does him no harm, whereas every sin is more hurtful to the sinner than to the sinned against.

III. THREE LEVELS
OF REALITY

While Augustine has no metaphysics in the Aristotelian sense of a discipline that transcends the considerations of physics, he does offer a general view of reality that is distinctive and important. All natures are placed on three levels: God is at the top; the human soul stands in the middle; all bodies are on the lowest level. God is wholly immutable: He can suffer no change, either in time or place. Bodies, on the contrary, are completely mutable: they grow older in time and are buffeted about in place. Souls are mutable in time but immutable in place. It might be noted that angels, as created and finite spirits, belong on the same level as souls; that is one reason why Augustine makes angels co-citizens with men, in the two "Cities" which we shall examine in Chapter IX. There are only these three kinds of natures: divine, psychic and corporeal.

As an intermediary nature between the divine and the corporeal, the human soul is initially in a condition of instability, or tension, between what lies below and above. We have noted in Chapter II how man's mental gaze may turn upward or downward. Such "turning" is an affair of will: if man turns his attention up to God, this is *conversio* (a key source of the idea of religious conversion); but if man turns away from God, it does not matter to what else he turns, this is *aversio* or *perversio*. It is not that bodies are morally evil, but simply that Augustine thinks that a person cannot look both ways at once and with equal interest. One is either for God or against Him. Those who judge that temporal, earthly matters are most important are thereby putting God in a position of secondary value. In the long run there will be but two kinds of men: those who love God and those who love something else. This duality will be important in Chapters IX and X. For the present, it is enough to situate it in terms of the threefold hierarchy of being.

God, on the highest level, dwells in eternity. It is not until the next century that Boethius will coin the standard theological definition of eternity (the total and simultaneous possession of unending life), but Augustine is quite clear on the utter unlikeness of eternity and time. With God are the eternal truths and principles, the *rationes aeternae,* which are like Platonic Forms residing in God's mind. They are actually the divine Ideas. Mutability, change, has no place on this highest level.

On the lowest level, all is subject to change. The created principles of vital changes, growth, reproduction and other biological activities, are certain infinitesimal "seeds" (*rationes seminales*), created by God in the very texture of matter. Seminal reasons are not bulky seeds, like beans or grains of wheat, but are hidden factors in beans, wheat, etc., which ensure that only beans grow from beans, and wheat from wheat. All such growths and changes take place in time, which is the duration (*manentia*) characteristic of creatures.

Other than principles of vital change, there would not seem to be any created, natural "forces" in the world of Augustine. He did not know the four-cause theory of Aristotle's *Physics* and *Metaphysics.* Causality meant efficient production to Augustine; in a very real sense, all efficacy in the inanimate universe of bodies is directly and immediately supplied by God. (See the section in Chapter V: "God Works Throughout Nature.") Of course, the teaching that divine Ideas are the eternal patterns of all created things is equivalent to a theory of exemplary causality; it is not treated as such by Augustine, however.

In a very important sense, Augustine's geography of being reduces to a two-level system: all natures are either Creator or creature, eternal or temporal, immutable or mutable, and so on. Yet man's soul must be fitted in between, as we have seen; it requires an intermediate sort of nature for its initial location.

All natures, from top to bottom, are good in themselves. Bodies are inferior to souls and infinitely below the divine —yet there is no suggestion in Augustinianism that corporeal things, or matter, are evil. Augustine saw evil as a real occurrence but not as a nature. Each instance of evil is like a wound in being, a lack or privation of some perfection that is expected to be present but is not. This privative explanation of evil should not be misunderstood. Augustine is not saying that evil is nothing, a mere negation, or an unreal abstraction. Few men have been more aware of the terrible importance of evil, both moral and physical. Reacting to

Manicheism which tried to assign a positive nature to evil, Augustine stressed the idea that evil is a hole or gap in nature, in order, or in goodness. Like any hole, it is there and one can fall into it and hurt oneself—but there is no stuff that holes are made of, nor are there evil natures.

CREATOR, HUMAN SOUL, BODY*

Now every creature of God is good [1 Tim. 4:4]
2.18. and every man, in so far as he is a man, is a creature—but not by virtue of the fact that he is a sinner. So, God is the Creator of both human body and soul. Neither of these is evil, nor does God hate either of them: for He hates none of the things that He has made. But the conscious soul (*animus*) is better than the body; while God, the Maker and Founder of both, is still more excellent and He hates nothing in man except sin. Sin for man is a disorder and perversion: that is, a turning away (*aversio*) from the most worthy Creator and a turning toward (*conversio*) the inferior things that He has created.

NATURES ON THREE LEVELS†

As I know you well, I ask you to accept and ponder
2. the following brief sentences on a great theme. There is a nature which is susceptible of change with respect to both place and time, namely, the corporeal. There is another nature which is in no way susceptible of change with respect to place, but only with respect to time, namely, the spiritual. And there is a third Nature which can be changed neither in respect to place nor in respect to time: that is, God. Those natures of which I have said that they are mutable in some respect are called creatures; the Nature which is immutable is called Creator. Seeing, however, that we affirm the existence of anything only in so far as it continues and is one (in consequence of which, unity is the condition essential to beauty in every form), you cannot fail to distinguish, in this classification of natures, which exists in the highest possible manner, and which occupies the low-

* *Questions for Simplicianus,* I, 2.18; trans. V.J.B.
† *Letter* 18, to Coelestinus; trans. Dods.

est place, yet is within the range of existence, and which occupies the middle place, greater than the lowest, but coming short of the highest. That highest is essential blessedness; the lowest, that which cannot be either blessed or wretched; and the intermediate nature lives in wretchedness when it stoops towards that which is lowest, and in blessedness when it turns towards that which is highest. He who believes in Christ does not sink his affections in that which is lowest, is not proudly self-sufficient in that which is intermediate, and thus he is qualified for union and fellowship with that which is highest; and this is the sum of the active life to which we are commanded, admonished, and by holy zeal impelled to aspire.

SOUL, RULED BY GOD, RULES ITS BODY*

12. These operations are either used with the preceding passions of the body—such as when forms break in upon the light of our eyes, or sound flows into our ears, or fumes to the nose, tastes to the palate and to the rest of the body whatever solid and corporeal things are moved toward it from the outside. Or these operations occur when in the body itself something migrates or moves from one spot to another spot, or the whole body itself is moved by its own or another's weight.

13. These are the operations which the soul uses in the preceding feelings of the body, which please the soul agreeing with them, offend the soul resisting them. When, however, the soul suffers anything from these feelings, its own operations, it suffers from itself, not from the body. Plainly this happens when it adjusts itself to the body. Therefore, it is less with itself because the body is always less than the soul itself.

And therefore the soul, being turned from its Lord to its slave, necessarily weakens; and again, being turned from its slave to its Lord, necessarily progresses and gives to this same slave a most easy life and therefore a life very little toilsome and troublesome, to which no attention is forced on account of its great quiet. Thus there exists that disposition of

* On Music, VI, 5, 12-13; trans. Tafford P. Maher, S.J., The De Musica VI of St. Augustine, Translated and Philosophically Annotated (St. Louis University Master's Thesis, 1939), pp. 87-89. Used with permission.

the body which is called health. Here again it has no need of our intention, not because then the soul does nothing in the body, but because it does nothing more easily. Now in all of our works we work in so far more attentively as we work with more difficulty. This health, moreover, will be more firm and certain when, in its own time and order, the body will have been restored to its former stability. (a) And this resurrection of the body, before it is most fully understood, is wholesomely believed. For it is necessary that the soul be ruled by a Superior and rule the inferior. That Superior is God alone; that inferior is the body alone—if you look to all in the whole and entire soul. Therefore, as the entire soul cannot be without its Lord, so it cannot excel without its slave. But, as the Lord is greater than the soul, so the slave is less. And so, intent upon its Lord, the soul understands His eternal things, and then more fully *is*. The more also its slave *is,* in its kind, through the soul. However, on the other hand, neglecting the Lord, the soul, intent upon its carnal slave by which it is led into concupiscence, feels its movements which the slave offers to it and it *is* less: not so much less, however, than its slave is less, even when it most is in its proper nature. But through the fault of its mistress, the body is less than it was since the soul was greater before its fall.

SOUL: ABOVE THE SENSIBLE, BELOW GOD*

But in spite of all those who cling tenaciously to 3.3. the writings of these philosophers, I will say most confidently that, in these Christian times, no one can doubt what religion ought to be embraced most readily, or which is the sure path to truth and happiness. Suppose that Plato himself were alive and did not disdain my questions, or, better still, suppose that one of his disciples during his actual life had addressed him somewhat as follows: "You have persuaded me that truth cannot be perceived by bodily eyes, but by the intelligence alone; that every soul which clings to the truth becomes happy and complete; that nothing keeps us farther from the truth than a life given over to the pleasures of the flesh and a mind

* *The True Religion,* 3.3; trans. C.A. Hangartner, S.J., *De vera religione (Chapters 1-17)* (St. Louis University Master's Thesis, 1945), pp. 9, 11. Used with permission.

crowded with the deceiving impressions of sensible objects, impressions which arise from the sensible world, are transmitted by the body, and give rise to the most varied beliefs and errors. We must try, therefore, to achieve perfect mental health, that we may attain to the vision of the immutable pattern of things, to the beauty which is always constant with itself and everywhere the same, beauty never distorted by changes of place or time, but standing out one and the same under all circumstances, the beauty whose very existence men discredit, but which in fact has the most true, the highest form of existence. All other things are born, die, pass in constant flux, and slip away—yet, in so far as they exist, they have certainly been produced by that eternal God in accordance with His truth. It is given only to the rational and intelligent souls among all these creatures to enjoy the contemplation of his eternal nature, to be moved and adorned by it, and to be able to merit eternal life.

GOD, MUTABLE SPIRITS, AND BODIES*

1. The highest good, than which there is no higher, is God, and consequently He is unchangeable good, hence truly eternal and truly immortal. All other good things are only from Him, not of Him. For what is of Him, is Himself. And consequently if He alone is unchangeable, all things that He has made, because He has made them out of nothing, are changeable. For He is so omnipotent, that even out of nothing, that is out of what is absolutely nonexistent, He is able to make good things both great and small, both celestial and terrestrial, both spiritual and corporeal. But because He is also just, He has not put those things that He has made out of nothing on an equality with that which He begat out of Himself. Because, therefore, no good things whether great or small, through whatever gradations of things, can exist except from God; but since every nature, so far as it is nature, is good, it follows that no nature can exist save from the most high and true God: because all things even not in the highest degree good, but related to the highest good, and again, because all good things, even those of most recent origin, which are far from the highest good, can have their existence only from the highest good. Therefore every spirit, though subject to

* *The Nature of the Good,* 1-25; trans. Dods.

change, and every corporeal entity, is from God, and all this, having been made, is nature. For every nature is either spirit or body. Unchangeable spirit is God, changeable spirit, having been made, is nature, but is better than body; but body is not spirit, unless when the wind, because it is invisible to us and yet its power is felt as something not inconsiderable, is in a certain sense called spirit.

2.   But for the sake of those who, not being able to understand that all nature, that is, every spirit and every body, is naturally good, are moved by the iniquity of spirit and the mortality of body, and on this account endeavor to bring in another nature of wicked spirit and mortal body, which God did not make, we determine thus to bring to their understanding what we say can be brought. For they acknowledge that no good thing can exist save from the highest and true God, which also is true and suffices for correcting them, if they are willing to give heed.

3.   For we Catholic Christians worship God, from whom are all good things whether great or small; from whom is all measure great or small; from whom is all form great or small; from whom is all order great or small. For all things in proportion as they are better measured, formed, and ordered, are assuredly good in a higher degree; but in proportion as they are measured, formed, and ordered in an inferior degree, are they the less good. These three things, therefore, measure, form, and order— not to speak of innumerable other things that are shown to pertain to these three—these three things, therefore, measure, form, order, are as it were generic goods in things made by God, whether in spirit or in body. God is, therefore, above every measure of the creature, above every form, above every order, nor is He above by local spaces, but by ineffable and singular potency, from whom is every measure, every form, every order. These three things, where they are great, are great goods, where they are small, are small goods; where they are absent, there is no good. And again, where these things are great, there are great natures; where they are small, there are small natures; where they are absent, there is no nature. Therefore all nature is good.

4.   When accordingly it is inquired, whence is evil, it must first be inquired, what is evil, which is nothing else than corruption, either of the measure, or the form, or the order, that belong to nature. Nature therefore which has been corrupted is called evil, for assuredly when

incorrupt it is good; but even when corrupt, so far as it is nature it is good, so far as it is corrupted it is evil.

5. But it may happen, that a certain nature which has been ranked as more excellent by reason of natural measure and form, though corrupt, is even yet better than another incorrupt which has been ranked lower by reason of an inferior natural measure and form: as in the estimation of men, according to the quality which presents itself to view, corrupt gold is assuredly better than incorrupt silver, and corrupt silver than incorrupt lead; so also in more powerful spiritual natures a rational spirit even corrupted through an evil will is better than an irrational though incorrupt, and better is any spirit whatever even corrupt than any body whatever though incorrupt. For better is a nature which, when it is present in a body, furnishes it with life, than that to which life is furnished. But however corrupt may be the spirit of life that has been made, it can furnish life to a body, and hence, though corrupt, it is better than the body though incorrupt.

6. But if corruption take away all measure, all form, all order from corruptible things, no nature will remain. And consequently every nature which cannot be corrupted is the highest good, as is God. But every nature that can be corrupted is also itself some good; for corruption cannot injure it, except by taking away from or diminishing that which is good.

7. But to the most excellent creatures, that is, to rational spirits, God has offered this, that if they will not they cannot be corrupted; that is, if they should maintain obedience under the Lord their God, so should they adhere to his incorruptible beauty; but if they do not will to maintain obedience, since willingly they are corrupted in sins, unwillingly they shall be corrupted in punishment, since God is such a good that it is well for no one who deserts Him, and among the things made by God the rational nature is so great a good, that there is no good by which it may be blessed except God. Sinners, therefore, are ordained to punishment; which ordination is punishment for the reason that it is not conformable to their nature, but it is justice because it is conformable to their fault.

8. But the rest of things that are made of nothing, which are assuredly inferior to the rational soul, can be neither blessed nor miserable. But because in pro-

portion to their fashion and appearance are things themselves good, nor could there be good things in a less or the least degree except from God, they are so ordered that the more infirm yield to the firmer, the weaker to the stronger, the more impotent to the more powerful; and so earthly things harmonize with celestial, as being subject to the things that are preeminent. But to things falling away, and succeeding, a certain temporal beauty in its kind belongs, so that neither those things that die, or cease to be what they were, degrade or disturb the fashion and appearance and order of the universal creation: as a speech well composed is assuredly beautiful, although in it all syllables and sounds rush past as it were in being born and in dying.

9. What sort of punishment, and how great, is due to each fault, belongs to Divine judgment, not to human; which punishment assuredly when it is remitted in the case of the converted, there is great goodness on the part of God; and when it is deservedly inflicted, there is no injustice on the part of God; because nature is better ordered by justly smarting under punishment, than by rejoicing with impunity in sin; which nature nevertheless, even thus having some measure, form, and order, in whatever extremity there is as yet some good, which things, if they were absolutely taken away, and utterly consumed, there will be accordingly no good, because no nature will remain.

10. All corruptible natures therefore are natures at all only so far as they are *from* God, nor would they be corruptible if they were *of* Him; because they would be what He himself is. Therefore of whatever measure, of whatever form, of whatever order, they are, they are so because it is God by whom they were made; but they are not immutable, because it is nothing of which they were made. For it is sacrilegious audacity to make nothing and God equal, as when we wish to make what has been born of God such as what has been made by Him out of nothing.

11. Wherefore neither can God's nature suffer harm, nor can any nature under God suffer harm unjustly: for when by sinning unjustly some do harm, an unjust will is imputed to them; but the power by which they are permitted to do harm is from God alone, who knows, while they themselves are ignorant, what they ought to suffer, whom He permits them to harm.

12. All these things are so perspicuous, so assured, that if they who introduce another nature which God did not make, were willing to give attention, they would not be filled with so great blasphemies, as that they should place so great good things in supreme evil, and so great evil things in God. For what the truth compels them to acknowledge, namely, that all good things are from God alone, suffices for their correction, if they were willing to give heed, as I said above. Not, therefore, are great good things from one, and small good things from another; but good things great and small are from the supremely good alone, which is God.

13. Let us, therefore, bring before our minds good things however great, which it is fitting that we attribute to God as their author, and these having been eliminated let us see whether any nature will remain. All life both great and small, all power great and small, all safety great and small, all memory great and small, all virtue great and small, all intellect great and small, all tranquillity great and small, all plenty great and small, all sensation great and small, all light great and small, all suavity great and small, all measure great and small, all beauty great and small, all peace great and small, and whatever other like things may occur, especially such as are found throughout all things, whether spiritual or corporeal, every measure, every form, every order both great and small, are from the Lord God. All which good things whoever should wish to abuse, pays the penalty by divine judgment; but where none of these things shall have been present at all, no nature will remain.

14. But in all these things, whatever are small are called by contrary names in comparison with greater things; as in the form of a man because the beauty is greater, the beauty of the ape in comparison with it is called deformity. And the imprudent are deceived, as if the former is good, and the latter evil, nor do they regard in the body of the ape its own fashion, the equality of members on both sides, the agreement of parts, the protection of safety, and other things which it would be tedious to enumerate.

15. But that what we have said may be understood, and may satisfy those too slow of comprehension, or that even the pertinacious and those repugnant to the most manifest truth may be compelled to confess what is true, let them be asked, whether corruption can harm the body of an ape? But if it can, so that it may become more hideous, what diminishes but the good of beauty? Whence as long as the nature of the body subsists, so long something will remain. If, accordingly, good having been consumed, nature is consumed, the nature is therefore good. So also we say that slow is contrary to swift, but yet he who does not move at all cannot even be called slow. So we say that a heavy voice is contrary to a sharp voice, or a harsh to a musical; but if you completely remove any kind of voice, there is silence where there is no voice, which silence, nevertheless, for the simple reason that there is no voice, is usually opposed to voice as something contrary thereto. So also lucid and obscure are called as it were two contrary things, yet even obscure things have something of light, which being absolutely wanting, darkness is the absence of light in the same way in which silence is the absence of voice.

Yet even these privations of things are so ordered in 16. the universe of nature, that to those wisely considering they not unfittingly have their vicissitudes. For by not illuminating certain places and times, God has also made the darkness as fittingly as the day. For if we by restraining the voice fittingly interpose silence in speaking, how much more does He, as the perfect framer of all things, fittingly make privations of things? Whence also in the hymn of the three children, light and darkness alike praise God, [Dan. 3:72] that is, bring forth praise in the hearts of those who well consider.

No nature, therefore, as far as it is nature, is evil; 17. but to each nature there is no evil except to be diminished in respect of good. But if by being diminished it should be consumed so that there is no good, no nature would be left; not only such as the Manicheans introduce, where so great good things are found that their exceeding blindness is wonderful, but such as anyone can introduce.

For neither is that material, which the ancients called 18. Hyle, to be called an evil. I do not say that which Manicheus with most senseless vanity, not knowing what he says, denominates Hyle, namely, the former of corporeal beings; whence it is rightly said to him, that he introduces another god. For nobody can form and create corporeal beings but God alone; for neither are they created unless there subsist with them measure, form, and order, which I think that now even they themselves confess to be good things,

and things that cannot be except from God. But by *Hyle*
I mean a certain material absolutely formless and without
quality, whence those qualities that we perceive are formed,
as the ancients said. For hence also wood is called in Greek
hyle, because it is adapted to workmen, not that itself may
make anything, but that it is the material of which something may be made. Nor is that *Hyle,* therefore, to be called
an evil which cannot be perceived through any appearance,
but can scarcely be thought of through any sort of privation
of appearance. For this has also a capacity of forms; for if it
cannot receive the form imposed by the workman, neither
assuredly may it be called material. Hence if form is some
good, whence those who excel in it are called beautiful,
(*forma-formosus*) as from appearance they are called handsome, (*species-speciosus*) even the capacity of form is undoubtedly something good. As because wisdom is a good,
no one doubts that to be capable of wisdom is a good.
And because every good is from God, no one ought to
doubt that even matter, if there is any, has its existence from
God alone.

19. Magnificently and divinely, therefore, our God said
to his servant: "I am that I am," and "Thou shalt
say to the children of Israel, He who is sent me to
you." [Exod. 3:14] For He truly is because He is unchangeable. For every change makes what was not, to be: therefore
He truly is, who is unchangeable; but all other things that
were made by Him have received being from Him each in
its own measure. To Him who is highest, therefore, nothing can be contrary, save what is not; and consequently as
from Him everything that is good has its being, so from Him
is everything that by nature exists; since everything that exists by nature is good. Thus every nature is good, and everything good is from God; therefore every nature is from God.

20. But pain, which some suppose to be in an especial
manner an evil, whether it be in mind or in body,
cannot exist except in good natures. For the very
fact of resistance in any being leading to pain, involves a
refusal not to be what it was, because it was something good;
but when a being is compelled to something better, the
pain is useful, when to something worse, it is useless. Therefore in the case of the mind, the will resisting a greater power
causes pain; in the case of the body, sensation resisting a
more powerful body causes pain. But evils without pain
are worse: for it is worse to rejoice in iniquity than to be-

wail corruption; yet even such rejoicing cannot exist save from the attainment of inferior good things. But iniquity is the desertion of better things. Likewise in a body, a wound with pain is better than painless putrescence, which is especially called the corruption which the dead flesh of the Lord did not see, that is, did not suffer, as was predicted in prophecy: "Thou shalt not suffer Thy Holy one to see corruption." [Ps. 15:10] For who denies that He was wounded by the piercing of the nails, and that He was stabbed with the lance? [John 19:18, 34] But even what is properly called by men corporeal corruption, that is, putrescence itself, if as yet there is anything left to consume, increases by the diminution of the good. But if corruption shall have absolutely consumed it, so that there is no good, no nature will remain, for there will be nothing that corruption may corrupt; and so there will not even be putrescence, for there will be nowhere at all for it to be.

21. Therefore now by common usage things small and mean are said to have measure, because some measure remains in them, without which they would no longer be moderate-sized, but would not exist at all. But those things that by reason of too much progress are called immoderate, are blamed for very excessiveness; but yet it is necessary that those things themselves be restrained in some manner under God who has disposed all things in extension, number, and weight. [Wisd. 11:21]

22. But God cannot be said to have measure, lest He should seem to be spoken of as limited. Yet He is not immoderate by whom measure is bestowed upon all things, so that they may in any measure exist. Nor again ought God to be called measured, as if He received measure from anyone. But if we say that He is the highest measure, by chance we say something, if indeed in speaking of the highest measure we mean the highest good. For every measure in so far as it is a measure is good; whence nothing can be called measured, modest, modified, without praise, although in another sense we use *measure* for *limit,* and speak of no *measure* where there is no *limit,* which is sometimes said with praise as when it is said: "And of His kingdom there shall be no limit." For it might also be said, "There shall be no measure," so that measure might be used in the sense of limit; for He who reigns in no measure, assuredly does not reign at all.

23. Therefore a bad measure, a bad form, a bad order, are either so called because they are less than they should be, or because they are not adapted to those things to which they should be adapted, so that they may be called bad as being alien and incongruous; as if anyone should be said not to have done in a good measure because he has done less than he ought, or because he has done in such a thing as he ought not to have done, or more than was fitting, or not conveniently; so that the very fact of that being reprehended which is done in a bad measure, is justly reprehended for no other cause than that the measure is not there maintained. Likewise a form is called bad either in comparison with something more handsome or more beautiful, this form being less, that greater, not in size but in comeliness; or because it is out of harmony with the thing to which it is applied, so that it seems alien and unsuitable. As if a man should walk forth into a public place naked, which nakedness does not offend if seen in a bath. Likewise also order is called bad when order itself is maintained in an inferior degree. Hence not order, but rather disorder, is bad; since either the ordering is less than it should be, or not as it should be. Yet where there is any measure, any form, any order, there is some good and some nature; but where there is no measure, no form, no order, there is no good, no nature.

24. Those things which our faith holds and which reason in whatever way has traced out, are fortified by the testimonies of the divine Scriptures, so that those who by reason of feebler intellect are not able to comprehend these things, may believe the divine authority, and so may deserve to know. But let not those who understand, but are less instructed in ecclesiastical literature, suppose that we set forth these things from our own intellect rather than what are in those Books. Accordingly, that God is unchangeable is written in the *Psalms:* "Thou shalt change them and they shall be changed; but Thou thyself art the same." [Ps. 101:27] And in the *Book of Wisdom,* concerning wisdom: "Remaining in herself, she renews all things." [Wisd. 7:27] Whence also the Apostle Paul: "To the invisible, incorruptible, only God." [1 Tim 1:17] And the Apostle James: "Every best giving and every perfect gift is from above, descending from the Father of light, with whom there is no changeableness, neither obscuring of influence." [Jas. 1:17]

Likewise because what He begat of Himself is what He Himself is, it is said in brief by the Son Himself: "I and the Father are one." [John 10:30] But because the Son was not made, since through Him were all things made, thus it is written: "In the beginning was the Word, and the Word was with God, and God was the Word; this was in the beginning with God. All things were made through Him, and without Him was made nothing"; [John 1:1-3] that is, without Him was not anything made.

25. For no attention should be paid to the ravings of men who think that *nothing* should be understood to mean *something,* and moreover think to compel anyone to vanity of this kind on the ground that *nothing* is placed at the end of the sentence. Therefore, they say, it was made, and because it was made, nothing is itself something. They have lost their senses by zeal in contradicting, and do not understand that it makes no difference whether it be said: "Without Him was made nothing," or "without Him nothing was made." For even if the order were the last mentioned, they could nevertheless say, that nothing is itself something because it was made. For in the case of what is in truth something, what difference does it make if it be said "Without him a house was made," so long as it is understood that something was made without him, which something is a house? So also because it is said: "Without Him was made nothing," since nothing is assuredly not anything, when it is truly and properly spoken, it makes no difference whether it be said: "Without Him was made nothing," or "Without Him nothing was made," or "Nothing was made." But who cares to speak with men who can say of this very expression of mine "It makes no difference," "Therefore it makes some difference, for nothing itself is something"? But those whose brains are not addled see it as a thing most manifest that this something is to be understood when it says "It makes no difference," as when I say "It matters in no respect." But these, if they should say to anyone, "What hast thou done?" and he should reply that he has done nothing, would, according to this mode of disputation, falsely accuse him saying, "Thou hast done something, therefore, because thou hast done nothing; for nothing is itself something." But they have also the Lord Himself placing this word at the end of a sentence, when He says: "And in secret have I spoken nothing." [John 18:20] Let them read, therefore, and be silent.

DIVINE, PSYCHIC, AND BODILY NATURE*

5. Let these two theologies, then, the fabulous and the civil, give place to the Platonic philosophers, who have recognized the true God as the author of all things, the source of the light of truth, and the bountiful bestower of all blessedness. And not these only, but to these great acknowledgers of so great a God, those philosophers must yield who, having their mind enslaved to their body, supposed the principles of all things to be material; as Thales, who held that the first principle of all things was water; Anaximenes, that it was air; the Stoics, that it was fire; Epicurus, who affirmed that it consisted of atoms, that is to say, of minute corpuscules; and many others whom it is needless to enumerate, but who believed that bodies, simple or compound, animate or inanimate, but nevertheless bodies, were the cause and principle of all things. For some of them—as, for instance, the Epicureans—believed that living things could originate from things without life; others held that all things living or without life spring from a living principle, but that, nevertheless, all things, being material, spring from a material principle. For the Stoics thought that fire, that is, one of the four material elements of which this visible world is composed, was both living and intelligent, the maker of the world and of all things contained in it— that it was in fact God. These and others like them have only been able to suppose that which their hearts enslaved to sense have vainly suggested to them. And yet they have within themselves something which they could not see: they represented to themselves inwardly things which they had seen without, even when they were not seeing them, but only thinking of them. But this representation in thought is no longer a body, but only the similitude of a body; and that faculty of the mind by which this similitude of a body is seen is neither a body nor the similitude of a body; and the faculty which judges whether the representation is beautiful or ugly is without doubt superior to the object judged of. This principle is the understanding of man, the rational soul; and it is certainly not a body, since that similitude of a body which it beholds and judges of is itself not a body. The soul is neither earth, nor water, nor air, nor fire, of which

* *City of God,* VIII, 5-6; trans. Dods.

58

four bodies, called the four elements, we see that this world is composed. And if the soul is not a body, how should God, its Creator, be a body? Let all those philosophers, then, give place, as we have said, to the Platonists, and those also who have been ashamed to say that God is a body, but yet have thought that our souls are of the same nature as God. They have not been staggered by the great changeableness of the soul—an attribute which it would be impious to ascribe to the divine nature—but they say it is the body which changes the soul, for in itself it is unchangeable. As well might they say, "Flesh is wounded by some body, for in itself it is invulnerable." In a word, that which is unchangeable can be changed by nothing, so that that which can be changed by the body cannot properly be said to be immutable.

6. These philosophers, then, whom we see not undeservedly exalted above the rest in fame and glory, have seen that no material body is God, and therefore they have transcended all bodies in seeking for God. They have seen that whatever is changeable is not the most high God, and therefore they have transcended every soul and all changeable spirits in seeking the supreme. They have seen also that, in every changeable thing, the form which makes it that which it is, whatever be its mode or nature, can only *be* through Him who truly *is*, because He is unchangeable. And therefore, whether we consider the whole body of the world, its figure, qualities, and orderly movement, and also all the bodies which are in it; or whether we consider all life, either that which nourishes and maintains, as the life of trees, or that which, besides this, has also sensation, as the life of beasts; or that which adds to all these intelligence, as the life of man; or that which does not need the support of nutriment, but only maintains, feels, understands, as the life of angels—all can only *be* through Him who absolutely *is*. For to Him it is not one thing to *be,* and another to live, as though He could *be,* not living; nor is it to Him one thing to live, and another thing to understand, as though He could live, not understanding; nor is it to Him one thing to understand, another thing to be blessed, as though He could understand and not be blessed. But to Him to live, to understand, to be blessed, are to *be.* They have understood, from this unchangeableness and this simplicity, that all things must have been made by Him, and that He could Himself have been made by none. For

they have considered that whatever *is* is either body or life, and that life is something better than body, and that the nature of body is sensible, and that of life intelligible. Therefore they have preferred the intelligible nature to the sensible. We mean by sensible things such things as can be perceived by the sight and touch of the body; by intelligible things, such as can be understood by the sight of the mind. For there is no corporeal beauty, whether in the condition of a body, as figure, or in its movement, as in music, of which it is not the mind that judges. But this could never have been, had there not existed in the mind itself a superior form of these things, without bulk, without noise of voice, without space and time. But even in respect of these things, had the mind not been mutable, it would not have been possible for one to judge better than another with regard to sensible forms. He who is clever, judges better than he who is slow, he who is skilled than he who is unskillful, he who is practiced than he who is unpracticed; and the same person judges better after he has gained experience than he did before. But that which is capable of more and less is mutable; whence able men, who have thought deeply on these things, have gathered that the first form is not to be found in those things whose form is changeable. Since, therefore, they saw that body and mind might be more or less beautiful in form, and that, if they wanted form, they could have no existence, they saw that there is some existence in which is the first form, unchangeable, and therefore not admitting of degrees of comparison, and in that they most rightly believed was the first principle of things which was not made, and by which all things were made. Therefore that which is known of God He manifested to them when His invisible things were seen by them, being understood by those things which have been made; also His eternal power and Godhead by whom all visible and temporal things have been created. [Rom. 1:19-20] We have said enough upon that part of theology which they call physical, that is, natural.

CAUSALITY: DIVINE, PSYSHIC, AND BODILY*

9.
... But it does not follow that, though there is for God a certain order of all causes, there must therefore be nothing depending on the free exercise of our

* *City of God,* V, 9; trans. Dods.

own wills, for our wills themselves are included in that order of causes which is certain to God, and is embraced by His foreknowledge, for human wills are also causes of human actions; and He who foreknew all the causes of things would certainly among those causes not have been ignorant of our wills. For even that very concession which Cicero himself makes is enough to refute him in this argument. For what does it help him to say that nothing takes place without a cause, but that every cause is not fatal, there being a fortuitous cause, a natural cause, and a voluntary cause? It is sufficient that he confesses that whatever happens must be preceded by a cause. For we say that those causes which are called fortuitous are not a mere name for the absence of causes, but are only latent, and we attribute them either to the will of the true God, or to that of spirits of some kind or other. And as to natural causes, we by no means separate them from the will of Him who is the author and framer of all nature. But now as to voluntary causes. They are referable either to God, or to angels, or to men, or to animals of whatever description, if indeed those instinctive movements of animals devoid of reason, by which, in accordance with their own nature, they seek or shun various things, are to be called wills. And when I speak of the wills of angels, I mean either the wills of good angels, whom we call the angels of God, or of the wicked angels, whom we call the angels of the Devil or demons. Also by the wills of men I mean the wills either of the good or of the wicked. And from this we conclude that there are no efficient causes of all things which come to pass unless voluntary causes, that is, such as belong to that nature which is the spirit of life. For the air or wind is called spirit, but, inasmuch as it is a body, it is not the spirit of life. The spirit of life, therefore, which quickens all things, and is the creator of everybody, and of every created spirit, is God Himself, the uncreated spirit. In His supreme will resides the power which acts on the wills of all created spirits, helping the good, judging the evil, controlling all, granting power to some, not granting it to others. For, as He is the creator of all natures, so also is He the bestower of all powers, not of all wills; for wicked wills are not from Him, being contrary to nature, which is from Him. As to bodies, they are more subject to wills: some to our wills, by which I mean the wills of all living mortal creatures, but more to the wills of men than of beasts. But all of them are most of all subject to the will of God, to whom all wills also are subject, since they have no power except what He has bestowed upon them. The cause of things, therefore, which makes but is not made, is God; but all other causes both make and are made. Such are all created spirits, and especially the rational. Material causes, therefore, which may rather be said to be made than to make, are not to be reckoned among efficient causes, because they can only do what the wills of spirits do by them.

DIVINE IDEAS AS PROTOTYPES*

46.1.   Plato is known as the first to have named the Ideas. Not that if this name were nonexistent before he established it, the things that he called Ideas would not have existed, or would not have been understood by anyone—but they were probably called by different names by different people. It is permitted to give to any known thing that lacks an accepted name, whatever name one wishes. . . . But enough has previously been said about the name; let us examine the thing which is principally to be considered and understood, leaving each person free, as far as the terms are concerned, to give whatever name he wishes to the object of his knowledge.

2.   So, in Latin we may call Ideas forms or species, to make it clear that we are translating word for word. But, if we call them "reasons," we are departing somewhat from a strict translation; reasons are called *logoi* in Greek and not Ideas. However, if a person chose to use this term, he would not be far from the real meaning. In fact, Ideas are the primary forms, or the permanent and immutable reasons of real things, and they are not themselves formed; so they are, as a consequence, eternal and ever the same in themselves, and they are contained in the divine intelligence. And since they never come into being or go out of it, everything that can come into being and go out of it, and everything that does come into being and goes out of it, may be said to be formed in accord with them.

It is denied that the soul can look upon them, unless it be rational, in that part whereby it excels, that is, in its mind and reason, as it were in its face or interior and intellectual eye. And for this vision not everyone is suitable but only that rational soul which is holy and pure, that one

* *Eighty-three Different Questions,* q. 46, 1-2; trans. V.J.B.

which keeps the eye in which such objects are seen, healthy, clear, serene and like unto those objects to which its view is directed. What religious man, infused with the true religion, even though not yet able to contemplate these objects, would nevertheless dare to deny and even refuse to confess that all things that are—that is, whatsoever things are constituted with a nature of their own in their proper kinds— were created by God as their source, so that they might exist? And that all living things are alive by virtue of the same source? And that the whole of things is preserved, and the very order in which they change, as they manifest their temporal courses according to a definite pattern, is maintained and governed, by the laws of the highest God? When this is established and admitted, who will dare to say that God established all things in an irrational manner? Now if this cannot be said or accepted in any proper sense, the conclusion remains that all things were founded by means of reason. Not that a man is based on the same reason as a horse; this would be an absurd notion. So, each one of these is created in accord with its own reason. Now, where would we think that these reasons are, if not in the mind of the Creator? For He did not look to anything placed outside Himself as a model for the construction of what he created; to think that He did would be irreligious.

Now, if these reasons for all things to be created, or already created, are contained in the divine mind, and if there can be nothing in the divine mind unless it be eternal and immutable, and if Plato called these primary reasons of things Ideas—then not only do Ideas exist but they are true because they are eternal and they endure immutably in this way; and it is by participation in these that whatever exists is produced, however its way of existing may be.

GOD SET SPIRITUAL CREATION ABOVE THE CORPOREAL*

Living, then, in immutable eternity, He has created 20.39. all things together, and from them periods of time flow, places are filled, and the centuries unroll in the temporal and local motions of real things. Among these things, He has established some as spiritual and others as corporeal, giving form to the matter that He Himself created without

* *Literal Commentary on Genesis,* VIII, 20.39; 25.46; 26.48; trans. V.J.B.

form but capable of being formed—matter which was made by no other being but which did have a Maker. This matter preceded its formation, not in time but in its origin. Now, He set the spiritual creature above the corporeal one, because the spiritual could be moved only through time, while the corporeal was movable through both time and place. For example, the mind is moved through time when it recalls what had been forgotten, or learns what it did not know, or wills what it had rejected—but the body is moved through place, either from earth to sky, from sky to earth, from west to east, or in any other similar way. Now, it is impossible for anything that moves through place to avoid being moved, by the same fact, through time; however, not everything that moves through time must also be moved through place.

So, just as the substance that is moved only through time takes precedence over the substance that is moved through both time and place, so does that substance which is moved neither in place nor in time take precedence even over it. As a result, just as a body moves through time and place, while the motion of a created spirit is only through time—so, He moves the created spirit through time but the Creator Spirit moves neither through time nor through place. However, the created spirit moves itself through time and its body through time and place; while the Creator Spirit moves Himself apart from time and place, and the created spirit through time apart from place, but body through time and place. . . .

25.46. So, the nature of the whole corporeal universe is not helped in a corporeal way by anything extrinsic to it. The reason for this is that outside it no body exists; if there were, it would not include the whole of bodies. From within, however, it is assisted incorporeally; for God moves it in such a way that it remains entirely natural (since all things are from Him, through Him, and in Him). Yet the parts of this universe are helped both intrinsically, in an incorporeal way (or rather, they are made so that they may exist as natures, and they were extrinsically helped, in a corporeal way, so that they may become better; thus the provision of food, agriculture, medicine and even the decorative arts, is made not simply for protection and greater growth but also so that man may live more decently. . . .

26.48. With these points established, [it is evident that] God, the omnipotent and all-supporting, Who is unmoved in time or place and ever the same in the

immutability of eternity, truth, and will, moves spiritual creation in the course of time, and also moves corporeal creation through both time and place.

EVIL: THE PRIVATION OF THE GOOD*

10.   By the Trinity, thus supremely and equally and unchangeably good, all things were created; and these
are not supremely and equally and unchangeably
good, but yet they are good, even taken separately. Taken as
a whole, however, they are very good, because their ensemble
constitutes the universe in all its wonderful order and beauty.

11.   And in the universe, even that which is called evil,
when it is regulated and put in its own place, only en-
hances our admiration of the good; for we enjoy and
value the good more when we compare it with the evil. For
the Almighty God, who, as even the heathen acknowledge,
has supreme power over all things, being Himself supremely
good, would never permit the existence of anything evil
among His works, if He were not so omnipotent and good
that He can bring good even out of evil. For what is that
which we call evil but the absence of good? In the bodies of
animals, disease and wounds mean nothing but the absence
of health; for when a cure is effected, that does not mean
that the evils which were present—namely, the diseases
and wounds—go away from the body and dwell elsewhere:
they altogether cease to exist; for the wound or disease is
not a substance, but a defect in the fleshly substance—the
flesh itself being a substance, and therefore something good,
of which those evils—that is, privations of the good which
we call health—are accidents. Just in the same way, what are
called vices in the soul are nothing but privations of natural
good. And when they are not transferred elsewhere: when
they cease to exist in the healthy soul, they cannot exist anywhere else.

12.   All things that exist, therefore, seeing that the Creator of them all is supremely good, are themselves
good. But because they are not, like their Creator,
supremely and unchangeably good, their good may be diminished and increased. But for good to be diminished is an evil,
although, however much it may be diminished, it is neces-

* *Enchiridion,* 10-12; trans. Dods.

sary, if the being is to continue, that some good should remain to constitute the being. For however small or of whatever kind the being may be, the good which makes it a being cannot be destroyed without destroying the being itself. An uncorrupted nature is justly held in esteem. But if, still further, it be incorruptible, it is undoubtedly considered of still higher value. When it is corrupted, however, its corruption is an evil, because it is deprived of some sort of good. For if it be deprived of no good, it receives no injury; but it does receive injury, therefore it is deprived of good. Therefore, so long as a being is in process of corruption, there is in it some good of which it is being deprived; and if a part of the being should remain which cannot be corrupted, this will certainly be an incorruptible being, and accordingly the process of corruption will result in the manifestation of this great good. But if it do not cease to be corrupted, neither can it cease to possess good of which corruption may deprive it. But if it should be thoroughly and completely consumed by corruption, there will then be no good left, because there will be no being. Wherefore corruption can consume the good only by consuming the being. Every being, therefore, is a good; a great good, if it can not be corrupted; a little good, if it can: but in any case, only the foolish or ignorant will deny that it is a good. And if it be wholly consumed by corruption, then the corruption itself must cease to exist, as there is no being left in which it can dwell.

IV. MAN'S SOUL

It could be argued that Augustine's greatness as a thinker rests as much on his psychology as on any other facet of his thought. Oddly, his approach to the study of man and his soul is very empirical. Like a modern psychologist or phenomenologist, Augustine usually starts with some concrete fact or event in man's conscious life, describes it, and then asks himself what it means. His remarkable analysis of auditory sensation in the sixth Book *On Music* deserves to be better known. It begins with the experience of hearing a spoken line of poetry and proceeds to a mathematical interpretation of the various stages in this psychological event. I know of no other such description of an auditory sensation in the history of philosophy or psychology. Nearly all similar studies have concentrated on visual or tactile experience.

Augustine's interest in human consciousness stemmed, of course, from his mature conviction that incorporeal activity is much more important than corporeal events. As a very young man, he had found it impossible to think what a spiritual substance might be. The seventh Book of the *Confessions* tells how he first conceived God as a huge, amorphous mass—like a giant sponge extending throughout the world and beyond it. Platonic philosophy showed him how to think of a real but incorporeal substance, in terms of the dynamic source of activities rather than of that which occupies space. From this point onward, Augustine was convinced that immaterial natures are better than, and more real than, bodies. It is in terms of this background that we should approach his statement (*On the Moral Behavior of the Catholic Church*, I, 27, 52) that man is "a soul using a body" (*anima utens corpore*). In much the same context, he defined the human soul as "a rational substance designed to rule the body" (*Magnitude of the Soul*, 13, 22). Later, more mature writings (such as *The Trinity*) will put more stress on the unity of man as a whole, but there is always the impression that he

67

thought of man's soul and body as two substances loosely bound together. Even his last works contrast the basic nature of soul and body. A body is always something extended in three dimensions (*The Soul and Its Origin,* IV, 21, 35), while soul is by definition, it would seem, unextended.

Functionally, Augustine distinguishes (in the first selection that follows) various degrees of actuality in the existence of the soul. *To be, to live, to sense,* and *to understand* form a graded series of more and more noble acts. Even within the area of sense perception, he sets internal sensing above the external function and discusses the ranking of the various external sense functions.

Out of the analysis of hearing (already mentioned) arises a famous general definition of sensation as "a modification of the body which does not, of itself, escape the soul" (*passio corporis per seipsam non latens animam;* see *On the Magnitude of the Soul,* 25, 48, and our second selection in this chapter). This means that sense perception is an action of the soul through the body, and in no way a production of anything in consciousness from the activity of bodily things. Briefly, his theory is a one-way interactionism: soul can move body, but no body can produce any modification in any soul. This is one of the few instances of a purely active theory of sensation in Western philosophy.

Augustine's is not a faculty psychology; there are no distinct operative powers in the Augustinian soul. Unfortunately, many scholars have failed to grasp this, particularly those trained in the traditions of Thomism. When Augustine describes the functions of man's soul in terms of memory, understanding, and will (*memoria, intelligentia, voluntas*), he is not at all thinking of different powers. Rather, as he clearly states in our third selection of this chapter, the whole soul is memory, the whole soul is intelligence, and the whole soul is will. This is a trinitarian psychology in which the diversity of functions of remembering, knowing, and willing does not entail any real difference within the nature of the soul. For those familiar with Aristotelian or Scholastic philosophy, the point may be put as follows: Augustine pays little attention to the theory of substance and its accidents; he takes it that the activities of the soul stem directly from its own nature, without any accidental potencies intervening. This is what makes Augustine's psychology an ideal base for his meditations on the divine Trinity.

His ability as a describer of the inner aspects of human consciousness is nowhere more obvious than in the noted passage on memory and its contents, printed here from the *Confessions*. Existentalists and phenomenologists now stress the close examination of the immediate data of consciousness; this has become the favorite starting point for these schools of contemporary philosophy. Augustine's descriptive interiorism is a recognized anticipation of this trend.

Finally, a word should be said on the three types of "vision" represented in our last selection of this chapter, from the *Literal Commentary on Genesis*. The lowest kind is the seeing of bodies through the medium of corporeal light and by means of the eyes of the body: it is the soul that is seeing, but he calls it *corporeal* vision. The second type of vision is accomplished by the soul viewing images of bodily things: this is *spiritual* vision (named from a special meaning of "spirit" which Augustine explains in our selection). Cogitation is the name given to the activity of thinking on this second, imaginative level. On the highest plane of vision, the soul sees intelligible truths without the help of any images: this is *intellectual* vision. In effect, Augustine is claiming that man is capable of imageless thought. The higher visions do not depend on the inferior ones: we do not have here any suggestion that the meanings seen by intellectual vision are "abstracted" from prior or concomitant sensations. On the contrary, intellectual cognition comes from above the soul, not from things below it. It should be added that the soul as will (that is, as active) functions on all three levels of vision. One's attention must be turned to the objects appropriate to each level: this directing of the gaze of the soul is accomplished by volitional effort. I see or hear because I wish to do so. Augustine does not separate cognition, feeling, desiring, loving, and so on, as many other psychologists do. These functions are fused in the unity of human psychic experience.

EXISTENCE, LIFE, SENSE, AND REASON*

7. Let us then pursue the following order of inquiry: first, how is it manifest that God is; next, whether goods, whatsoever their kind or degree, are from Him; finally, whether free will is to be accounted a good.

* *On Free Choice*, II, 3, 7-8, 10; trans. C.M. Sparrow, *St. Augustine on Free Will* (Charlottesville, University of Virginia Studies, 1947), pp. 38-43. Used with permission.

When we have answered these it will be clear enough, I think, whether free will was rightly given to man. Wherefore, in order that we may take our start from the most obvious things, I ask you whether you yourself exist, or whether you think you may be under an illusion as to that; although surely if you did not exist you could not possibly have an illusion.

E. Go on rather to other matters.

A. It is evident, then, that you exist; and since that could not be evident unless you were living, it is also evident that you live. Do you understand that these two things are very true?

E. I understand thoroughly.

A. Therefore this third thing is evident: you understand.

E. It is evident.

A. Which of these three do you think is most excellent?

E. Understanding.

A. Why do you think so?

E. Because while there are three things: to exist, to live, to understand; even a stone exists, and a beast lives, yet I do not think that a stone lives, or that a beast understands. But he who understands assuredly both exists and lives; wherefore I do not hesitate to judge that one more excellent in which all three are present, than that in which two or one are lacking. For though what lives certainly also exists, it does not follow that it also understands: of such sort, I judge, is the life of a beast. If something exists, moreover, it by no means follows that it lives and understands; for I may acknowledge that a corpse exists, but no one would say that it lives. But if the thing does not live, much less does it understand.

A. We see then that of these three, two are wanting to the corpse, one to the beast, and none to man.

E. True.

A. We also hold to be most excellent of the three which man has with the two others; namely, understanding, whose possession implies both existence and life.

E. Surely.

8. *A.* Tell me now, whether you know that you have those everyday bodily senses: seeing and hearing, and smelling, and tasting, and touching?

E. I do.

A. What do you think pertains to the sense of sight; I mean what do you think we perceive by sight?

E. Anything corporeal.

A. Do you think we also perceive hardness and softness by sight?

E. No.

A. What then properly pertains to the eyes, and is perceived by them?

E. Color.

A. What to the ears?

E. Sound.

A. What to smell?

E. Odor.

A. What to taste?

E. Flavor.

A. What to touch?

E. Softness and hardness, smoothness and roughness, and many such things.

A. How about the shapes of bodies: large, small, square, round, and such? Do we not perceive them both by touch and by sight, so that we cannot properly assign them either to touch or sight alone, but only to both?

E. That is clear.

A. You see then that certain senses have individually their own proper objects about which they tell us, and that certain others have some objects in common.

E. I see that too.

A. Now can we by means of any of these senses distinguish what is proper to each sense, and what all or certain senses have in common?

E. By no means: we judge that by a sort of interior sense.

A. Is that perhaps reason itself, which the beasts have not? For it is by reason, I think, that we grasp these things, and so know that we have senses.

E. I think rather that by reason we comprehend that there is a certain interior sense, to which all things are referred by the five ordinary senses. For the sense by which a beast sees is one thing, and that by which it seeks or avoids what it perceives by sight is another; for the first sense is in the eyes, but that other is in the soul itself. By it animals seek and appropriate what they like, and avoid and reject what they do not; not only what they see, but what they hear or perceive by the other senses. Nor can this sense be called sight or hearing or smell or taste or touch, but is something other than presides over all of them together. While we comprehend this by reason, as I have said, we cannot nevertheless call it reason, since the beasts also evidently have it.

A. I recognize that, whatever it is, and do not hesi-
9.   tate to call it the interior sense. But unless it goes
       beyond what is brought to us by our bodily senses, it
cannot attain to knowledge. For what we know, we hold in the
grasp of reason. But, not to mention other things, we know
that we cannot perceive colors by hearing, nor voices by
sight. And when we know this, we know it neither by our
eyes nor by our ears, nor by that interior sense which the
beasts also have. For one cannot believe that they know that
ears do not perceive light, nor eyes voices, since we discern
such things only by rational attention and thought.

E. I cannot say that I see that clearly. For what if they do
discern also by that interior sense, which you admit they
have, that colors cannot be perceived by hearing, nor voices
by sight?

A. Well, do you think that they can distinguish from one
another the color that is perceived, and the sense that is in
the eye, and that interior sense within the soul, and the
reason by which these are defined and enumerated one by
one?

E. By no means.

A. Could reason, then, distinguish these four from one another, and set bounds to them by definitions, if color were
not referred to it by the sense of the eyes, and that sensation again by the interior sense that presides over it, and
that same interior sense by itself, assuming that there is not
yet another something interposed?

E. I do not see how else it could.

A. And do you see that color is perceived by the sense of
the eyes, but that the sensation itself is not perceived by
the same sense? For you do not see the seeing itself by the
same sense by which you see color.

E. Not at all.

A. Try also to distinguish these; for I think you will not
deny that color is one thing, and seeing color another, and
that it is yet another, when color is not present, to have
the sense by which it could be seen if it were present.

E. I distinguish those too, and grant that they are different.

A. Do you see any of these three with your eyes, except
color?

E. Nothing else.

A. Tell me then how you do see the other two; for if you
did not see them, you could not distinguish them.

E. I know nothing further. I know that I do, nothing more.

A. You do not know then whether this is reason itself, or

that life which we call the interior sense, and which is superior to the bodily senses, or something else?

E. No.

A. You know at least that these things can be defined only by reason; and that reason cannot do this unless they are presented to it for examination.

E. That is true.

A. Whatever, therefore, that other thing is, by means of which we perceive everything that we know, it is in the service of reason, to which it presents and reports whatever it touches, so that the things perceived may be distinguished by their properties, and grasped not merely for perception, but for knowledge as well.

E. That is so.

A. Well, how about this reason, which distinguishes from one another its servants and the things they bring before it, and likewise recognizes the difference between itself and these things, and assures itself of its superiority to them? Does it comprehend itself by means of anything other than itself, that is, reason? Or would you know that you had reason if you did not perceive it by reason?

E. Most true.

A. So then, when we perceive a color we do not likewise by the sense itself perceive that we perceive; nor when we hear a sound do we also hear our hearing; nor when we smell a rose has the smelling fragrance too; nor tasting something does the tasting itself have flavor in the mouth; nor touching a thing can we also touch the sense of touch. Therefore it is clear that those five senses cannot be perceived by any one sense among them, although by them all corporeal things are perceived.

E. That is clear.

A. I think it is clear that the interior sense perceives not only the things referred to it by the five senses, but also the sensations themselves. For otherwise an animal would not stir, either to pursue or to run away from anything, if it did not perceive that it had the sensation—not as knowledge, for that is reason's province, but only in order to move—which it certainly does not perceive by any one of those five. If this is still not clear, it will become clear by considering some one sense, say sight. For one could not open his eyes, or turn his gaze upon what he seeks to see, unless when his eyes were closed, or not turned toward it, he perceived that he did not see. But if, not seeing, he perceives that he does not see, he must also perceive that he sees when he does see; for the fact that when he sees a thing he does not move his eyes in search of it shows that he perceives both.

But whether this life that perceives that it perceives corporeal things perceives itself too, is not so clear; except that anyone who looks within himself finds that every living thing flees death. But since death is the opposite of life, it must be that life perceives itself, since it flees its own opposite. But if this be still not clear, let us pass it over, so that we may move on toward our goal only by evidence that is certain and manifest. For this much is clear: we perceive corporeal things by our bodily senses, but we cannot by the sense itself perceive a sense. By the interior sense we perceive both that we are perceiving corporeal things through the bodily sense, and also the bodily sense itself. But by reason all those other things and also reason itself become known and are held together in knowledge. Is this clear to you?

E. Perfectly clear.

SENSATION AS AN ACTIVITY OF THE SOUL*

Master: Immediately I shall say what I think. But
5.9. you—you either follow or even precede, if you are able, when you notice me delay and hesitate. Now, I do not think that this body is animated by the soul unless by the intention of its Maker. Nor do I think that the soul suffers anything from the body, but acts with the body and in it, subjected divinely to its domination. Nevertheless, I think that the soul operates sometimes with ease, sometimes with difficulty, in so far as corporeal nature gives way, more or less, to it in accordance with its merits. Therefore, whatever corporeal things are put into or taken out of this body from without, produce something, not in the soul but in the body, which either is opposed to its work or agrees with it. And so, when the soul strives against the reluctant body and with difficulty molds the matter subjected to it for the ways of its working, it becomes more attentive to the activity on account of the difficulty—and this difficulty is called sensation on account of the attention (since it does

* *On Music,* VI, 5, 9-10; trans. T. P. Maher, *The De Musica VI of St. Augustine* (St. Louis University Master's Thesis, 1939), pp. 81-84. Used with permission.

not escape the notice of the soul). This perception is called pain or labor. But when that which is brought in or lies close, agrees, the soul easily brings the whole of it, or of it as much as it needs, into the journeyings of its working. And this action by which it joins its body extrinsically to a suitable object is not hidden, since the action is carried on more attentively on account of some adventitious circumstance and, moreover, on account of the suitability it is sensed with pleasure. But when those things by which it restores the losses of the body are absent, extreme want follows. When by that difficulty of action it becomes more attentive, and when such an operation of it does not lie hidden from the soul, it is called hunger or thirst or something similar. When, however, what has been eaten is above measure, and difficulty of working is born from the weight of the food, neither does this happen without attention. Further, when such an action is not hidden, sluggishness is felt. It even functions attentively when it ejects the superfluity—if gently, with delight; if roughly, with pain. The soul attentively acts in the morbid disturbance of the body, seeking to aid the body as it slips and disintegrates. Again, when this action is not hidden, the soul is said to feel illness and disease.

10. And lest I make it too long, it seems to me that the soul, when it feels in the body, is not affected in anything from it but acts more attentively in its affections, and then these actions are either easy, on account of the agreeableness, or difficult on account of the disagreeableness, and they do not escape the soul. This is all that is called sensation. But that sense which, even when we do not sense still is present, is an instrument of the body, which is such a disposition that the soul be in it more prepared to direct the passions of the body with attention, so that it joins like things to like and repels what is harmful. Furthermore, as I think, it directs—in the eyes, something akin to light; in the ears, breezes, the most gentle and mobile; in the nose, something misty; in the mouth, moist; and in the touch, earthy and muddy. But whether by this or by some other distribution, these things are united—the soul acts quietly, when those inner components of its integrated health occur in some sort of intimate state of agreement. But when those are used which affect the body with some change, if I may speak thus, the soul then brings out more attentive actions as suited to the proper place and instrument. In that instance it is said to hear, or to smell, or to taste, or to sense by touching, and by these actions it gladly associates the compatible things, with difficulty resists the incompatible. These operations the soul puts over against the passions of the body when it senses and itself does not receive the same feelings.

MEMORY, UNDERSTANDING, AND WILL*

11.17. Putting aside, then, for a little while all other things of which the mind is certain concerning itself, let us especially consider and discuss these three—memory, understanding, will. For we may commonly discern in these three the character of the abilities of the young also, since the more tenaciously and easily a boy remembers, and the more acutely he understands, and the more ardently he studies, the more praiseworthy is he in point of ability. But when the question is about anyone's learning, then we ask not how solidly and easily he remembers, or how shrewdly he understands, but what it is that he remembers, and what it is that he understands. And because the mind is regarded as praiseworthy, not only as being learned, but also as being good, one gives heed not only to what he remembers and what he understands, but also to what he wishes; not how ardently he wishes, but first what it is he wishes, and then how greatly he wishes it. For the mind that loves eagerly is then to be praised, when it loves that which ought to be loved eagerly. Since then we speak of these three—ability, knowledge, use—the first of these is to be considered under the three heads, of what a man can do in memory, and understanding, and will. The second of them is to be considered in regard to that which any one has in his memory and in his understanding, whither he has attained by a studious will. But the third, viz. use, lies in the will, which handles those things that are contained in the memory and understanding, whether it refer them to anything further, or rest satisfied with them as an end. For to use is to take up something into the power of the will; and to enjoy is to use with joy, not any longer of hope, but of the actual thing. Accordingly, every one who enjoys, uses; for he takes up something into the power of the will, wherein he also is

* On the Trinity, X, 11.17-18; trans. Dods.

satisfied as with an end. But not everyone who uses, enjoys if he has sought after that which he takes up into the power of the will, not on account of the thing itself but on account of something else.

18. Since then these three, memory, understanding, will, are not three lives but one life, nor three minds but one mind, it follows certainly that neither are they three substances but one substance. Since memory, which is called life, and mind, and substance, is so called in respect to itself, but it is called memory relatively to something. And I should say the same also of understanding and of will, since they are called understanding and will relatively to something, but each in respect to itself is life, and mind, and essence. And hence these three are one, in that they are one life, one mind, one essence; and whatever else they are severally called in respect to themselves, they are called also together not plurally but in the singular number. But they are three in that wherein they are mutually referred to each other; and if they were not equal, and this not only each to each but also each to all, they certainly could not mutually contain each other; for not only is each contained by each, but also all by each. For I remember that I have memory, and understanding, and will; and I understand that I understand, and will, and remember; and I will that I will, and remember, and understand; and I remember together my whole memory, and understanding, and will. For that of my memory which I do not remember is not in my memory; and nothing is so much in the memory as memory itself. Therefore I remember the whole memory. Also, whatever I understand I know that I understand, and I know that I will whatever I will; but whatever I know I remember. Therefore I remember the whole of my understanding, and the whole of my will. Likewise, when I understand these three things, I understand them together as whole. For there is none of things intelligible which I do not understand, except what I do not know; but what I do not know, I neither remember, nor will. Therefore, whatever of things intelligible I do not understand, it follows also that I neither remember nor will. And whatever of things intelligible I remember and will, it follows that I understand. My will also embraces my whole understanding and my whole memory, whilst I use the whole that I understand and remember. And, therefore, while all are mutually comprehended by each, and as wholes, each as a whole is equal to each as a whole, and each as a whole at the same time to all as wholes; and these three are one, one life, one mind, one essence.

THE WONDERS OF MEMORY*

So, I shall also pass above this power of my nature,
8.12. ascending by degrees toward Him who made me,
and I come into the fields and broad palaces of memory, where there are treasures of innumerable images, brought in from all sorts of sense objects. There is stored away whatever we cogitate on, too, either by adding to, or taking away from, or changing in any way the things which sense perception has contacted, and anything else kept or put back there, which forgetfulness has not yet engrossed and buried.

When I am in it, I can request that whatever I wish be brought forward. Some things come forth immediately; others are hunted after for a longer time, yet they are dug out as it were from some more concealed containers; still others rush out in a mob, when something else is sought and looked for, jumping forth in the middle as if to say: "Would we do, perhaps?" These I drive away from the face of my remembrance with the hand of my heart, until what I want becomes clear and enters into sight from the secret places. Other things come up as they are required, in easy and uninterrupted sequence. The first ones give way to those which follow and, in leaving, are stored up to come forth again when I desire it. All of this goes on when I recite something memorized.

In it all things are kept distinct and classified. They
13. are carried in, each by its own channel—light, for
instance, and all colors and shapes of bodies through the eyes; through the ears, all kinds of sounds; all odors through the channel of the nostrils; all flavors through the channel of the mouth; and then, by the sensitivity of the whole body, what is hard or soft, hot or cold, smooth or rough, heavy or light, whether outside or inside the body. All these the great recess of memory, and its indescribably hidden and mysterious chasms, take in, to be called to mind and reviewed, when need arises. All these things go in, each

* *Confessions,* X, 8-26; trans. FOC 5, 273-297.

by its own gateway, and are there stored away. The things
themselves do not go in, of course, but the images of sensible things are ready there for the cogitation which recalls
them.

Just how these are fashioned who can say, though it is
evident by which senses they are caught up and stored
away within? For, even while I dwell in darkness and silence,
I can, if I wish, produce colors in my memory, and distinguish between white and black and between any others as
I wish. Nor do sounds rush in and disturb the object drawn
in through the eyes, when I am considering it; yet, they are
there, also, and lie hidden in separation, as it were. I can
summon these, too, if it pleases me, and they are present
at once; with tongue at rest and silent throat, I can sing as
much as I wish. The images of colors, despite the fact that
they are present, do not intervene or break in when another
store, which has flowed in through the ears, is reviewed.
Thus, I can remember at will the other things which have
been taken in and piled up through the other senses. I can
distinguish the fragrance of lilies from that of violets, while
smelling nothing, and I can prefer honey to a decoction of
musk, smooth to rough, and not by tasting or touching anything at the time, but by recollecting.

14.   I do this inside, in the immense palace of my memory. In it, sky, earth, and sea are present before me,
together with all the things I could perceive in
them, except for those which I have forgotten. In it, I
even encounter myself and I bring myself to mind: what,
when and where I did something, and how I felt when I
did it. In it are all the things which I remember, either
those personally experienced or those taken on faith. Out of
the same supply, even, I can take now these, now those
likenesses of things (whether those experienced or those derived from experience) and combine them with things of
the past, and from these I can even think over future actions, happenings, and hopes—and all these, again, as if in
the present. "I shall do this or that," I say within myself
in this huge recess of my mind, filled with the images of
things so many and so great, and this or that follows in
consequence. "Oh, if this or that could happen!" "May God
prevent this or that!"—I say these things to myself, and,
while I say them, the images of all the things I am saying
are present from the same storehouse of memory. I could
not say anything at all about them, if they were lacking.

15. Great is this power of memory, exceeding great, O my God, a vast and unlimited inner chamber. Who has plumbed its depths? Yet, this is a power of my mind and it belongs to my nature; I myself do not grasp all that I am. Is, then, the mind too narrow to hold itself, so that the questions arise: Where is this thing which belongs to it and it cannot grasp? Would it be outside it and not in it? How, then, does it not grasp it? A mighty wonder rises before me, and on this point astonishment seizes me.

Yet, men go to admire the mountains' peaks, giant waves in the sea, the broad courses of rivers, the vast sweep of the ocean, and the circuits of the stars—and they leave themselves behind! They feel no wonder that I did not see with my eyes all these things when I was talking about them. Yet, I could not have talked of them unless I could see within, in my memory, in their vast expanses, as if I were seeing them externally, the mountains, waves, rivers and stars which I have seen, and the ocean which I take on faith. Yet, I did not by vision take these things into me, when I saw them with my eyes. They are not themselves with me but just their images. And I know for each what was impressed on me by each sense of the body.

9.16. These are not the only things which the vast capacity of my memory bears. Here, also, are all those things which have been grasped from the liberal disciplines and which have not yet been forgotten—put aside, as it were, in an inner place which is not a place. Nor do I carry the images of these, but the things themselves. For, what literature is, what skill in discussion is, how many kinds of questions there are, whatever things like this I know, are present in my memory in a special way. I have not left the thing outside and just retained the image—nor has it existed as a sound and then passed away, like a spoken word impressed through the ears, through a vestigial image, by which in recollection it again sounds, as it were, when it is not actually sounding—nor, as an odor, while passing and disappearing on the breezes, affects the sense of smell, from which it sends in its image to the memory, for us to recall when remembering —nor as food, which of course causes no taste when already in the stomach, yet is tasted, in a way, in memory—nor as some object perceived by touching it with the body, which the memory pictures even when it is separated from us. In fact, these things are not introduced into the memory, but their images alone are grasped with marvelous speed, and are put away in wonderful compartments, and come forth in a wondrous way through remembering.

10.17. However, when I hear that there are three kinds of questions—Whether a thing is? What it is? What kind it is?—I keep the images of the sounds by which these words are constituted, of course, and I know that they have passed away through the air, accompanied by noise, and now do not exist. But the things themselves which are signified by these sounds I did not attain by any sense of the body, nor did I see them anywhere else than in my mind; yet I have stored up in memory, not their image but the things themselves.

If they can, let them tell me whence these things have come into me. For I have gone over all the entrances of my flesh and have not found out by which one they came in. Of course, the eyes say: "If they are colored, we have reported them"; the ears say: "If they emitted sound, they have been made known by us"; the nostrils say: "If they were odorous, they passed through us"; so also the sense of taste says: "If it is not a matter of taste, do not ask me"; touch says: "If it has no bodily bulk, I did not touch it; if I did not touch it, I did not make it known."

From what source, and by what route, did these things enter into my memory? I do not know how. When I learned these things, I did not believe in another man's heart; rather, I recognized them in my own and I approved them as true. I committed them to it as to a repository, from which I could take them out when I desired. Therefore, they were there even before I learned them, but they were not in the memory. Where, then, and why did I know them when they were spoken, saying: "It is so, it is true," unless because they were already in memory, but so far removed, buried in its deeper enclosures, that, unless they had been dug out by something that suggested them, I should perhaps have been unable to think them.

11.18. Therefore we find that to learn things of this kind —whose images we do not acquire through sensation, but which we discern in themselves within us, without images and as they are—is nothing else than, by cogitation, to make a kind of collation of the haphazard and unarranged contents of memory and, through one's act of awareness, to command that they be placed close at hand, as it were, in this same memory, where they formerly lay scattered about and unnoticed, that they may eventually come easily to the attention of a mind already familiar with them.

How many things of this kind my memory holds which are already found out and, as I say, placed ready at hand, as it were—things which we are said to have learned and to know! If I cease to recall them to mind for even a short period of time, they are again submerged and slip off, as it were, into the more removed recesses, so that they must again be excogitated, as if new, from the same place as before—there is no other place for them—and they must be drawn together [*cogenda*] again, so that they may be known. That is, they must be collected as if from a condition of being dispersed; hence one speaks of cogitating. For, *cogo* [draw together] and *cogito* [cogitate] are related as are *ago* [do] and *agito* [do constantly] and as *facio* [make] and *factito* [make frequently]. But the mind has made this word its own property, so that what is collated, that is, drawn together, in the mind, but not in another place, is now properly said to be cogitated.

12.19. Again, memory contains the reasons and innumerable laws of numbers and dimensions, none of which any bodily sense impresses; for these are neither colored nor resonant nor odorous nor tasty nor tangible. I have heard the sounds of words by which they are signified when there is a discussion about them, but these sounds are one thing and the objects are another. For the sounds are different in Greek from what they are in Latin, but the things are neither Greek nor Latin, nor do they belong to any kind of language. I have seen the lines of craftsmen—even the thinnest ones, like a strand from a spider's web; but these [mathematical lines] are quite different. They are not the images of those lines which my fleshly eye has reported to me. They are known by whoever recognizes them interiorly, without cogitation about any body whatever. I have perceived, also, the numbers which we reckon in all the bodily senses, but the ones *by which* we do the counting are quite different. They are not images of these, and so they really exist. Let him laugh at my saying this, the man who does not see them. I shall pity him for laughing at me.

13.20. I hold all these things in memory, and I also remember the way I learned them. I have heard and keep in memory the many things most falsely said against them in arguments. Now, even though they are false, the fact that I remember them is not false. I remember, too, that

I distinguished between those truths and these errors which are said in opposition. In one way I see that I am now distinguishing these two things, and in another way I remember that I have often made this distinction when I cogitated on them. Therefore I both remember that I have often understood these things and, as for the fact that I now perceive and understand them, this I store up in memory, so that afterwards I may remember that I now did understand. And so I remember that I remembered, just as later, if I recall that I could now remember these things, I shall certainly recall it through the power of memory.

The same memory contains also the feelings of my *14.21.* mind, not in the way that the mind itself possesses them when it undergoes them, but quite differently, in the way that the power of memory is related to itself. For I can remember having experienced joy, yet not be joyful; I recall my past sorrow, without being sorrowful; I recollect that I formerly was in fear, without present fear; and I have remembrance of former desire, without present desire. Sometimes, on the contrary, I reminisce about my departed sorrow with present joy, and my joy with present sorrow.

There is nothing to be wondered at in this, in regard to the body; the mind is one thing, the body another. Thus, if I remember with joy a past pain of the body, that is not so astonishing; however, this is different with the mind, since the mind is memory itself. Thus, when we give something to be memorized, we say: "See that you keep this in mind"; and when we forget, we say: "It was not in my mind" and "It slipped my mind"—for we call the memory itself, mind.

Since this is so, then how is it that, when I remember with joy my past sorrow, my mind possesses joy and my memory sorrow? And when the mind is joyful from the fact that joy is present in it, how is it then that the memory is not sorrowful from the fact that sorrow is present in it? Does memory, perhaps, not belong to the mind? Who would claim this?

Without doubt, memory is something like a stomach for the mind; so joy and sorrow are like sweet and bitter food. When they are committed to memory, conveyed down, as it were, into the stomach where they come to be stored, they cannot be tasted. It is ridiculous to consider these things similar, yet they are not entirely dissimilar.

But look, when I say that there are four passions of *22.* the mind, I bring forth from memory desire, joy, fear, and sorrow. Whatever I could say in a discussion about them, by dividing each into the species within the genus of each and by defining them, it is in the memory that I find what to say and from there that I bring it forth. However, I do not suffer any of these passions when I take note of them by remembering. Yet, before they were recalled by me and reviewed, they were there. For that reason, it was possible to draw them out of it through remembrance.

It may be, then, that these are produced from memory in the process of recall, just as food is from the stomach in the process of rumination. But why is the sweetness of joy, or the bitterness of sorrow, not perceived in the mouth of cogitation by the man engaged in discussion, that is, the man who is reminiscing? Is this the point of dissimilarity, since they surely are not wholly alike? Who would willingly speak of things of this sort, if every time we mention sorrow or fear we were forced to undergo sorrow or fear? Yet we would not speak of them unless we found in our memory not only the sounds of their names according to images impressed by the senses of the body, but also the notions of the things themselves, which we did not receive through any avenue of the flesh. The mind itself, in sensing, through the experience of its own passions, committed them to memory; or the memory retained them for itself, even though they were not committed to it.

Whether through images or not, who can easily say? *15.23.* In fact, I can name a stone, I can name the sun, while the things themselves are not present to my senses. Of course, their images are at hand in my memory. I can name bodily pain, and it is not present in me when there is no suffering. Yet unless its image were present in my memory, I would not know what I am talking about, and I would not distinguish it from pleasure, in a discussion. I can name the health of the body, while I am healthy in my body; the thing itself is indeed present in me. Yet, in fact, unless its image were also present in my memory, I would not recall at all what the sound of this name meant. Nor would sick people know what was said, when health is named, unless the same image were kept by the power of memory, although the thing itself were absent from the body.

I can name the numbers by which we count; see, they are in my memory: not their images, but themselves. I can name the image of the sun and it is present in my memory. I do not recall an image of an image, but simply the image; it is present to me when I remember. I can name the memory and I recognize what I am naming. Where do I recognize it unless in memory itself? Now, could it be present to itself through its own image, and not through itself?

16.24. Now, when I name oblivion, and likewise recognize what I am naming, what would be the source of my recognition if I did not remember it? I am not talking about the sound of the name, but the thing which it signifies. Now, if I had forgotten this meaning, I should not be able at all to recognize what the sound's function is. Therefore, when I remember my memory, the very memory is present to itself in itself, but when I remember oblivion, both memory and oblivion are present—memory, as that from which I recall; oblivion, as that which I recall. But what is oblivion except the privation of memory? How then can it be present, so that I may remember it, when I cannot remember while it is present? But if we keep in memory what we remember, and if, without remembering oblivion, we could not possibly know the meaning of this word when we heard it, then oblivion is retained in memory. Therefore, it is present so that we will not forget, and when it is present, we do forget.

Or is one to understand from this that it is not present in memory through itself, when we remember it, but rather through its image—because, if oblivion were present in itself, would not the result be that we would forget, not that we would remember? Now, who will eventually work this out? Who will understand how it is?

25. Certainly, O Lord, I am working hard on it, and my work is being done on myself; I have become unto myself a soil of difficulty, and of too much sweat. For we are not now gazing curiously at the sky's expanses nor are we measuring the distances between the stars, nor are we trying to weigh the earth; I am the one who is remembering, I am the mind. It is not so astonishing if whatever I am not is far distant from me, but what is nearer to me than myself? And notice, the power of my memory is not understood by me, yet at the same time I cannot speak of myself without it. What should I say, when it is a certitude to me that I do remember oblivion? Or should I say that what I remember is not in my memory? Or should I say that oblivion is in my memory just for this—that I may not forget? Both are most absurd.

What of a third possibility? On what basis may I say that the image of oblivion is kept in my memory, not oblivion itself, when I do remember it? On what basis, too, may I say this, since, when any image of a thing is impressed on memory, it is first necessary for the thing itself to be present, from which the image can be impressed? For, thus do I remember Carthage; thus, all the places where I have been; thus, the faces of the men I have seen and the things reported by the other senses; thus, the health of the body itself or its pain. When these things were at hand, my memory took the images from them, which, as being present, I might see directly and review in my mind when I remembered the things in their absence.

If, then, oblivion is held in memory through its image and not through itself, it must certainly have been present itself, in order that its image might be grasped. Now, when it was present, how did it write its image in the memory, when oblivion erases by its presence even what it finds already known? Yet I am certain that I do remember in some manner or other, though this manner be incomprehensible and inexplicable, even oblivion itself, whereby the object we remember is consigned to destruction.

17.26. Great is the power of memory; its deep and boundless multiplicity is something fearful, O my God! And this is the mind, and I am this myself. What then am I, O my God? What is my nature? A life of many aspects and many ways, strikingly immeasurable.

Look into the fields, hollows, and innumerable caverns of my memory, filled beyond number with innumerable kinds of things, either by means of images as in the case of all bodies, or by means of their own presence as in the case of the arts, or by means of some sort of notions or impressions as in the case of the feelings of the mind (which the memory keeps even when the mind is not undergoing them, though whatever is in the memory is in the mind!). I run through all these things, and I flit here and there. I even go as deep as I can, yet there is no limit. So great is the power of memory, so great is the power of life in man who lives mortally!

What shall I do, Thou true Life of mine, O my God? I shall pass over even this power of mine which is called memory; I shall pass over it to reach Thee, sweet Light. What dost Thou say to me? Behold, going up through my mind to Thee, who dwellest above me, I shall even pass over this power of mine which is called memory, desiring to attain Thee where Thou canst be attained, and to cleave to Thee where it is possible to be in contact with Thee.

For even beasts and birds have memory; otherwise, they

could not find their lairs and nests, or the many other
things to which they become accustomed. And they could not
grow accustomed to any thing, unless through memory. Therefore, I shall even pass over memory to attain Him who has
set me apart from the four-footed beasts and made me "wiser
than the fowls of the air." [Job 35:11] I shall even pass over
memory, so that I may find Thee—where, O truly good and
serene Sweetness—where shall I find Thee? But if I find
Thee without memory, I am without remembrance of Thee.
And how indeed may I find Thee, if I am without remembrance of Thee?

18.27. The woman who had lost her drachma and looked
for it with a lamp would not have found it, unless
she retained some remembrance of it. For, when it
had been found, how would she know whether it was the
one, if she retained no remembrance of it? I remember
many lost things which I have looked for and found. From
this I know that, when I was looking for one of them, and
people would say to me: "Perhaps this is it? Maybe this
one?" I would continue to say: "It is not," until the thing I
was seeking was shown to me. Unless I had some remembrance of it, whatever it was, I should not have found it,
even if it were shown to me, for I should not have recognized
it. That is always the way it is, when we look for some lost
thing and find it. Yet, of course, when by chance something is lost from sight, not from memory—any visible body,
for example—its image is retained within, and it is sought
until it comes back within view. And, when it is found, it is
recognized from the image which is within. We do not say
that we have found what we lost, if we do not recognize it,
and we cannot recognize it, if we do not remember it. It disappeared indeed from before our eyes, but it was retained
in memory.

19.28. What? When the memory itself loses something, as
happens when we forget and try to remember, pray,
where do we look for it, unless in the memory itself?
And in it, if one thing is presented in place of another, we
reject it until the thing we are looking for turns up. When it
does turn up, we say: "This is it." We would not say that
unless we recognized it, and we would not recognize it unless we remembered. Yet we certainly had forgotten it.

Or had it disappeared, not completely but only in part?
And is the other part sought by means of that which is re-

tained, because the memory felt that its object of consideration was not as complete as usual, and, feeling the defect in a
habit which was as it were defective in some part, it strove
to get back what was missing?

For instance, if a man who is known comes before our eyes
or into our thoughts, and we are trying to recall his name,
which we have forgotten, then any other name which occurs
fails to be connected, because it has not been customary for
our thought of him to go along with it; hence it is rejected
until that name occurs which our customary way of thinking
of the man accepts as not inappropriate. And from what
source does it occur, if not from memory itself? For when
we recognize it, on being reminded by someone else, it is
from there that it comes. So we do not accept it as something
new, but, in recalling it, we judge that what has been said is
the right name. But if it is entirely wiped out of mind, then
we do not remember even when reminded. And if we even
remember that we have forgotten it, then we have not yet
completely forgotten. Therefore, we would not be able to
look for something that has been lost, if we had altogether
forgotten it.

20.29. Now, how do I look for Thee, O Lord? When I
look for Thee, my God, I am looking for the happy
life. May I seek Thee, so that my soul may live.
[Isa. 55:3] For my body has life from my soul, and my soul
has life from Thee. How then do I seek the happy life? It is
not mine, until I can say: "Enough, there it is." Here then I
ought to say how I do look for it, whether through remembrance, as though I had forgotten it and I still retained the
fact that I had forgotten, or through a desire to learn it as
something unknown, either something I never knew, or which
I have so forgotten that I have no remembrance even that I
have forgotten it. Surely the happy life is this: What all men
desire and [such that] there is absolutely no one who does
not desire it? Where did they know it, this object which they
desire in such a way? Where did they see it, to love it so?
Certainly we do possess it, but how I know not.

There is one certain way whereby each man, when he
possesses this object, is then happy, and there also are those
who are happy in hope. The latter possess it in an inferior
way, compared to those who are already really happy, yet
they are better off than those others who are happy neither
in reality nor in hope. Still, unless this third kind of people
possessed it, in some way, they would not desire to be happy;

that they have such a desire is most certain. Somehow or other they came to know it, and so they possess it in some kind or other of knowledge. My problem concerning this is whether it may be in the memory; for if it is there, then we were at one time happy, either all individually, or all in that man who was the first to sin, in whom also we all died from whom we are all born amidst unhappiness. I do not ask this question now, but I do ask whether the happy life is in the memory.

Now, we would not love it, unless we knew it. We hear this word and we all admit that we seek this thing, for we are not delighted merely by the sound. When a Greek hears this word in Latin, he is not delighted, for he does not know what has been said. Yet we Latins are delighted, as he is, too, if he hears it in Greek, for the thing itself is neither Greek nor Latin, this thing which Greeks and Latins and men of every tongue yearn to obtain. So, it is known to all men who, if they could be asked whether they desire to be happy, would reply in one voice, without any hesitation, that they do. This would be impossible, unless the thing itself, of which this is the name, were kept in their memory.

Now, is this the same as the case of the man, who, having seen Carthage, remembers it? No! The happy life is not seen with the eyes, since it is not a body. Is it like the example of our remembering numbers? No! One who possesses these in knowledge does not seek to obtain further, but we possess the happy life in knowledge, and so we love it, yet wish to attain it further so that we may *be* happy.

Is it like the instance where we remember the art of oratory? No! For, though, when this word has been heard, people recall to mind the thing itself, even those who are not yet eloquent—and many do desire to be (whence it is apparent that eloquence exists in their knowledge), but, on the other hand, they have observed through the senses of the body that other people are eloquent and they are delighted and long to be likewise; they would not be delighted except from interior knowledge and they would not desire to be likewise unless they were so delighted. However, we do not have personal experience of the happy life in other people, through any sense of the body.

Is it like the way in which we remember joy? Perhaps so. For I remember my joy even when sad, just as I do the happy life when I am unhappy, and I have never seen or heard or smelled or tasted or touched my joy by any sense of the body, but I have experienced it in my mind when I have been joyful. Its knowledge stuck in my memory, so that I am able to remember it, sometimes with contempt, sometimes with longing, depending on the difference between the things from which my joy came, as I remember it. For, I have been imbued with a certain joy arising from shameful things, and, as I now recall this, I feel disgust and curse it; at other times, it arises from good and virtuous things and I recall it with longing, even though, perhaps, they are no longer available, and therefore I am saddened as I recall my former joy.

31. Where then, and when, did I experience my happy life that I should now remember, love, and desire it? Not just I alone, or in the company of a few people, but absolutely all people want to be happy. Unless we knew it with certain knowledge, we would not will it with such a certain act of will. But how is this? If the question be asked of two men whether they wish to serve in the army, it is quite possible that one of them may reply that he wants to, the other that he does not. But if they are asked whether they wish to be happy, both will say at once and without any hesitation that they do desire it. Nor is there any different reason why one wishes to enter military service and the other does not than that they wish to be happy. One man, perhaps, finds his joy in one thing, another man in another? Even so, they agree that they all wish to be happy, just as they would agree, if asked the question, that they wish to possess joy. This joy they call the happy life. Even though one man attains it here, another there, still it is but one thing which all men strive to reach, so that they may be joyful. Now, since this is a thing which no man can deny experiencing, it is therefore recognized as found in the memory, when the name, happy life, is heard.

22.32. Far be it, O Lord, far be it from the heart of Thy servant who is confessing to Thee, far be it that I should consider myself happy by virtue of just any joy which I experience. For there is a joy which is not given to the wicked, but rather to them who serve Thee for Thine own sake; for such people, Thou Thyself art Joy. And this is the happy life, to rejoice unto Thee, from Thee, on account of Thee: this it is and there is none other. They who think that there is another pursue a different joy, and not the true one. Yet, their will is not turned away from some representation of joy.

Is it then uncertain that all men wish to be happy,
23.33. because those who do not wish to find their joy in
Thee—and this is the only happy life—do not, in
point of fact, desire the happy life? Or do all desire this, but,
because "the flesh lusts against the spirit, and the spirit
against the flesh ... so that they do not do what they wish,
[Gal. 5:17] they descend to that of which they are capable
and are content with it, for they do not desire that for which
they have insufficient capacity, to the extent that their
desire would render them capable of it?

Now, I ask all men whether they would prefer to get their
joy from truth rather than from falsity? They will hesitate
as little to say that they prefer it from truth as they hesitate
in saying that they wish to be happy. Indeed, the happy life
is joy arising from truth. For this is the joy coming from
Thee, who art the Truth, [John 14:6] O God; Thou art
"my light," [Ps. 26:1] the salvation of my countenance, O
my God. [Ps. 41:12] This happy life all men desire; this life,
which alone is happy, all men desire; the joy arising from
truth all men desire.

I have been acquainted with many men who wished to
deceive, but not one who wished to be deceived. Where
then did they get their knowledge of this happy life, unless
where they got their knowledge of truth too? For they love
the latter also, since they do not wish to be deceived. And,
when they love the happy life, which is nothing other than
joy arising from truth, they certainly love truth also. Nor
would they love it, unless some knowledge of it were in their
memory.

Why then do they not take their joy from it? Why are
they not happy? Because they are more keenly concerned
with other things, which have greater power to make them
unhappy, than this, which they faintly remember to make
them happy. "Yet a little while the light is" [John 12:35]
in men; let them walk, walk, lest darkness overtake them.

But why does "truth engender hatred" [Cf. Terence,
34.   Andria, 68] and Thy man who speaks the truth has
become an enemy to them, [John 8:40] when a
happy life is loved and it is nothing but joy arising from
truth? Is it that truth is so loved that, whoever love something else, they wish this object of love to be the truth, and,

since they did not want to be deceived, they do not want to be shown that they have been deceived? Therefore they hate the truth because of the same thing which they love in place of truth. They love truth when it enlightens; they hate it when it reproves. Since they do not wish to be deceived, and they do wish to deceive, they love it when it reveals its own self, and they hate it when it reveals themselves. Its retribution upon them stems from this: they who do not wish to be revealed by it, it both reveals against their will and is not itself revealed to them.

Thus, thus, even thus is the human mind, even thus is it blind and weak; it wishes to lie hidden, a foul and unattractive thing, but does not wish anything to be hidden to it. What befalls it is the contrary: it is not hidden before the truth, but the truth is hidden before it. Nevertheless, even while it is in such unhappiness, it prefers to rejoice in true things rather than in false. It will be happy then, if, with no hindrance interposed, it will come to rejoice in that through which all things are true, in the only Truth.

See how much I have traveled about in the spacious-
24.35. ness of my memory while looking for Thee, O Lord, and I have not found Thee outside it. Nor have I found anything about Thee which I did not keep in memory, ever since I learned of Thee. For, from the time that I learned of Thee, I did not forget Thee. Now, wherever I found the truth, there do I find my God, Truth Itself, and from the time that I learned of the Truth, I have not forgotten. Therefore, from the time that I learned about Thee, Thou dost dwell in my memory, and there do I find Thee when I remember Thee and delight in Thee. These are my holy delights which Thou hast given me in Thy mercy, having regard to my poverty.

But where dost Thou dwell in my memory, O
25.36. Lord; where dost Thou dwell there? What resting place hast Thou fashioned for Thyself? What sanctuary hast Thou built for Thyself? Thou hast granted this favor to my memory, to dwell in it, but in which part of it Thou dost dwell, this I now consider. When I recalled Thee to mind, I went above those parts of it which the beasts also possess, for I did not find Thee there among the images of bodily things. So I came to the parts of it in which I keep my mental feelings, but I did not find Thee there. So I entered into the seat of my very mind, and there is one for it in my memory, since the mind also remembers itself, and Thou

wert not there. Because, just as Thou art not a bodily image, nor the feeling of a living being, such as occurs when we are joyful, sorrowful, longing, fearful, mindful, forgetful, or anything else of this kind, so too Thou art not the mind itself. For Thou art the Lord God of the mind, and all these things are mutable, but Thou dwellest as an immutable Being above them all. So Thou hast deigned to reside in my memory, from the time that I have learned about Thee.

And why do I look for the place in it where Thou dost dwell, as if there really were places in it? What is certain is that Thou dwellest in it, for I remember Thee from the time that I have learned about Thee, and I do find Thee in it when I recall Thee to mind.

Where then did I find Thee in order to learn about
26.37. Thee? For Thou wert not already in my memory
before I learned of Thee. Where then did I find
Thee in order to learn about Thee, unless in Thyself above me? Yet there is no place. We go backward and we go forward, yet there is no place. O Truth, Thou dost preside over all things, even those which can take counsel with Thee, and Thou dost answer in the same time all who consult Thee, however diverse their questions. Thou dost answer clearly, but all do not hear clearly. All seek counsel concerning what they wish, but they do not always hear what they wish. He serves Thee best who does not so much expect to hear the thing from Thee which he himself desires, but rather to desire what he hears from Thee.

THREE LEVELS OF VISION*

To see an object not in an image but in itself, yet
6.15. not through the body, is to see with a vision sur-
passing all other visions. There are various ways of
seeing, and with God's help I shall try to explain them and show how they differ. When we read this one commandment: "Thou shalt love thy neighbor as thyself," we experience three kinds of vision: one through the eyes, by which we see the letters; a second through the spirit, by which

* *Literal Commentary on Genesis,* XII, 6.15-11.22, 30.58-31.59; trans. J.H. Taylor, S.J., *St. Augustine De Genesi ad Litteram, Bk XII* (St. Louis University Dissertation, 1948), pp. 25-29, 33, 39-43, 137-139. Used with permission.

we think of our neighbor even when he is absent; and a third through an intuition of the mind, by which we see and understand love itself. Of these three kinds of vision the first is clear to everyone: through it we see heaven and earth and in them everything that meets the eye. The second, by which we think of corporeal things that are absent, is not difficult to explain; for we think of heaven and earth and the visible things in them even when we are in the dark. In this case we see nothing with the eyes of the body but in the soul behold corporeal images: whether true images, representing the bodies that we have seen and still hold in memory, or fictitious images, fashioned by the power of thought. My manner of thinking about Carthage, which I know, is different from my manner of thinking about Alexandria, which I do not know. The third kind of vision, by which we see and understand love, embraces those objects which have no images at once resembling them, yet differing from them. A man, a tree, the sun, or any other bodies in heaven or on earth are seen in their own proper form when present and are thought of, when absent, in images impressed upon the soul. There are two ways of seeing them: one through the bodily senses, the other through the spirit, in which images are contained. But in the case of love, is it seen in one manner, when present, in the form in which it exists, and in another manner, when absent, in an image resembling it? Certainly not. But in proportion to the clarity of our intellectual vision, love itself is seen by one more clearly, by another less so. If, however, we think of some corporeal image, it is not love that we behold.

7.16. These are the three kinds of visions about which we had something to say in the preceding books as occasion arose, though we did not there specify their number. Now that we have briefly explained them, since the question under consideration demands a somewhat fuller discussion of them, we must give them definite and appropriate names, in order to avoid the encumbrance of constant circumlocution. Hence let us call the first kind of vision corporeal, because it is perceived through the body and presented to the senses of the body. The second will be spiritual, for whatever is not a body, and yet is something, is rightly called spirit; and certainly the image of an absent body, though it resembles a body, is not itself a body any more than is the act of vision by which it is perceived. The third kind will be intellectual, from the word "intellect," since *mentale* [mental] from *mens* [mind], because it is just a newly coined word, is too ridiculous for us to employ....

8.19. It is not from any of these meanings we have mentioned, in which spirit is used, that we take the word spiritual to designate the kind of vision we are now treating. It is rather from that singular use of the word, found in the *Epistle to the Corinthians,* in which spirit is obviously distinguished from mind. "For," says the Apostle, "if I pray in a tongue, my spirit prays, but my understanding is unfruitful. . . ."

9.20. I am using the word spirit, therefore, in the sense in which the Apostle uses it, where he distinguishes it from the mind: "I will pray with the spirit, but I will pray with the mind also." Here he implies that signs of things are formed in the spirit, and that an understanding of the signs shines forth in the mind. According to this distinction, then, I have designated as spiritual the kind of vision by which we represent in thought the images of bodies even in their absence.

10.21. But the intellectual type of vision, which is proper to the mind, is on a higher plane. The word intellect, as far as I know, cannot be used in a wide variety of meanings, such as we found in the case of the word spirit. But whether we say intellectual or intelligible, we mean one and the same thing, though some have wished to make a distinction between the two, designating as intelligible that reality which can be perceived by the intellect alone, and as intellectual the mind which understands. But whether there exists any being perceivable by the intellect alone, but not itself endowed with intellect—this is a large and difficult question. On the other hand I do not believe there is any one who either thinks or says that there exists a thing which perceives with the intellect and is at the same time incapable of being perceived by the intellect. For mind is not seen except by mind. Therefore, since it can be seen, it is intelligible, and since it can also see, it is intellectual, according to the distinction just mentioned. Putting aside then the extremely difficult question about a thing which would only be understood but not possess understanding, we here use intellectual and intelligible in the same sense.

11.22. These three kinds of vision, therefore, namely, corporeal, spiritual, and intellectual, must be considered separately so that the reason may ascend from the lower to the higher. We have already proposed above an example by which all three kinds are illustrated in one sentence. For when we read: "Thou shalt love thy neighbor as thyself," the letters are seen corporeally, the neighbor is thought of spiritually, and love is beheld intellectually. But the letters when absent can also be thought of spiritually, and the neighbor when present can be seen corporeally. But love can neither be seen in its own essence with the eyes of the body nor be thought of in the spirit by means of an image like a body; but only in the mind, that is, in the intellect, can it be known and perceived. Corporeal vision indeed does not oversee any operations of the other two kinds of vision; rather the object perceived by it is announced to the spiritual vision, which acts as an overseer. For when an object is seen by the eyes, an image of it is immediately produced in the spirit. But this representation is not perceived unless we remove our eyes from the object that we were gazing at through the eyes and find an image of it within our soul. And if indeed the spirit is irrational, as in the beasts, the announcement made by the eyes goes just as far as the spirit. But if the soul is rational, the announcement is made also to the intellect, which presides over the spirit. And so, after the eyes have taken their object in and announced it to the spirit, in order that an image of it may be produced there, then, if it is symbolic of something, its meaning is either immediately understood by the intellect or sought out; for there can be neither understanding nor searching except by the functioning of the mind....

30.58. But in the ordinary course of our daily life there are other objects that arise in various ways from our spirit itself or are, after a fashion, suggested to the spirit by the body, according as we have been influenced by the flesh or by the mind. Thus men in their waking hours think of their troubles, turning over in their minds the likenesses of bodily things; and so in their sleep, too, they frequently dream of something they need. The reason for this is that greed is the motive force of their business dealings; and when they happen to go to sleep hungry and thirsty, they are often after food and drink with open mouth. Now, in my opinion, when these objects are compared with the revelations of angels, they ought to be assigned the same relative value that we give, in the corporeal order, to earthly bodies in comparison with celestial bodies.

31.59. So also among the objects of the intellect; there are some that are seen in the soul itself: for example, the virtues (to which the vices are opposed), either virtues which will endure, such as piety, or virtues that are useful for this life and not destined to remain in the next, as faith, by which we believe what we do not see, and hope, by which we await with patience the life that shall be, and patience itself, by which we bear every adversity until we arrive at the goal of our desires. These virtues, of course, and other similar ones, which are quite necessary for us now in living out our exile, will have no place in the blessed life, for the attainment of which they are necessary. And yet even they are seen with the intellect; for they are not bodies, nor have they forms similar to bodies. But distinct from these objects is the light by which the soul is illumined, in order that it may see and truly understand everything, either in itself or in the light. For the light is God himself, whereas the soul is a creature; yet, since it is rational and intellectual, it is made in His image. And when it tries to behold the Light, it trembles in its weakness and finds itself unable to do so. Yet from this source comes all the understanding it is able to attain. When, therefore, it is thus carried off and, after being withdrawn from the senses of the body, is made present to this vision in a more perfect manner (not by a spatial relation, but in a way proper to its being), it also sees above itself that Light in whose illumination it is enabled to see all the objects that it sees and understands in itself.

V. THE WORLD OF BODIES

While St. Augustine always felt that physical things are the least important of all creatures, he was fascinated with the wonders of nature. Much of his information may have been unreliable (he was certainly not a physical scientist), but his attitude in the selections that follow makes one conclusion clear: no type of later "Augustinianism" which teaches a contempt for bodies is faithful to the spirit of the Bishop of Hippo. It is not necessary for a Christian to know geography, biology, or physics, to be saved—but, then, it is not necessary to know theology, either.

Recent archaeological discoveries by French scientists in Algeria (see van der Meer) show that Augustine's personal observations were accurate enough. The outdoor mosaics on the waterfront at Carthage have now been partly recovered; they confirm the description found in the sixteenth book of the *City of God.*

Much of Augustine's speculation in cosmology is found in the *Literal Commentary on Genesis,* a treatise not yet fully translated into English. Discussing the creation of the world in the first six days, Augustine there develops his own theory of matter and form. Neither term has the meaning that is found in Aristotelianism. There is no theory of potency and act in Augustine's thought; so matter simply means the original stuff that God created out of nothing. It is called both "matter" (*materia*) and "material" (*materies*) and is described as initially formless. This does not mean that it is entirely without character, but that formless matter is somewhat amorphous, imperfect, ill-defined in its nature. Form (*forma* or *species*) is often taken in the sense of shape or external appearance. No distinction is made between substantial and accidental forms: earth is "formed" as it grows into a tree; lumber is "formed" when made into a table; a human being is "formed" by becoming more virtuous and wise. This notion of form is much closer to Plato than to Aristotle.

Special mention should be made of measure, number and weight as formal determinants. Here again, a biblical text (Wisdom 11:21), to the effect that God has arranged all things in accordance with these three principles, is the simple source of much complicated speculation. Measure (*mensura, modus*) is sometimes associated with the cognitive function of mind (*mens*), and it is also treated as a principle of being. Number (*numerus*) is related to *species* and is a sort of metaphysical determinant: all existing things are numbered. Weight (*pondus*) is connected with order, in its dynamic sense: all natures incline toward their appointed ends because they are weighted. Weight is a determinant of will, of love, or any sort of tendency.

In our last chapter, we shall see a famous psychological interpretation of time, as the extension of mental events, but this does not prevent Augustine from regarding cosmic or physical time as real. One of our present passages ("Place, Time, and the Physical World") shows bodily events occurring in time and requiring some sort of framework of space.

We have already observed some of the features of the theory of seminal reasons. Several selections in this chapter deal with these seedlike principles. While the terminology stems from Stoic usage (*logoi spermatikoi*), the Augustinian teaching on *rationes seminales* is largely an outgrowth of the creation account in Genesis. If God made all things in the first six days, then in some sense everything that will ever appear in the cosmos is already existing in the original stuff of the universe. Augustine is almost forced to postulate tiny, invisible "seeds" which are the originals of all trees, horses, human bodies, and so on, that will grow into extended beings during the course of time. Nothing really new comes into existence after the first six days; all creatures are in existence at all times, sometimes in their "seeds," at other times as grown out of their *rationes seminales*.

This theory explains only the development and movement of *living* creatures. It is barely possible that Augustine thought that all created things are living. However, if he ever recognized nonvital events in physical nature (the movement of winds, the flow of rivers), Augustine would account for these, not by supposing physical forces or created causes, but by appealing to the power of God working directly upon bodies. God makes the wind blow and the water run. (See the selection: "God Works Throughout Nature.")

The human body is beautifully formed and is useful to man in many of his earthly activities. However, it is ani-

mated, vitalized, energized by man's soul; as a body, it has
no power of its own. All human activities, then, are ultimately
of a psychic character—even walking, talking, and similar
actions. No body is an efficient cause.

Many of Augustine's views on the bodily world have lost
their original significance. Certainly, much of modern science
represents a departure from his whole point of view. He was
not a "naturalist" in any sense of the term. Yet the themes
touched on in this chapter are typically Augustinian and
have a place in the history of man's efforts to understand
his environment.

ALL BODILY NATURES ARE GOOD*

4.   But it is ridiculous to condemn the faults of beasts
and trees, and other such mortal and mutable things
as are void of intelligence, sensation, or life, even
though these faults should destroy their corruptible nature; for
these creatures received, at their Creator's will, an existence
fitting them, by passing away and giving place to others, to
secure that lowest form of beauty, the beauty of seasons,
which in its own place is a requisite part of this world. For
things earthly were neither to be made equal to things heavenly, nor were they, though inferior, to be quite omitted from
the universe. Since, then, in those situations where such
things are appropriate, some perish to make way for others
that are born in their room, and the less succumb to the
greater, and the things that are overcome are transformed
into the quality of those that have the mastery, this is the
appointed order of things transitory. Of this order the beauty
does not strike us, because by our mortal frailty we are so
involved in a part of it, that we cannot perceive the whole,
in which these fragments that offend us are harmonized with
the most accurate fitness and beauty. And therefore, where
we are not so well able to perceive the wisdom of the Creator,
we are very properly enjoined to believe it, lest in the
vanity of human rashness we presume to find any fault with
the work of so great an Artificer. At the same time, if we
attentively consider even these faults of earthly things, which
are neither voluntary nor penal, they seem to illustrate the
excellence of the natures themselves, which are all originated

* *City of God,* XII, 4; trans. Dods.

and created by God; for it is that which pleases us in this nature which we are displeased to see removed by the fault —unless even the natures themselves displease men, as often happens when they become hurtful to them, and then men estimate them not by their nature, but by their utility; as in the case of those animals whose swarms scourged the pride of the Egyptians. But in this way of estimating, they may find fault with the sun itself; for certain criminals or debtors are sentenced by the judges to be set in the sun. Therefore it is not with respect to our convenience or discomfort, but with respect to their own nature, that the creatures are glorifying to their Artificer. Thus even the nature of the eternal fire, penal though it be to the condemned sinners, is most assuredly worthy of praise. For what is more beautiful than fire flaming, blazing, and shining? What more useful than fire for warming, restoring, cooking, though nothing is more destructive than fire burning and consuming? The same thing, then, when applied in one way, is destructive, but when applied suitably, is most beneficial. For who can find words to tell its uses throughout the whole world? We must not listen, then, to those who praise the light of fire but find fault with its heat, judging it not by its nature, but by their convenience or discomfort. For they wish to see, but not to be burnt. But they forget that this very light, which is so pleasant to them, disagrees with and hurts weak eyes; and in that heat which is disagreeable to them, some animals find the most suitable conditions of a healthy life.

All natures, then, inasmuch as they are, and have therefore a rank and species of their own, and a kind of internal harmony, are certainly good. And when they are in the places assigned to them by the order of their nature, they preserve such being as they have received. And those things which have not received everlasting being, are altered for better or for worse, so as to suit the wants and motions of those things to which the Creator's law has made them subservient; and thus they tend in the divine providence to that end which is embraced in the general scheme of the government of the universe. So that, though the corruption of transitory and perishable things brings them to utter destruction, it does not prevent their producing that which was designed to be their result. And this being so, God, who supremely is, and who therefore created every being which has not supreme existence (for that which was made of nothing could not be equal to Him, and indeed could not be at all had He not made it), is not to be found fault with on ac-

count of the creature's faults, but is to be praised in view of
the natures He has made.

INVISIBLE SEEDS IN THE ELEMENTS*

Yet it is not on this account to be thought that the
8.13. matter of visible things is subservient to the bidding
of those wicked angels; but rather to that of God,
by whom this power is given, just so far as He, who is unchangeable, determines in His lofty and spiritual abode to
give it. For water and fire and earth are subservient even to
wicked men, who are condemned to the mines, in order
that they may do therewith what they will, but only so far as
is permitted. Nor in truth are those evil angels to be called
creators, because by their means the magicians, withstanding
the servant of God, made frogs and serpents; for it was not
they who created them. But in truth some hidden seeds of
all things that are born corporeally and visibly are concealed in the corporeal elements of this world. For those seeds
that are visible at once to our eyes from fruits and living
things, are quite distinct from the hidden seeds of those
former seeds; whence, at the bidding of the Creator, the
water produced the first swimming creatures and fowl, and
the earth the first buds after their kind, and the first living
creatures after their kind. For neither at that time were
those seeds so drawn forth into products of these several kinds,
as that the power of production was exhausted in those products; but for the most part, suitable combinations of circumstances are wanting, whereby they may be enabled to burst
forth and complete their species. For consider, the very least
shoot is a seed; for, if fitly consigned to the earth, it produces
a tree. But of this shoot there is a yet more subtle seed in some
grain of the same species, and this so far visible to us. But
of this grain also there is further still a seed, which, although
we are unable to see with our eyes, yet we can conjecture
its existence from our reason; because, except there were
some such power in those elements, there would not so generally be produced from the earth things which had not been
sown there; nor yet so many animals, without any previous
commixture of male and female, whether on the land, or in
the water, which yet grow, and by commingling bring forth

* *On the Trinity*, III, 8.13; trans. Dods.

others, while themselves sprang up without any union of parents. And certainly bees do not conceive the seeds of their young by commixture, but gather them as they lie scattered over the earth with their mouth. For the Creator of these invisible seeds is the Creator of all things Himself: since whatever comes forth to our sight by being born, receives the first beginnings of its course from hidden seeds, and takes the successive increments of its proper size and its distinctive forms from these as it were original rules.

THE ELEMENTS CONTAIN SEMINAL REASONS*

17.32. The elements of this bodily world have their own precise force and quality, what each of them can or cannot do, what can be made from what, or cannot. From these elements, as the original principles of things, all things that are generated take their origin and development, each in its proper time; and they receive their terminations and decreases, each according to its kind. Hence it comes about that a bean does not grow from a grain of wheat, or wheat from a bean, or a man from a beast, or a beast from a man. Above this natural change and course of things, the power of the Creator keeps to Himself the ability to make out of all these things something other than what their seminal reasons, as it were, contain—but not something that He did not place in them, so that He might produce it out of them or accomplish it by His own power. For He is omnipotent, not by virtue of thoughtless power but by virtue of His wisdom.

MEASURE, NUMBER, AND WEIGHT †

3.7. For this reason, when we read that He completed all things in six days and we think over the number six, we discover that it is perfect, and moreover, that the orderly course of creation ran in such a way that there was evidently a sort of step-by-step distinction of the parts of creation whereby this number was perfected. So the thought came to mind of the statement in another place in Scripture,

* *Literal Commentary on Genesis,* IX, 17.32; trans. V.J.B.
† *Literal Commentary on Genesis,* IV, 3.7; trans. V.J.B.

"He hath arranged all things according to measure, number and weight." [Wisd. 11:21] And thus may the soul think as well as it can, having asked the help of God Who both provides and energizes its powers, whether these three items, measure, number, and weight, according to which it was written that God arranged all things, were anywhere in existence before the whole of creation was made, or whether these three were themselves created, or, if they existed previously, where were they?

Indeed, before creation there was nothing other than the Creator. So they were in Him. But how? In fact, we also read that the things that were created were in Him: now, were these three identical with Him, while the other things were present in Him by Whom they are ruled and governed? Then, how were they identical with Him? For God is neither measure nor number nor weight, nor is He all these together. Is it according to what we know as measure in the things that we measure, and as number in the things that we number, and as weight in the things that we weigh—but surely God is not these? Or is it according to that original standard that provides a measure for everything, and the number that offers a species to everything, and the weight that draws everything to rest and stability—He is identical with these three, originally, truly, and especially, for He limits all, He shapes all, and He orders all? Through the heart and tongue of man, how was there any other way of understanding the statement that Thou hast arranged all things according to measure, number, and weight, than that Thou hast arranged all things within Thyself?

It is a great feat, granted to few, to rise above all things that can be measured, in order to see the measure that is without measure; to go beyond all that may be numbered, to see number without number; to surpass all that can be weighed, to see weight without weight. For this meaning cannot be thought in terms of these as observed in stones only, and in pieces of wood and bulky things like that, or in bodily things of whatever size, either on earth or in the heavens. Measure is some sort of principle of action, to prevent an unalterable and unregulated process; number pertains to the dispositions and powers of the soul, whereby it is properly gathered in from the deformity of unwisdom to the form of wisdom; and weight applies to will and love, when it becomes evident how much and what weight is to be given to feelings of desire or dislike, or of preference or rejection. But this measure of the soul and mind is determined by another measure, and this number is formed by another number, and this weight is balanced by another weight. Now, the measure without measure is that one to which its derivatives are compared, but which has itself no other origin; number without number is that whereby all things are formed, but it is not itself formed; weight without weight is that whereby those beings whose rest is pure joy are carried to their rest, but it is not itself carried toward any other being.

Of course, whoever knows these terms, measure, number, and weight, only in the visible sphere has but a servile knowledge. So, let him rise above everything that is so known, or if he is not yet able, let him not stick to these meanings which can only be thought in a base sense. To the extent that these principles are dear to a man on the level of higher things, they are less dear to him on the level of lower things. And if a person does not care to transfer those terms that he learned from lower and less worthy things to those sublime entities through whose contemplation he strives to order his mind, then he should not be pressed to do so. As long as the point is understood that needs to be understood, it is not of much concern how it is expressed. Yet one should recognize that there is such a likeness between lower things and higher ones; for it is not different for reason to have a right inclination on one level or another, and it does tend upward.

CONCERNING FORMLESS MATTER*

3.3. Now, certainly, this "earth was invisible and unorganized," [Gen. 1:2, Old Latin] some sort of deep abyss above which there was no light, because no visible appearance belonged to it. For this reason Thou didst command it to be written, "that darknesses were upon the deep" [Gen. 1:2]: what else is this than the absence of light? For where would light be, if it existed, unless it were above, in the sense of dominating and enlightening? So, where the light did not yet exist, what else did it mean by darknesses being present than that light was absent? And so, darknesses were there above, because light was not there; just as where sound is not, there is silence. And what does it mean that silence is there, except that sound is not there? Hast not Thou taught this soul which is confessing to

* *Confessions,* XII, 3.3-9.9; trans. V.J.B.

Thee? Hast not Thou taught me that, before Thou didst form and distinguish into different kinds this unformed matter, there was not any definite thing, neither color, nor shape, nor body, nor spirit? Yet it is not that there was absolutely nothing: it was a certain formlessness without any species.

4.4.   Now, what should one call this, so that some meaning may be conveyed even to those of slower perceptions, unless one use some familiar term? In fact, what can be found, in all the regions of the world, that is nearer to absolute formlessness than earth and abyss? For these are less formed in beauty, because of their low level, than the higher things which are translucent and all-resplendent. Why, then, may I not take the formlessness of matter, which Thou hadst made without beauty of form, and from which Thou mightest make the beautifully formed world, as being thus suitably expressed for men, when it is called "the earth invisible and unorganized"?

5.5.   Thus, when cogitation seeks to find what meaning may be attached to it, and says to itself: "It is not an intelligible form, such as life or such as justice, for it is the material of bodies; nor is it a sensible form because what may be seen and perceived in sensation is not present in the invisible and unorganized"—while human cogitation says this to itself, it is trying either to know it by means of ignorance or to ignore it by means of knowledge.

6.6.   Indeed, O Lord, if I may confess to Thee, with my mouth and pen, all that Thou hast taught me concerning matter in this sense, when formerly I heard its name and did not understand it—and those who told me about these things did not understand, either—I was thinking of it, in cogitation, as having innumerable and diverse species, and so I was not really thinking about it. My mind used to roll up foul and frightening forms into confused arrangements, but they were forms, nevertheless. So I called formless not something that lacked form, but something that had form of such a kind that, were it to become perceptible, my power of perception would turn away, as from something unaccustomed and unsuitable, and my human frailty would have been thrown into confusion.

But in truth what I used to consider in cogitation was formless, not through the privation of all form, but by comparison with more beautifully formed things. Then true reasoning suggested that I should remove altogether the last vestiges of any form whatsoever, if I desired to cogitate the genuinely formless. This I could not do. For I should more easily have agreed that it did not exist at all, a thing deprived of every form, than think of something in between form and nothing, something neither formed nor nothing, an unformed thing which is almost nothing.

My mind stopped questioning my imaginative spirit thereafter, for it was full of images of formed bodies, and it changed and varied these as it wished. And I directed my attention to bodies themselves, working more deeply into their mutability; by means of it, they cease to be what they were and start to be what they were not. I suspected that this transition from form to form was accomplished by means of some unformed thing and not by means of complete nothingness.

But I wanted to know, not merely to suspect; and if my voice and writing were to confess to Thee all that Thou hast opened up for me concerning this question, who among my readers would stay with it long enough to grasp it? Yet my heart shall not cease despite this to give honor to Thee and to sing Thy praises concerning these things which it is unable to put into words.

The mutability, then, of mutable things is itself capable of receiving all the forms into which mutable things are changed. And what is this? Is it mind? Is it body? Is it a species of mind or of body? If one could say: "nothing—thing" and "is—is not," I should say it thus; yet it would have to have some kind of being, in order to be able to receive these visible and organized forms.

Whatever it is, where did it come from but from
7.7.   Thee, from whom all things are, in so far as they
are? But the more distant a thing is from Thee, the more it is unlike Thee; nor does this have reference to place. . . .

Indeed, Thou, O Lord, didst make the world from
8.8.   formless matter, and this Thou didst make almost
nothing and out of nothing, that Thou mightest make great things from it, at which we, the sons of men, wonder. . . . Now, this earth which Thou hadst made was formless material, because it was invisible and unorganized, and the darknesses were above the abyss. From this invisible and unorganized earth, from this formlessness, from this almost-nothing, Thou wert to make all things by which this

mutable world subsists—yet it does not really subsist—in which that mutability is evident that enables periods of time to be perceived and distinguished by measurement. For periods of time come into being by means of the changes of things, as the forms, whose material is the aforementioned invisible earth, are diversified and altered.

Therefore the Spirit, the Teacher of Thy servant, is silent concerning periods of time, and says nothing about days when He mentions that Thou didst make heaven and earth in the beginning. Of course, the heaven of heaven which Thou madest in the beginning is some intellectual creature, which, though in no way coeternal with Thee, the Trinity, is nonetheless a participant in Thy eternity. By virtue of the sweetness of the most happy contemplation of Thee, it restrains its own mutability; and, without falling once since first it was made, it transcends every variable vicissitude of time by adhering closely to Thee.

9.9.

Nor, in fact, is this formlessness—the invisible and unorganized earth—itself numbered by means of days. For where there is no form, no order, nothing whatever comes or passes away; and where this does not occur, there are certainly no days, no alteration of temporal durations.

PLACE, TIME, AND THE PHYSICAL WORLD*

Next we must see what reply can be made to those who agree that God is the Creator of the world, but have difficulties about the time of its creation, and what reply also they can make to difficulties we might raise about the place of its creation. For, as they demand why the world was created then and no sooner, we may ask why it was created just here where it is, and not elsewhere.... While these, then, neither confine in any place, nor limit, nor distribute the divine substance, but, as is worthy of God, own it to be wholly though spiritually present everywhere, will they perchance say that this substance is absent from such immense spaces outside the world, and is occupied in one only (and that a very little one compared with the infinity beyond), the one, namely, in which is the world? I think they will not proceed to this absurdity. Since they maintain that there is but one world, of vast material bulk,

XI.5.

* *City of God*, XI, 5-6; trans. Dods.

indeed, yet finite, and in its own determinate position, and
that this was made by the working of God, let them give
the same account of God's resting in the infinite times before
the world as they give of His resting in the infinite spaces
outside of it. And as it does not follow that God set the world
in the very spot it occupies and no other by accident rather
than by divine reason, although no human reason can comprehend why it was so set, and though there was no merit in
the spot chosen to give it the precedence of infinite others, so
neither does it follow that we should suppose that God
was guided by chance when He created the world in that
and no earlier time, although previous times had been running by during an infinite past, and though there was no difference by which one time could be chosen in preference
to another. But if they say that the thoughts of men are idle
when they conceive infinite places, since there is no place beside the world, we reply that, by the same showing, it is vain
to conceive of the past times of God's rest, since there is no
time before the world.

6.   For if eternity and time are rightly distinguished by
this, that time does not exist without some movement and transition, while in eternity there is no
change, who does not see that there could have been no
time had not some creature been made, which by some motion could give birth to change—the various parts of which
motion and change, as they cannot be simultaneous, succeed
one another—and thus, in these shorter or longer intervals
of duration, time would begin? Since then God, in whose
eternity is no change at all, is the Creator and Ordainer of
time, I do not see how He can be said to have created the
world after spaces of time had elapsed, unless it be said
that prior to the world there was some creature by whose
movement time could pass. And if the sacred and infallible
Scriptures say that in the beginning God created the heavens
and the earth, in order that it may be understood that He
had made nothing previously—for if He had made anything
before the rest, this thing would rather be said to have been
made "in the beginning"—then assuredly the world was
made, not in time, but simultaneously with time. For that
which is made in time is made both after and before some
time—after that which is past, before that which is future.
But none could then be past, for there was no creature by
whose movements its duration could be measured. But simultaneously with time the world was made, if in the

world's creation change and motion were created, as seems
evident from the order of the first six or seven days. For in
these days the morning and evening are counted, until, on the
sixth day, all things which God then made were finished,
and on the seventh the rest of God was mysteriously and
sublimely signalized. What kind of days these were it is extremely difficult, or perhaps impossible for us to conceive,
and how much more to say!

THE WONDERS OF NATURE*

4. If therefore the salamander lives in fire, as naturalists
have recorded, and if certain famous mountains of
Sicily have been continually on fire from the remot-
est antiquity until now, and yet remain entire, these are sufficiently convincing examples that everything which burns is
not consumed. As the soul, too, is a proof that not everything which can suffer pain can also die, why then do they
yet demand that we produce real examples to prove that it is
not incredible that the bodies of men condemned to everlasting punishment may retain their soul in the fire, may
burn without being consumed, and may suffer without perishing? For suitable properties will be communicated to the
substance of the flesh by Him who has endowed the things
we see with so marvellous diverse properties, that their very
multitude prevents our wonder. For who but God the Creator of all things has given to the flesh of the peacock its
antiseptic property? This property, when I first heard of it,
seemed to me incredible; but it happened at Carthage that a
bird of this kind was cooked and served up to me, and taking a suitable slice of flesh from its breast, I ordered it to
be kept, and when it had been kept as many days as make
any other flesh stinking, it was produced and set before me,
and emitted no offensive smell. And after it had been laid
by for thirty days and more, it was still in the same state;
and a year after, the same still, except that it was a little
more shrivelled, and drier. Who gave to chaff such power to
freeze that it preserves snow buried under it, and such power
to warm that it ripens green fruit?

But who can explain the strange properties of fire itself,
which blackens everything it burns, though itself bright; and
which, though of the most beautiful colors, discolors almost

* *City of God*, XXI, 4-5; trans. Dods.

all it touches and feeds upon, and turns blazing fuel into grimy cinders? Still this is not laid down as an absolutely uniform law; for, on the contrary, stones baked in glowing fire themselves also glow, and though the fire be rather of a red hue, and they white, yet white is congruous with light, and black with darkness. Thus, though the fire burns the wood in calcining the stones, these contrary effects do not result from the contrariety of the materials. For though wood and stone differ, they are not contraries, like black and white, the one of which colors is produced in the stones, while the other is produced in the wood by the same action of fire, which imparts its own brightness to the former, while it begrimes the latter, and which could have no effect on the one were it not fed by the other. Then what wonderful properties do we find in charcoal, which is so brittle that a light tap breaks it and a slight pressure pulverizes it, and yet is so strong that no moisture rots it, nor any time causes it to decay. So enduring is it, that it is customary in laying down landmarks to put charcoal underneath them, so that if, after the longest interval, any one raises an action, and pleads that there is no boundary stone, he may be convicted by the charcoal below. What then has enabled it to last so long without rotting, though buried in the damp earth in which [its original] wood rots, except this same fire which consumes all things?

Again, let us consider the wonders of lime; for besides growing white in fire, which makes other things black, and of which I have already said enough, it has also a mysterious property of conceiving fire within it. Itself cold to the touch, it yet has a hidden store of fire, which is not at once apparent to our senses, but which, experience teaches us, lies as it were slumbering within it even while unseen. And it is for this reason called "quick lime," as if the fire were the invisible soul quickening the visible substance or body. But the marvelous thing is, that this fire is kindled when it is extinguished. For to disengage the hidden fire the lime is moistened or drenched with water, and then, though it be cold before, it becomes hot by that very application which cools what is hot. As if the fire were departing from the lime and breathing its last, it no longer lies hid, but appears; and then the lime lying in the coldness of death cannot be requickened, and what we before called "quick," we now call "slaked." What can be stranger than this? Yet there is a greater marvel still. For if you treat the lime, not with water, but with oil, which is as fuel to fire, no amount of oil will heat it. Now if this marvel had been told us of some Indian mineral which we had no opportunity of experimenting upon, we should either have forthwith pronounced it a falsehood, or certainly should have been greatly astonished. But things that daily present themselves to our own observation we despise, not because they are really less marvelous, but because they are common; so that even some products of India itself, remote as it is from ourselves, cease to excite our admiration as soon as we can admire them at our leisure.

The diamond is a stone possessed by many among ourselves, especially by jewellers and lapidaries, and the stone is so hard that it can be wrought neither by iron nor fire, nor, they say, by anything at all except goat's blood. But do you suppose it is as much admired by those who own it and are familiar with its properties as by those to whom it is shown for the first time? Persons who have not seen it perhaps do not believe what is said of it, or if they do, they wonder as at a thing beyond their experience; and if they happen to see it, still they marvel because they are unused to it, but gradually familiar experience [of it] dulls their admiration. We know that the lodestone has a wonderful power of attracting iron. When I first saw it I was thunderstruck, for I saw an iron ring attracted and suspended by the stone; and then, as if it had communicated its own property to the iron it attracted, and had made it a substance like itself, this ring was put near another, and lifted it up, and as the first ring clung to the magnet, so did the second ring to the first. A third and a fourth were similarly added, so that there hung from the stone a kind of chain of rings, with their hoops connected, not interlinking, but attached together by their outer surface. Who would not be amazed at this virtue of the stone, subsisting as it does not only in itself, but transmitted through so many suspended rings, and binding them together by invisible links? Yet far more astonishing is what I heard about this stone from my brother in the episcopate, Severus bishop of Milevis. He told me that Bathanarius, once count of Africa, when the bishop was dining with him, produced a magnet, and held it under a silver plate on which he placed a bit of iron; then as he moved his hand with the magnet underneath the plate, the iron upon the plate moved about accordingly. The intervening silver was not affected at all, but precisely as the magnet was moved backwards and forwards below it, no matter how quickly, so was the iron attracted above. I have related what I myself have witnessed; I have related what I was told by one whom I trust as I trust my own eyes.

Let me further say what I have read about this magnet. When a diamond is laid near it, it does not lift iron; or if it has already lifted it, as soon as the diamond approaches, it drops it. These stones come from India. But if we cease to admire them because they are now familiar, how much less must they admire them who procure them very easily and send them to us? Perhaps they are held as cheap as we hold lime, which, because it is common, we think nothing of, though it has the strange property of burning when water, which is wont to quench fire, is poured on it, and of remaining cool when mixed with oil, which ordinarily feeds fire.

5. Nevertheless, when we declare the miracles which God has wrought, or will yet work, and which we cannot bring under the very eyes of men, skeptics keep demanding that we shall explain these marvels to reason. And because we cannot do so, inasmuch as they are above human comprehension, they suppose we are speaking falsely. These persons themselves, therefore, ought to account for all these marvels which we either can or do see. And if they perceive that this is impossible for man to do, they should acknowledge that it cannot be concluded that a thing has not been or shall not be because it cannot be reconciled to reason, since there are things now in existence of which the same is true. I will not, then, detail the multitude of marvels which are related in books, and which refer not to things that happened once and passed away, but that are permanent in certain places, where, if any one has the desire and opportunity, he may ascertain their truth; but only a few I recount. The following are some of the marvels men tell us: The salt of Agrigentum in Sicily, when thrown into the fire, becomes fluid as if it were in water, but in the water it crackles as if it were in the fire. The Garamantae have a fountain so cold by day that no one can drink it, so hot by night no one can touch it. In Epirus, too, there is a fountain which, like all others, quenches lighted torches, but, unlike all others, lights quenched torches. There is a stone found in Arcadia, and called asbestos, because once lit it cannot be put out. The wood of a certain kind of Egyptian fig-tree sinks in water, and does not float like other wood; and, stranger still, when it has been sunk to the bottom for some time, it rises again to the surface, though nature requires that when soaked in water it should be heavier than ever. Then there are the apples of Sodom, which grow indeed to an appearance of ripeness, but, when you touch them

with hand or tooth, the peel cracks, and they crumble into dust and ashes. The Persian stone pyrites burns the hand when it is tightly held in it, and so gets its name from fire. In Persia, too, there is found another stone called selenite, because its interior brilliancy waxes and wanes with the moon. Then in Cappadocia the mares are impregnated by the wind, and their foals live only three years. Tilon, an Indian island, has this advantage over all other lands, that no tree which grows in it ever loses its foliage.

These and numberless other marvels recorded in the history, not of past events, but of permanent localities, I have no time to enlarge upon and diverge from my main object; but let those skeptics who refuse to credit the divine writings give me, if they can, a rational account of them. For their only ground of unbelief in the Scriptures is, that they contain incredible things, just such as I have been recounting. For, say they, reason cannot admit that flesh burn and remain unconsumed, suffer without dying. Mighty reasoners, indeed, who are competent to give the reason of all the marvels that exist! Let them then give us the reason of the few things we have cited, and which, if they did not know they existed, and were only assured by us they would at some future time occur, they would believe still less than that which they now refuse to credit on our word. For which of them would believe us if, instead of saying that the living bodies of men hereafter will be such as to endure everlasting pain and fire without ever dying, we were to say that in the world to come there will be salt which becomes liquid in fire as if it were in water, and crackles in water as if it were in fire; or that there will be a fountain whose water in the chill air of night is so hot that it cannot be touched, while in the heat of day it is so cold that it cannot be drunk; or that there will be a stone which by its own heat burns the hand when tightly held, or a stone which cannot be extinguished if it has been lit in any part; or any of those wonders I have cited, while omitting numberless others? If we were to say that these things would be found in the world to come, and our skeptics were to reply, "If you wish us to believe these things, satisfy our reason about each of them," we should confess that we could not, because the frail comprehension of man cannot master these and suchlike wonders of God's working; and that yet our reason was thoroughly convinced that the Almighty does nothing without reason, though the frail mind of man cannot explain the reason; and that while we are in many instances uncertain what He intends, yet that it is always most certain that nothing which He intends is impossible to Him; and that when He declares His mind, we believe Him whom we cannot believe to be either powerless or false. Nevertheless these cavilers at faith and exactors of reason, how do they dispose of those things of which a reason cannot be given, and which yet exist, though in apparent contrariety to the nature of things? If we had announced that these things were to be, these skeptics would have demanded from us the reason of them, as they do in the case of those things which we are announcing as destined to be. And consequently, as these present marvels are not nonexistent, though human reason and discourse are lost in such works of God, so those things we speak of are not impossible because inexplicable; for in this particular they are in the same predicament as the marvels of earth.

GOD WORKS THROUGHOUT NATURE*

5.11.   Since the divine power governs the whole of creation, spiritual and corporeal, the waters of the sea are summoned and poured out upon the face of the earth on certain days of every year. But when this was done at the prayer of the holy Elias, the divine power was manifest in the great showers of rain which so rapidly followed, and by which that miracle was granted and dispensed; because so long and so continuous a course of fine weather had gone before, and because in the very hour in which the servant of God prayed, the air itself had not by any aspect of moisture shown signs of the coming of rain [3 Kings 18:45]. Thus too, God works ordinarily in the case of storms of thunder and lightning; but because these were wrought in an unusual manner on Mount Sinai, and then sounds were not uttered with a confused noise, but so that it appeared by most sure proofs that certain signs were given by them, they were miracles [Exod. 19:16]. Who but God draws up the sap through the root of the vine to the bunch of grapes, and makes the vine? God, who while man plants and waters, Himself giveth the increase [1 Cor. 3:7]. But when at the command of the Lord water was turned into wine with extraordinary quickness, the divine power was made manifest by the confession even of the foolish

* *On the Trinity,* III, 5.11-6.11; trans. Dods.

[John 2:9]. Who but God ordinarily clothes the trees with leaves and flowers? But when the rod of Aaron the priest blossomed, the Godhead in some way conversed with doubting humanity [Num. 17:8]. Again, earthly matter certainly serves in common to the production and formation of wood of all kinds and of the flesh of animals; and who makes them but He who said, Let the earth bring forth these things [Gen. 1:24], and who governs and directs, by the same word of His, those things which He has created? But when He changed the same matter from the rod of Moses to the flesh of a serpent, immediately and quickly [Exod. 4:3], that change, which was unusual, although of a thing that was changeable, was a miracle. But who is it that gives life to every living thing at its birth, save He who also gave life to that serpent at the moment at which there was need of it?

6.11.   And who is it that restored their proper souls to the dry bones when the dead rose again [Ezek. 37:15], but He who gives life to the flesh in the mother's womb, that those may come into being who yet must some time die? But when such things happen in, as it were, a continuous stream of everflowing succession, passing from the hidden to the visible, and from the visible to the hidden, by a regular and beaten track, then they are called natural; but when for the admonition of men they are intruded by an unusual form of change, they are called miracles.

MAN'S NATURAL ENDOWMENTS*

24.   But we must now contemplate the rich and countless blessings with which the goodness of God, who cares for all He has created, has filled this very misery of the human race, which reflects His retributive justice. . . . He alone, coupling and connecting in some wonderful fashion the spiritual and corporeal natures, the one to command, the other to obey, makes a living being. And this work of His is so great and wonderful, that not only man, who is a rational animal, and consequently more excellent than all other animals of the earth, but even the most diminutive insect, cannot be considered attentively without astonishment and without praising the Creator.

* City of God, XXII, 24; trans. Dods.

It is He, then, who has given to the human soul a mind, in which reason and understanding lie as it were asleep during infancy, and as if they were not destined, however, to be awakened and exercised as years increase, so as to become capable of knowledge and of receiving instruction, fit to understand what is true and to love what is good. It is by this capacity the soul drinks in wisdom, and becomes endowed with those virtues by which, in prudence, fortitude, temperance, and righteousness, it makes war upon error and the other inborn vices, and conquers them by fixing its desires upon no other object than the supreme and unchangeable Good. And even though this be not uniformly the result, yet who can competently utter or even conceive the grandeur of this work of the Almighty, and the unspeakable boon He has conferred upon our rational nature, by giving us even the capacity of such attainment? For over and above those arts which are called virtues, and which teach us how we may spend our life well, and attain to endless happiness —arts which are given to the children of the promise and the kingdom by the sole grace of God which is in Christ—has not the genius of man invented and applied countless astonishing arts, partly the result of necessity, partly the result of exuberant invention, so that this vigor of mind, which is so active in the discovery not merely of superfluous but even of dangerous and destructive things, betokens an inexhaustible wealth in the nature which can invent, learn, or employ such arts? What wonderful—one might say stupefying—advances has human industry made in the arts of weaving and building, of agriculture and navigation! With what endless variety are designs in pottery, painting, and sculpture produced, and with what skill executed! What wonderful spectacles are exhibited in the theaters, which those who have not seen them cannot credit! How skillful the contrivances for catching, killing, or taming wild beasts! And for the injury of men, also, how many kinds of poisons, weapons, engines of destruction, have been invented, while for the preservation or restoration of health the appliances and remedies are infinite! To provoke appetite and please the palate, what a variety of seasonings have been concocted! To express and gain entrance for thoughts, what a multitude and variety of signs there are, among which speaking and writing hold the first place! what ornaments has eloquence at command to delight the mind! what wealth of song is there to captivate the ear! how many musical instruments and strains of harmony have been devised! What skill has been attained in measures and numbers! with what sagacity have the movements and connections of the stars been discovered! Who could tell the thought that has been spent upon nature, even though, despairing of recounting it in detail, he endeavored only to give a general view of it? In fine, even the defense of errors and misapprehensions, which has illustrated the genius of heretics and philosophers, cannot be sufficiently declared. For at present it is the nature of the human mind which adorns this mortal life which we are extolling, and not the faith and the way of truth which lead to immortality. And since this great nature has certainly been created by the true and supreme God, who administers all things He has made with absolute power and justice, it could never have fallen into these miseries, nor have gone out of them to miseries eternal—saving only those who are redeemed—had not an exceeding great sin been found in the first man from whom the rest have sprung.

Moreover, even in the body, though it dies like that of the beasts, and is in many ways weaker than theirs, what goodness of God, what providence of the great Creator, is apparent! The organs of sense and the rest of the members, are not they so placed, the appearance, and form, and stature of the body as a whole, is it not so fashioned, as to indicate that it was made for the service of a reasonable soul? Man has not been created stooping towards the earth, like the irrational animals; but his bodily form, erect and looking heavenwards, admonishes him to mind the things that are above. Then the marvellous nimbleness which has been given to the tongue and the hands, fitting them to speak, and write, and execute so many duties, and practice so many arts, does it not prove the excellence of the soul for which such an assistant was provided? And even apart from its adaptation to the work required of it, there is such a symmetry in its various parts, and so beautiful a proportion maintained, that one is at a loss to decide whether, in creating the body, greater regard was paid to utility or to beauty. Assuredly no part of the body has been created for the sake of utility which does not also contribute something to its beauty. And this would be all the more apparent, if we knew more precisely how all its parts are connected and adapted to one another, and were not limited in our observations to what appears on the surface; for as to what is covered up and hidden from our view, the intricate web of veins and nerves, the vital parts of all that lies under the skin, no one can discover it. For although, with a cruel zeal for science, some medical men, who are called anatomists, have dissected the bodies of the dead, and sometimes even of sick persons who died under their knives, and have inhumanly pried into the secrets of the human body to learn the nature of the disease and its exact seat, and how it might be cured, yet those relations of which I speak, and which form the concord, or, as the Greeks call it, "harmony," of the whole body outside and in, as of some instrument, no one has been able to discover, because no one has been audacious enough to seek for them. But if these could be known, then even the inward parts, which seem to have no beauty, would so delight us with their exquisite fitness, as to afford a profounder satisfaction to the mind—and the eyes are but its ministers—than the obvious beauty which gratifies the eye. There are some things, too, which have such a place in the body, that they obviously serve no useful purpose, but are solely for beauty, as *e.g.* the teats on a man's breast, or the beard on his face; for that this is for ornament, and not for protection, is proved by the bare faces of women, who ought rather, as the weaker sex, to enjoy such a defense. If, therefore, of all those members which are exposed to our view, there is certainly not one in which beauty is sacrificed to utility, while there are some which serve no purpose but only beauty, I think it can readily be concluded that in the creation of the human body comeliness was more regarded than necessity. In truth, necessity is a transitory thing; and the time is coming when we shall enjoy one another's beauty without any lust—a condition which will specially redound to the praise of the Creator, who, as it is said in the psalm, has "put on praise and comeliness." [Ps. 103: 1]

THE PHYSICAL WORLD AND THE CHRISTIAN*

9. When, then, the question is asked what we are to believe in regard to religion, it is not necessary to probe into the nature of things, as was done by those whom the Greeks call *physici;* nor need we be in alarm lest the Christian should be ignorant of the force and number of the elements—the motion, and order, and eclipses of the heavenly bodies; the form of the heavens; the species and the natures of animals, plants, stones, fountains, rivers, mountains; about chronology and distances; the signs of coming

* *Enchiridion,* 9; trans. Dods.

storms; and a thousand other things which those philosophers either have found out, or think they have found out. For even these men themselves, endowed though they are with so much genius, burning with zeal, abounding in leisure, tracking some things by the aid of human conjecture, searching into others with the aids of history and experience, have not found out all things; and even their boasted discoveries are oftener mere guesses than certain knowledge. It is enough for the Christian to believe that the only cause of all created things, whether heavenly or earthly, whether visible or invisible, is the goodness of the Creator, the one true God; and that nothing exists but Himself that does not derive its existence from Him; and that He is the Trinity—to wit, the Father, and the Son begotten of the Father, and the Holy Spirit proceeding from the same Father, but one and the same Spirit of Father and Son.

VI. APPROACHING GOD
THROUGH UNDERSTANDING

Augustine's thought is theocentric: all his explanations focus upon God as that on which all else depends. It is essential in the study of Augustinianism to know about God from the very beginning. One cannot bracket the problem of divine existence and go on first to study psychology, physics or history. All order, all events, all meanings, stem from God. An atheistic Augustinian is an impossibility.

We have seen in our opening chapter that there are two roads to truth: that of faith and that of reason. For Augustine, God is first accepted on the basis of belief. He lived close enough to the time of Christ to feel that His life and deeds were undeniable facts of history. Never for a moment did Augustine doubt the divinity of Christ. He believed in the Holy Trinity.

He wished to understand, to see as clearly as possible, the meaning of his beliefs. That is why we find in the writings of Augustine anticipations of practically all the reasonings that have been used by later writers on natural theology. The arguments from universal consent of all men, from order in the universe, from degrees of perfection, from general awareness of moral duties—these and others are touched on by Augustine. (For detailed references, see Vega.) In many passages, Augustine speaks of physical creation's pointing to God as its Maker. Some are printed below.

Yet there is another sort of demonstration that is more peculiarly Augustinian. It is found in many of his works, but it is most strikingly expressed in the treatise *On Free Choice*. Our second selection here gives the meat of his reasoning, but one would have to read the whole second Book of this treatise to appreciate the full context. Essentially, Augustine says this: we start with a fact of human consciousness (I make a judgment that is eternally and immutably true, say, seven plus three equals ten); then we ask what is the ground or justification for such a judgment. He thinks that it cannot rest on any feature of bodies, for they are neither eternal nor immutable. But this judgment is. Nor can it be grounded on man's soul: the soul is not eternal, nor is it wholly immutable. There must then be some reality above the soul which will guarantee, account for, the eternity and immutable truth of such judgments. This eternal and immutable being, higher than the soul, either is God—or, if there be a still higher being, then He is God. This is the structure of the Augustinian argument.

Two things should be observed concerning it. The thinking starts from conscious experience and not from the physical world. Augustine considers the mental to be at once more real than the physical and nearer to God; hence, the mind is a superior point of departure for his argument. In the second place, this "demonstration" is not an exercise in logic; rather, it is one person taking another person by the hand and guiding him so that he may eventually see God for himself. Human reason needs to be exercised and directed (in this a human teacher may help), but, in the final analysis, my reason must see for itself. No other person can see for me; no other person can will or understand for me. To grasp a truth is a highly personal experience. Augustine's argument is not intended to substitute for that experience but to lead to it. In the long run, one either sees that God is—or one does not. The second part of the alternative seems almost incredible to Augustine: that a thinking person could fail to understand that there must be a highest Truth, Beauty, Goodness.

As to what God is, what sort of nature is divine, Augustine knows that this question cannot be answered by man. Two of our selections, from *The Trinity*, speak of the difficulties in thinking and speaking of God. Augustine worked out a list of many important divine attributes (*The Trinity*, Books VI-VII) and concluded that "Wisdom" is one of the best names for God. There is still another name which Augustine read in the old Latin version of the Psalms and which he considers to be peculiarly appropriate to God. This is the "Selfsame" (*Idipsum*), an expression of transcendent self-identity which is beyond explanation. The third from last selection, below, is a good example of the rapturous way in which Augustine treats this divine name.

The last brief passage ("Late Have I Loved Thee") is very important to this chapter. It reminds us that Augustine's approach to God is by no means purely cognitive. Augustinanism is a matter of love and feeling, perhaps more than it is of knowledge. The soul's journey to God is not an intellectual exercise but a progress in man's heart—and an ontological perfecting of his whole being.

CREATION IS A GREAT BOOK*

Some people read books in order to find God. Yet there is a great book, the very appearance of created things. Look above you; look below you! Note it; read it! God, whom you wish to find, never wrote that book with ink. Instead, He set before your eyes the things that He had made. Can you ask for a louder voice than that? Why, heaven and earth cry out to you: "God made me!"

THE JOURNEY OF THE SOUL TO GOD†

33.
Wherefore you will certainly not deny that there is an immutable truth, containing all things that are immutably true, which you cannot say is yours or mine or any one man's, but that in some wonderful way a mysterious and universal light, as it were, is present and proffers itself to all in common. But who would say that that which is commonly present to all who reason and understand belongs properly to the nature of any one of them? For you remember, I think, what we said a little while ago about the bodily senses namely, that those things which we perceive in common by the sense of the eyes or ears, such as colors and sounds, do not pertain to the nature of our eyes or ears, but are there for all to perceive in common. So too it will not do for you to say that those things which we see in common, each with his own mind, pertain to the nature of the mind of either one of us. For what the eyes of two persons see at the same time, cannot be said to be the eyes of this man or of that, but is some third thing to which the gaze of both is turned.

E. That is manifestly true.

* Sermon, Mai 126.6; trans. V.J.B.
† On Free Choice, II, 12, 33-34; 15, 39-40; 16, 41-42; trans. C.M. Sparrow, St. Augustine on Free Will (Charlottesville: University of Virginia Studies, 1947), pp. 64-73. Used with permission.

34. Do you think then that this truth, which we have been discussing at such length, and in which, single though it be, we have discerned so many things, is more excellent than our minds, or equal to them, or is it even inferior?

But if it were inferior we would judge not according to it, but concerning it; just as we judge of bodies because they are below us, and say commonly not only that they are so or not so, but that they ought to be so or not so. So too of our minds we know not only that the mind is so, but frequently also that it should be so. And of bodies to be sure we judge thus when we say: this is not as white as it should be, or not as square, and many similar things. But of minds: it is less apt than it should be, or less gentle, or less vehement, according as the manner of our character shows itself. And we judge of these things according to those inner rules of truth that we discern in common, but no one judges in any way of the rules themselves. For when anyone says that eternal things are better than temporal, or that seven and three are ten, no one says that it ought to be so, but knowing that it is so, he does not correct it as an examiner, but rejoices in it as a discoverer.

If again the truth were equal to our minds, it would be also mutable. For our minds perceive it sometimes more and sometimes less, and thereby acknowledge themselves mutable, while it, continuing in itself, is neither enhanced when we see it more, nor diminished when we see it less, but whole and uncorrupted it makes glad those who turn to it, and punishes with blindness those who turn away. But what then, if also we judge of those same minds according to that truth, while we can in no way judge of it? For we say of our mind: it understands less than it should or it understands as much as it should. But a mind should understand in the measure that it is able to draw near to and cleave to immutable truth. Wherefore, if that truth be neither inferior nor equal to our minds, it remains that it is higher and more excellent. . . .

39. You conceded, however, that if I should show you something higher than our minds, you would confess that it is God, if there were nothing yet higher. Accepting this concession of yours, I said that it would be enough if I should prove this. For if there is something yet more excellent than truth, that rather is God; but if not, then truth itself is God. Whether therefore there is this more

excellent thing, or whether there is not, you cannot deny that God is, which was the question set for our discussion and treatment. For if you are disturbed by what we have received in faith from the sacred teaching of Christ, that God is the Father of Wisdom, remember that we have also accepted in faith that equal to the eternal Father is the Wisdom begotten of Him. Wherefore nothing more need be asked, but only held with steadfast faith. For God is; and He is truly and supremely. This, I think, we not only hold now undoubted by faith, but know also by a sure, albeit still rather tenuous form of knowledge, which for the question in hand is enough to explain the other things that pertain to the matter. Unless, that is, you have something to say in objection.

E. Nay, I accept these things, and am completely filled with an incredible joy, which I cannot express in words, and I cry out that they are most sure. I cry out moreover with an inner voice, by which I wish to be heard by truth itself, and to cleave to it, because I concede it to be not only good but the supreme good and the maker of happiness.

A. Rightly so; and I too rejoice greatly. But I would ask whether we are now wise and happy, or whether we as yet only incline that way, so that it may come forth and be ours?

E. I think rather that we incline to it.

A. Whence then do you understand these things, at whose certainty and truth you cried out that you rejoiced? And do you grant that they pertain to wisdom? Or is any fool able to know wisdom?

E. So long as he is a fool he cannot.

A. You then are wise, or else you do not know wisdom.

E. I am certainly not yet wise, but neither would I call myself a fool in so far as I know wisdom, since these things which I know are certain, and I cannot deny that they pertain to wisdom.

A. Tell me, pray, will you not admit that he who is not just is unjust, and he who is not prudent is imprudent, and he who is not temperate is intemperate? Can there be any doubt as to this?

E. I admit that when a man is not just he is unjust and would give the same reply as to the prudent and temperate man.

A. Why, then, when he is not wise, is he not foolish?

E. I admit that too; when one is not wise, he is a fool.

A. Well then, which of these are you?

E. Whichever you call me; I should not dare to call myself wise, and I see that it follows from those things that I conceded, that I should not hesitate to say I am a fool.

A. Therefore the fool knows wisdom. For he would not be sure, as we said just now is the case, that he wished to be wise, and that he ought to wish it, if there were not inherent in his mind a notion of wisdom as having to do with those matters, concerning which you answered when asked about them separately, and which pertain to wisdom, and in the knowledge of which you rejoiced.

E. It is as you say.

41.   What else therefore do we do when we study to be wise, except to concentrate our whole soul with all the ardor we can upon what we touch with our mind, and as it were place it there and fix it unshakeably; so that it may no longer enjoy privately what has entangled it in passing things, but freed from all influence of times or places may lay hold on that which is ever one and the same. For just as the soul is the whole life of the body, the happy life of the soul is God. While we do this, and until we have completed it, we are on the way

And it is granted to us to rejoice in these true and sure goods, albeit they are as yet but flickering lights on this dark road. For is not this what is written about wisdom, when we are told how she deals with her lovers when they come to her: *She showeth herself joyfully to them along the ways, and runneth to meet them with all providence.* [Wisd. 6:17] For whithersoever you turn, by certain marks imprinted on her works she speaks to you, and when you slip back into eternal things, she again calls you within by the very forms of those things outside; so that you see that whatever delights you in the body, or allures through the bodily senses, is numbered. And you ask why this is, and return within yourself and understand that you cannot approve or find fault with that which you touch with your bodily senses, unless you have at hand certain laws of beauty, to which you may refer whatever beautiful things you may perceive externally.

42.   Look on earth and sky and sea, and whatsoever things are in them or shine from above or creep beneath or fly or swim; they have forms because they have numbers: take these away, they will be nothing. From what then are they, if not from number, seeing that they have being only in so far as they have number?

And even human artificers, makers of all corporeal forms, have numbers in their art to which they fit their works; and they move hands and tools in the fashioning till that which is formed outside, carried back to the light of numbers which is within, so far as may be attains perfection, and through the mediating sense pleases the inner judge looking upon the heavenly numbers.

Then seek what moves the limbs of the artificer himself: it will be number; for they too are moved in the rhythm of numbers. And if you take away the work from the hands, and from the mind the intention of making something, and that motion is directed toward pleasure, you will have a dance. Seek then what it is that gives pleasure in a dance; number will answer, "Behold, it is I."

Look now upon the beauty of the formed body; numbers are held in space. Examine the beauty of mobility in the body; numbers move around in time. Go into the art whence these proceed, seek in it time and place: never will it be, nowhere will it be; yet number lives in it, nor is its region of spaces, nor its age of days; and yet when they who would be artists apply themselves to learning the art, they move their bodies through space and time, and even their mind through time—with the passing of time, to be sure, they become more skillful. Transcend, therefore, the artist's mind also, to see the sempiternal number. Now wisdom will flash forth to you from her innermost throne, and from the very sanctuary of truth. If she dazzles and blinds your as yet too feeble vision, turn back the eye of the mind into that path where she showed herself joyfully; but remember then that you have put off the vision which, when you are stronger and sounder, you may seek again.

THE SOUL'S ASCENT TO GOD*

10.16. Being thence admonished to return to myself, I entered even into my inward self, Thou being my Guide, and able I was, for Thou wert become my Helper. And I entered and beheld with the eye of my soul (such as it was), above the same eye of my soul, above my mind, the Light Unchangeable. Not this ordinary light, which all flesh may look upon, nor as it were a greater of the same kind, as though the brightness of this should be manifold brighter, and with its greatness take up all space. Not such was this light, but other, yea, far other from all these. Nor was it above my soul, as oil is above water, nor

* *Confessions*, VII, 10.16-17.23; trans. E. B. Pusey, in Library of the Fathers (Oxford, 1838).

yet as heaven above earth: but above to my soul, because It made me; and I below It, because I was made by It. He that knows the Truth, knows what that Light is; and he that knows It, knows eternity. Love knoweth it. O Truth Who art Eternity! and Love Who art Truth! and Eternity Who art Love! Thou art my God, to Thee do I sigh night and day. Thee when I first knew, Thou liftedst me up, that I might see there was what I might see, and that I was not yet such as to see. And Thou didst beat back the weakness of my sight, streaming forth Thy beams of light upon me most strongly, and I trembled with love and awe: and I perceived myself to be far off from Thee, in the region of unlikeness, as if I heard this Thy voice from on high: "I am the food of grown men; grow and thou shalt feed upon Me; nor shalt thou convert Me, like the food of thy flesh, into thee, but thou shalt be converted into Me." And I learned that Thou for iniquity chastenest man, and Thou madest my soul to consume away like a spider. And I said, "Is Truth therefore nothing because it is not diffused through space finite or infinite?" And Thou criedst to me from afar: "Yea verily, I AM that I AM." And I heard, as the heart heareth, nor had I room to doubt, and I should sooner doubt that I live, than that Truth is not, which is clearly seen, being understood by those things which are made.

And I beheld the other things below Thee, and I 11.17. perceived that they neither altogether are, nor altogether are not, for they are, since they are from Thee, but are not, because they are not what Thou art. For that truly is which remains unchangeably. It is good then for me to hold fast unto God; for if I remain not in Him, I cannot in myself; but He, remaining in himself, reneweth all things. And Thou art the Lord my God, since Thou standest not in need of my goodness.

And it was manifested unto me, that those things be 12.18. good which yet are corrupted; which neither were they sovereignly good, nor unless they were good, could be corrupted: for if sovereignly good, they were incorruptible; if not good at all, there were nothing in them to be corrupted. For corruption injures, but unless it diminished goodness, it could not injure. Either then corruption injures not, which cannot be; or, which is most certain, all which is corrupted is deprived of good. But if they be deprived of all good, they shall cease to be. For if they shall be, and can now no longer be corrupted, they shall be better than before, because they shall abide incorruptibly. And what more monstrous than to affirm things to become better by losing all their good? Therefore, if they shall be deprived of all good, they shall no longer be. So long therefore as they are, they are good: therefore, whatsoever is, is good. That evil then which I sought whence it is, is not any substance: for were it a substance, it should be good. For either it should be an incorruptible substance, and so a chief good: or a corruptible substance, which unless it were good could not be corrupted. I perceived therefore, and it was manifested to me, that Thou madest all things good, nor is there any substance at all which Thou madest not; and for that Thou madest not all things equal, therefore are all things; because each is good, and altogether very good, because our God made all things very good.

And to Thee is nothing whatsoever evil: yea, not
13.19. only to Thee, but also to Thy creation as a whole,
because there is nothing without, which may break in and corrupt that order which Thou hast appointed it. But in the parts thereof some things, because unharmonizing with other some, are accounted evil: whereas those very things harmonize with others, and are good; and in themselves are good. . . .

There is no soundness in them, whom aught of Thy
14.20. creation displeaseth: as neither in me, when much
which Thou hast made displeased me. And because my soul durst not be displeased at my God, it would fain not account that Thine, which displeased it. Hence it had gone into the opinion of two substances, and had no rest, but talked idly. And returning thence, it had made to itself a God, through infinite measures of all space; and thought it to be Thee, and placed it in its heart; and had again become the temple of its own idol, to Thee abominable. But after Thou hadst soothed my head, unknown to me, and closed mine eyes that they should not behold vanity, I ceased somewhat of my former self, and my frenzy was lulled to sleep; and I awoke in Thee, and saw Thee infinite, but in another way, and this sight was not derived from the flesh.

And I looked back on other things, and I saw
15.21. that they owed their being to Thee, and were all
bounded in Thee but in a different way; not as being in space, but because Thou containest all things in Thine

hand in Thy Truth, and all things are true so far as they be; nor is there any falsehood, unless when that is thought to be which is not. And I saw that all things did harmonize, not with their places only, but with their seasons. And that Thou, who only art Eternal, didst not begin to work after innumerable spaces of times spent; for that all spaces of times, both which have passed and which shall pass, neither go nor come but through Thee, working and abiding.

16.22. And I perceived and found it nothing strange that bread which is pleasant to a healthy palate is loathsome to one distempered: and to sore eyes light is offensive, which to the sound is delightful. And Thy righteousness displeaseth the wicked; much more the viper and reptiles, which Thou hast created good, fitting in with the inferior portions of Thy creation, with which the very wicked also fit in; and that the more, by how much they be unlike Thee; but with the superior creatures, by how much they become more like to Thee. And I inquired what iniquity was, and found it to be no substance, but the perversion of the will, turned aside from Thee, O God, the Supreme, towards these lower things, and casting out its bowels and puffed up outwardly.

17.23. And I wondered that I now loved Thee, and no phantasm for Thee. And yet did I not press on to enjoy my God, but was borne up to Thee by Thy beauty, and soon borne down from Thee by mine own weight, sinking with sorrow into these inferior things. This weight was carnal custom. Yet dwelt there with me a remembrance of Thee; nor did I any way doubt that there was One to Whom I might cleave, but that I was not yet such as to cleave to Thee: for that the body which is corrupted presseth down the soul, and the earthly tabernacle weigheth down the mind that museth upon many things. And most certain I was that Thy invisible works from the creation of the world are clearly seen, being understood by the things that are made, even Thy eternal power and Godhead. For examining whence it was that I admired the beauty of bodies celestial or terrestrial, and what aided me in judging soundly on things mutable, and pronouncing, "This ought to be thus, this not"; examining, I say, whence it was that I so judged, seeing I did so judge, I had found the unchangeable and true Eternity of Truth, above my changeable mind.

And thus by degrees, I passed from bodies to the soul, which through the bodily senses perceives, and thence to its inward faculty, to which the bodily senses represent things external, whitherto reach the faculties of beasts; and thence again to the reasoning faculty, to which what is received from the senses of the body is referred to be judged. Which finding itself also to be in me a thing variable, raised itself up to its own understanding, and drew away my thoughts from the power of habit, withdrawing itself from those troops of contradictory phantasms, that so it might find what that light was whereby it was bedewed, when, without all doubting, it cried out, "That the unchangeable was to be preferred to the changeable"; whence also it knew That Unchangeable, which unless it had in some way known, it had no sure ground to prefer it to the changeable. And thus with the flash of one trembling glance it arrived at THAT WHICH IS. And then I saw Thy invisible things understood by the things which are made. But I could not fix my gaze thereon; and, my infirmity being struck back, I was thrown again on my wonted habits, carrying along with me only a loving memory thereof, and a longing for what I had as it were perceived the odor of, but was not yet able to feed on.

THE WHOLE WORLD PROCLAIMS ITS MAKER*

12.   *I have gone round and have offered in His tabernacle a sacrifice of jubilation*. We offer up a sacrifice of jubilation, we offer up a sacrifice of gladness, a sacrifice of rejoicing, a sacrifice of thanksgiving, which no words can express. But where do we offer it? In his own tabernacle, in Holy Church. And what is the sacrifice we offer? An overflowing and ineffable joy, beyond words, not to be expressed in speech. This is the sacrifice of jubilation. Where seek for it, how find it? By looking everywhere. *I have gone round*, says the Psalmist, *and have offered in His tabernacle a sacrifice of jubilation*. Let your mind roam through the whole creation; everywhere the created world will cry out to you: "God made me." Whatever pleases you in a work of art brings to your mind the artist who wrought it; much more, when you survey the universe, does the consideration of it evoke praise for its Maker. You look on the heavens; they are God's great work. You behold the earth; God made its numbers of seeds, its varieties of plants, its multitude of animals. Go round the heavens again and back to

* *On Psalm 26*, Serm. 2, 12; trans. ACW 29, 272-273.

the earth, leave out nothing; on all sides everything cries out to you of its Author; nay, the very forms of created things are as it were the voices with which they praise their Creator. But who can fathom the whole creation? Who shall set forth its praises? Who shall worthily praise heaven and earth, the sea, and all things that are in them? And these indeed are visible things. Who shall worthily praise the angels, thrones, dominations, principalities, and powers? Who shall worthily praise that power which works actively within ourselves, quickening the body, giving movement to the members, bringing the senses into play, embracing so many things in the memory, distinguishing so many things by the intelligence; who can worthily praise it? Now if in considering these creatures of God human language is so at a loss, what is it to do in regard to the Creator? When words fail, can aught but triumphant music remain? *I have gone round and have offered in His tabernacle a sacrifice of jubilation.*

ASCENDING TO THE SUPREME TRUTH*

29.52.   Now that we have discussed the advantages of authority to a length that at present seems sufficient, let us see to what extent reason can succeed in ascending from the visible to the invisible and from the temporal to the eternal. We must not be passive and thoughtless in our contemplation of the beauty of the Heavens, the order of the heavenly bodies, the splendor of the sun, the alternation of day and night, the monthly phases of the moon, the four seasons of the year corresponding to the four fundamental elements, the great power of the seeds in producing figures and numbers, all things preserving their proper order and nature, each in its own kind. Our consideration of these phenomena must not be one of thoughtless, passing curiosity, but should become a step towards the undying and the everlasting. And so we must next consider what is that vital nature which perceives all these things and which, because it gives life to the body, is necessarily superior to the body. For no mass whatsoever, no matter how it glitters in the light, is to be valued highly, if it be without life. And any living substance is by the law of nature exalted above any nonliving substance.

* *The True Religion,* 29.52-31.58; trans. G. R. Sheahan, S.J., *De vera religione (Chapters 18-38)* (St. Louis University Master's Thesis, 1946), pp. 49-63. Used with permission.

53. But since even irrational animals are admittedly alive and sentient, that power in the human soul is not noblest by which man perceives sensible objects, but that by which man makes judgments about those objects. For most brutes see more clearly and perceive things more keenly with their other bodily senses than does man. But to form judgments about things is not the part of mere sentient life, but of rational life—a life which brutes lack, and in which men excel. Now, it is certainly easy to see that the judge is nobler than what he judges. The judgment of a rational being is exercised not only on the objects of the senses, but on the senses themselves; for example: why an oar should appear broken in water, although it is intact, and why the eyes perceive it as broken. A glance of the eyes can report the fact, but by no means can it pass judgment. Thus it is evident that, just as sentient life surpasses nonlife, so rational life surpasses both.

30.54. Thus, too, since to make judgments is the proper activity of rational life, there is no nature more noble.

However, even a rational nature is clearly changeable; for at one time it turns out to be skillful, at another time unskillful. Moreover, the worth of its judgments is proportioned to its skillfulness, and its skillfulness is proportioned to the degree in which it partakes of art or learning or wisdom. Let us, then, look into the nature of this art. By art in this context I do not mean what is picked up by experimentation; I mean what is developed at the cost of much ratiocination. For a man displays no great learning in knowing that the preparation made from lime and sand clings more tenaciously to rubble than does mud, or in building with such good taste as to balance off designs that are alike, and to centralize those that are unique. However, this sense of proportion does come closer to reason and to truth. But here is a real problem: why does it displease us to have two windows placed, not one above the other, but side by side, when they are of different sizes, and could have been of equal size? Why, on the other hand, are we not equally displeased with the inequality when one is even twice the size of the other, so long as they are placed one above the other? Why, again, does their being two prevent our caring how much larger or smaller one is than the other? For when there are three, our eyes themselves seem to cry out that either there be complete equality, or that between the largest and smallest there be a middle one, as much larger than the smallest as it is smaller than the largest; and in such a way at first that nature herself seems to be the criterion of our judgment. And here we should take special notice of how a thing might have given us slight displeasure when examined alone, but when compared with something better is completely rejected. Thus we find that ordinary art is merely a remembrance of things experienced and enjoyed, coupled with the exercise of certain bodily actions; and that, if you lack this art, you can still evaluate its products—a far more noble activity, despite the fact that you may not be able to do the handiwork.

55.   But in all arts there is a symmetry which pleases us and which imparts to everything a perfect and beautiful unity. It achieves its unity and its proportion either by a likeness of equal parts or by a gradation of unequal parts. But who could find the supreme proportion and likeness in material bodies; and who would dare assert, after diligent consideration, that any body is really and essentially one? For all bodies are changing by passage from one degree of beauty to another, or from one place to another; and they are composed of parts each with its own location, and through these parts they are separated in space. Furthermore, the real proportion and likeness, and the real and primary unity, are not perceived by the eyes of the body, or by any of the other senses, but by the intellect. For what would be the basis for a search for any proportion in material bodies, or for a conviction that their proportion differs by far from the perfect proportion, unless the perfect proportion itself were seen by the mind, even if it is the uncreated that we call perfect.

56.   But all things which are beautiful to the senses, whether they are brought forth by nature or worked out by artistry, are beautiful because of their order in place and in time, as, for example, a body or the motion of a body. Thus that proportion and unity, known only to the mind, and serving as a criterion for the mind to pass judgment upon corporeal beauty, as reported to it by the senses, does not fluctuate in place and in time. For it is wrong to say that it is a criterion for judging the rotundity of a wheel but not of a bowl, or the rotundity of a bowl but not of a coin. The same is true when we consider the duration and movement of bodies: it is ridiculous to say that it is a criterion for judging proportioned years but not propor-

tioned months, or proportioned months, but not proportioned days. But whether something moves with consistent speed through these periods of time, or through hours or through shorter periods, the same one and unchangeable criterion is used. And since the measurements of lesser and greater shapes and motions have the same criterion of equality or likeness or conformity, the law itself is greater than all these potentially. But by measurement in place or time it is neither greater nor less. For if it were greater, than we would not judge the less by the entire criterion; and if it were less, we would not judge the greater by it. But we use the complete law of quadratics to judge both a square plaza and a square rock and a square board and a square jewel; and we use the complete law of proportions to judge the order in the motion of the feet of a running ant, and of the feet of a walking elephant. Who then could doubt that the criterion for judging intervals of place and of time is neither greater nor less, since potentially it is above all things? And since this law is in all arts and is absolutely unchangeable, and since even the human mind to which we have conceded the perception of such a law allows of the instability of error, it is sufficiently clear that superior to our minds there exists the law of truth.

31.57. But I must not refrain any longer from saying that the unchangeable nature which is superior to our rational nature is God, and that primary Life and primary Essence is identical with primary Wisdom. For this is that unchangeable Truth which is rightly called the law of all arts, and the art of the omnipotent Artisan. And so, since the soul perceives that it cannot pass judgment even on the beauty and motion of bodies by its own standard, it must at once admit that, although its nature is superior to the nature it judges, still its nature is inferior to the nature according to which it makes its judgment, and of which it cannot possibly judge. For I can say why the corresponding members of different bodies should mutually agree, because I happily contemplate the supreme proportion; however, I do not do so with the eyes of my body, but with those of my mind. That is why I judge more highly of sensible objects in proportion to the degree in which their natures approach to objects of my mind. But why those things are as they are, no one can say; neither would any one in his right mind say that they had to be so, as if they could possibly be otherwise.

58. But why sensible objects give pleasure, and why it is that when we get a better taste of them we love them more strongly, no one who rightly understands them will presume to explain. For just as we and all rational souls rightly judge of inferior things by the criterion of truth, so we are judged by that only Truth when we cling to it. But that Truth is not judged even by the Father, for it is not inferior to Him; therefore, what the Father judges, He judges by Truth itself.

PLATO'S VIEW OF GOD*

4. But, among the disciples of Socrates, Plato was the one who shone with a glory which far excelled that of the others, and who not unjustly eclipsed them all. By birth, an Athenian of honorable parentage, he far surpassed his fellow-disciples in natural endowments, of which he was possessed in a wonderful degree. Yet, deeming himself and the Socratic discipline far from sufficient for bringing philosophy to perfection, he traveled as extensively as he was able, going to every place famed for the cultivation of any science of which he could make himself master. Thus he learned from the Egyptians whatever they held and taught as important; and from Egypt, passing into those parts of Italy which were filled with the fame of the Pythagoreans, he mastered, with the greatest facility, and under the most eminent teachers, all the Italic philosophy which was then in vogue. And, as he had a peculiar love for his master Socrates, he made him the speaker in all his dialogues, putting into his mouth whatever he had learned, either from others, or from the efforts of his own powerful intellect, tempering even his moral disputations with the grace and politeness of the Socratic style. And, as the study of wisdom consists in action and contemplation, so that one part of it may be called active, and the other contemplative—the active part having reference to the conduct of life, that is, to the regulation of morals, and the contemplative part to the investigation into the causes of nature and into pure truth—Socrates is said to have excelled in the active part of that study, while Pythagoras gave more attention to its contemplative part, on which he brought to bear all the force of his great

* *City of God*, VIII, 4; trans. Dods.

intellect. To Plato is given the praise of having perfected philosophy by combining both parts into one. He then divides it into three parts—the first moral, which is chiefly occupied with action; the second natural, of which the object is contemplation; and the third rational, which discriminates between the true and the false. And though this last is necessary both to action and contemplation, it is contemplation, nevertheless, which lays peculiar claim to the office of investigating the nature of truth. Thus this tripartite division is not contrary to that which made the study of wisdom to consist in action and contemplation. Now, as to what Plato thought with respect to each of these parts—that is, what he believed to be the end of all actions, the cause of all natures, and the light of all intelligences—it would be a question too long to discuss, and about which we ought not to make any rash affirmation. For, as Plato liked and constantly affected the well-known method of his master Socrates, namely, that of dissimulating his knowledge or his opinions, it is not easy to discover clearly what he himself thought on various matters, any more than it is to discover what were the real opinions of Socrates. We must, nevertheless, insert into our work certain of those opinions which he expresses in his writings, whether he himself uttered them, or narrates them as expressed by others, and seems himself to approve of—opinions sometimes favorable to the true religion, which our faith takes up and defends, and sometimes contrary to it, as, for example, in the questions concerning the existence of one God or of many, as it relates to the truly blessed life which is to be after death. For those who are praised as having most closely followed Plato, who is justly preferred to all the other philosophers of the Gentiles, and who are said to have manifested the greatest acuteness in understanding him, do perhaps entertain such an idea of God as to admit that in Him are to be found the cause of existence, the ultimate reason for the understanding, and the end in reference to which the whole life is to be regulated. Of which three things, the first is understood to pertain to the natural, the second to the rational, and the third to the moral part of philosophy. For if man has been so created as to attain, through that which is most excellent in him, to that which excels all things—that is, to the one true and absolutely good God, without whom no nature exists, no doctrine instructs, no exercise profits—let Him be sought in whom all things are secure to us, let Him be discovered in whom all truth becomes certain to us, let Him be loved in whom all becomes right to us.

1.2. And we shall mutually pardon one another the more easily, if we know, or at any rate firmly believe and hold, that whatever is said of a nature, unchangeable, invisible, and having life absolutely and sufficient to itself, must not be measured after the custom of things visible and changeable and mortal, or not self-sufficient. But although we labor, and yet fail, to grasp and know even those things which are within the scope of our corporeal senses, or what we are ourselves in the inner man; yet it is with no shamelessness that faithful piety burns after those divine and unspeakable things which are above: piety, I say, not inflated by the arrogance of its own power, but inflamed by the grace of its Creator and Savior Himself. For with what understanding can man apprehend God, who does not yet apprehend that very understanding itself of his own, by which he desires to apprehend Him? And if he does already apprehend this, let him carefully consider that there is nothing in his own nature better than it; and let him see whether he can there see any outlines of forms, or brightness of colors, or greatness of space, or distance of parts, or extension of size, or any movements through intervals of place, or any such thing at all. Certainly we find nothing of all this in that than which we find nothing better in our own nature, that is, in our own intellect, by which we apprehend wisdom according to our capacity. What, therefore, we do not find in that which is our own best, we ought not to seek in Him who is far better than that best of ours; that so we may understand God, if we are able, and as much as we are able, as good without quality, great without quantity, a creator though He lack nothing, ruling but from no position, sustaining all things without "having" them, in His wholeness everywhere yet without place, eternal without time, making things that are changeable, without change of Himself and without passion. Whoso thus thinks of God, although he cannot yet find out in all ways what He is, yet piously takes heed, as much as he is able, to think nothing of Him that He is not.

2.3. He is, however, without doubt, a substance, or, if it be better so to call it, an essence, which the Greeks call onsia. For as wisdom is so called from

* *On the Trinity*, V, 1.2-2.3; trans. Dods.

the being wise, and knowledge from knowing; so from being (*esse*) comes that which we call essence. And who is there that IS, more than He who said to His servant Moses, "I am that I am"; and, "Thus shalt thou say unto the children of Israel, He who is hath sent me unto you"? [Exod. 3:14] But other things that are called essences or substances admit of accidents, whereby a change, whether great or small, is produced in them. But there can be no accident of this kind in respect to God; and therefore He who is God is the only unchangeable substance or essence, to whom certainly BEING itself, whence comes the name of essence, most especially and most truly belongs. For that which is changed does not retain its own being; and that which can be changed, although it be not actually changed, is able not to be that which it had been; and hence that which not only is not changed, but also cannot at all be changed, alone falls most truly, without difficulty or hesitation, under the category of BEING.

THE PROBLEM OF SPEAKING ABOUT GOD*

4.7. For the sake, then, of speaking of things that cannot be uttered, that we may be able in some way to utter what we are able in no way to utter fully, our Greek friends have spoken of one essence, three substances; but the Latins of one essence or substance, three persons; because, as we have already said, essence usually means nothing else than substance in our language, that is, in Latin. And provided that what is said is understood only in a mystery, such a way of speaking was sufficient, in order that there might be something to say when it was asked what the three are which the true faith pronounces to be three, when it both declares that the Father is not the Son, and that the Holy Spirit, which is the gift of God, is neither the Father nor the Son. When, then, it is asked what the three are, or who the three are, we betake ourselves to the finding out of some special or general name under which we may embrace these three; and no such name occurs to the mind, because the supereminence of the Godhead surpasses the power of customary speech. For God is more truly thought than He is uttered, and exists more truly than He is thought. For when

* *On the Trinity*, VII, 4.7-9; trans. Dods.

we say that Jacob was not the same as Abraham, but that Isaac was neither Abraham nor Jacob, certainly we confess that they are three, Abraham, Isaac, and Jacob. But when it is asked what three, we reply three men, calling them in the plural by a specific name; but if we were to say three animals, then by a generic name; for man, as the ancients have defined him, is a rational, mortal animal: or again, as our Scriptures usually speak, three souls, since it is fitting to call the whole from the better part, that is, to call both body and soul, which is the whole man, from the soul; for so it is said that seventy-five souls went down into Egypt with Jacob, instead of saying so many men. Again, when we say that your horse is not mine, and that a third belonging to some one else is neither mine nor yours, then we confess that there are three; and if any one ask what three, we answer three horses by a specific name, but three animals by a generic one. And yet again, when we say that an ox is not a horse, but that a dog is neither an ox nor a horse, we speak of a three; and if any one questions us what three, we do not speak now by a specific name of three horses, or three oxen, or three dogs, because the three are not contained under the same species, but by a generic name, three animals; or if under a higher genus, three substances, or three creatures, or three natures. But whatsoever things are expressed in the plural number specifically by one name, can also be expressed generically by one name. But all things which are generically called by one name cannot also be called specifically by one name. For three horses, which is a specific name, we also call three animals; but a horse, and an ox, and a dog, we call only three animals or substances, which are generic names, or anything else that can be spoken generically concerning them; but we cannot speak of them as three horses, or oxen, or dogs, which are specific names; for we express those things by one name, although in the plural number, which have that in common that is signified by the name. For Abraham, and Isaac, and Jacob, have in common that which is man; therefore they are called three men: a horse also, and an ox, and a dog, have in common that which is animal; therefore they are called three animals. So three several laurels we also call three trees; but a laurel and a myrtle and an olive, we call only three trees or three substances or three natures: and so three stones we call also three bodies; but stone and wood and iron we call only three bodies, or by any other higher generic name by which they can be called. Of the Father, therefore, the Son, and the

Holy Spirit, seeing that they are three, let us ask what three they are, and what they have in common. For the being the Father is not common to them, so that they should be interchangeably fathers to one another: as friends, since they are so called relatively to each other, can be called three friends, because they are so mutually to each other. But this is not the case in the Trinity, since the Father only is there father; and not Father of two, but of the Son only. Neither are they three Sons, since the Father there is not the Son, nor is the Holy Spirit. Neither three Holy Spirits, because the Holy Spirit also, in that proper meaning by which He is also called the gift of God, is neither the Father nor the Son. What three therefore? For if three persons, then that which is meant by person is common to them; therefore that name is either specific or generic to them, if we regard the custom of speech. But where there is no difference of nature, there things that are more in number are so expressed generically, that they can also be expressed specifically. For the difference of nature causes, that a laurel and a myrtle and an olive, or a horse and an ox and a dog, are not called by the specific name, the former of three laurels or the latter of three oxen, but by the generic name, the former of three trees and the latter of three animals. But here, where there is no difference of essence, it is necessary that these three should have a specific name, which yet is not to be found. For person is a generic name, insomuch that man also can be so called, although there is so great a difference between man and God.

8. Further in that very generic word, if on this account we say three persons, because that which person means is common to them (otherwise they can in no way be so called, just as they are not called three sons, because that which son means is not common to them), why do we not also say three Gods? For certainly, since the Father is a person and the Son a person and the Holy Spirit a person, therefore there are three persons: since then the Father is God and the Son God and the Holy Spirit God, why not three Gods? Or else, since on account of their ineffable union these three are together one God, why not also one person; that so we could not say three persons, although we call each a person singly, just as we cannot say three Gods, although we call each singly God, whether the Father or the Son or the Holy Spirit? Is it because Scripture does not say three Gods? But neither do we find that Scripture anywhere mentions three persons. Or is it because Scripture does not call

these three, either three or one person (for we read of the person of the Lord, but not of the Lord as a person), that therefore it was lawful through the mere necessity of speaking and reasoning to say three persons, not because Scripture says it, but because Scripture does not contradict it: whereas, if we were to say three Gods, Scripture would contradict it, which says, "Hear, O Israel; the Lord thy God is one God"? [Deut. 6:4] Why then is it not also lawful to say three essences; which, in like manner, as Scripture does not say, so neither does it contradict? For if essence is a specific name common to three, why are They not to be called three essences, as Abraham, Isaac, and Jacob are called three men, because man is the specific name common to all men? But if essence is not a specific name, but a generic one, since man and cattle and tree and constellation and angel are called essences, why are not these called three essences, as three horses are called three animals, and three laurels are called three trees, and three stones three bodies? Or if they are not called three essences but one essence, on account of the unity of the Trinity, why is it not the case that, on account of the same unity of the Trinity, they are not to be called three substances or three persons, but one substance and one person? For as the name of essence is common to them, so that each singly is called essence, so the name of either substance or person is common to them. For that which must be understood of persons according to our usage, this is to be understood of substances according to Greek usage; for they say three substances, one essence, in the same way as we say three persons, one essence or substance.

9. What therefore remains, except that we confess that these terms sprang from the necessity of speaking, when copious reasoning was required against the devices or errors of the heretics? For when human weakness endeavored to utter in speech to the senses of man what it grasps in the secret places of the mind, in proportion to its comprehension respecting the Lord God its creator, whether by devout faith or by any discernment whatsoever; it feared to say three essences, lest any difference should be understood to exist in that absolute equality. Again, it could not say that there were not three somewhats, for it was because Sabellius said this that he fell into heresy. For it must be devoutly believed, as most certainly known from the Scriptures, and must be grasped by the eye of the mind with undoubting perception, that there is both Father and Son and

Holy Spirit, and that the Son is not the same with the Father, nor the Holy Spirit the same with the Father or the Son. It sought then what three it should call them, and answered substances or persons; by which names it did not intend diversity to be meant, but singleness to be denied: that not only unity might be understood therein from the being called one essence, but also Trinity from the being called three substances or persons. For if it is the same thing with God to be as to subsist, they were not to be called three substances, in such sense as they are not called three essences; just as, because it is the same thing with God to be as to be wise, as we do not say three essences, so neither three wisdoms.

GOD IS THE SELFSAME*

3.5. Let the remainder of the text remove all doubt, for we should not take a carnal meaning of: "Jerusalem which is built as a city; of which His participation is in the selfsame." So now, brethren, whoever lifts up the gaze of his mind, whoever puts aside the obscurity of the flesh, whoever cleanses the eye of his heart, let him rise up and see the selfsame. What is the selfsame? How may I express it, except as the selfsame? Brethren, if you are able, understand the selfsame. For, whatever other expression I use, I do not express the selfsame. Let us attempt, however, by means of some approximations of words and meanings, to extend the weakness of our minds so as to think upon the selfsame.

What is the selfsame? That which always exists in the same way; that which is not now one thing and again a different thing. What is that which is? That which is eternal. For, that which is always in one way and then in another is not, for it does not endure; it is not altogether nonexistent, but it does not exist in the highest sense. And what is that which is, except He Who when He sent Moses forth said to him, "I am Who am"? What is this, except He Who when His servant said, "Behold, Thou sendest me; if the people say to me, Who sent you?, what shall I reply?" would give no other name than, "I am Who am." He added this statement, "Say then to the sons of Israel, He Who is hath sent me to you." [Exod. 3:13-15] You cannot grasp it; it is a great deal to understand, a great deal to take in.

* On Psalm 121, 3.5; trans. V.J.B.

A DIVINE INVOCATION*

2. O God, Framer of the universe, grant me first rightly to invoke Thee; then to show myself worthy to be heard by Thee; lastly, deign to set me free. God, through whom all things, which of themselves were not, tend to be. God, who withholdest from perishing even that which seems to be mutually destructive. God, who, out of nothing, hast created this world, which the eyes of all perceive to be most beautiful. God, who dost not cause evil, but causest that it be not most evil. God, who to the few that flee for refuge to that which truly is, showest evil to be nothing. God, through whom the universe, even taking in its sinister side, is perfect. God, from whom things most widely at variance with Thee effect no dissonance, since worser things are included in one plan with better. God, who art loved, wittingly or unwittingly, by everything that is capable of loving. God, in whom are all things, to whom nevertheless neither the vileness of any creature is vile, nor its wickedness harmful, nor its error erroneous. God, who hast not willed that any but the pure should know the truth. God, the Father of truth, the Father of wisdom, the Father of the true and crowning life, the Father of blessedness, the Father of that which is good and fair, the Father of intelligible light, the Father of our awakening and illumination, the Father of the pledge by which we are admonished to return to Thee.

3. Thee I invoke, O God, the Truth, in whom and from whom and through whom all things are true which anywhere are true. God, the Wisdom, in whom and from whom and through whom all things are wise which anywhere are wise. God, the true and crowning Life, in whom and from whom and through whom all things live which truly and supremely live. God, the Blessedness, in whom and from whom and through whom all things are blessed which anywhere are blessed. God, the Good and Fair, in whom and from whom and through whom all things are good and fair which anywhere are good and fair. God, the intelligible Light, in whom and from whom and through

* Soliloquies, I, 2-6; trans. Dods.
144

whom all things intelligibly shine which anywhere intelligibly shine. God, whose kingdom is that whole world of of which sense has no ken. God, from whose kingdom a law is even derived down upon these lower realms. God, from whom to be turned away is to fall: to whom to be turned back is to rise again: in whom to abide is to stand firm. God, from whom to go forth is to die: to whom to return is to revive: in whom to have our dwelling is to live. God, whom no one loses, unless deceived: whom no one seeks, unless stirred up: whom no one finds, unless made pure. God, whom to forsake is one thing with perishing; towards whom to tend is one thing with living: whom to see is one thing with having. God, towards whom faith rouses us, hope lifts us up, with whom love joins us. God, through whom we overcome the enemy, Thee I entreat. God, through whose gift it is that we do not perish utterly. God, by whom we are warned to watch. God, by whom we distinguish good from ill. God, by whom we flee evil and follow good. God, through whom we yield not to calamities. God, through whom we faithfully serve and benignantly govern. God, through whom we learn those things to be another's which aforetime we accounted ours, and those things to be ours which we used to account as belonging to another. God, through whom the baits and enticements of evil things have no power to hold us. God, through whom it is that diminished possessions leave ourselves complete. God, through whom our better good is not subject to a worse. God, through whom death is swallowed up in victory. God, who dost turn us to Thyself. God, who dost strip us of that which is not, and arrayest us in that which is. God, who dost make us worthy to be heard. God, who dost fortify us. God, who leadest us into all truth. God, who speakest to us only good, who neither terrifiest into madness nor sufferest another so to do. God, who callest us back into the way. God, who leadest us to the door of life. God, who causest it to be opened to them that knock. God, who givest us the bread of life. God, through whom we thirst for the draught, which being drunk we never thirst. God, who dost convince the world of sin, of righteousness, and of judgment. God, through whom it is that we are not commoved by those who refuse to believe. God, through whom we disapprove the error of those who think that there are no merits of souls before Thee. God, through whom it comes that we are not in bondage to the weak and beggarly elements. God, who cleansest us and preparest us for Divine rewards, to me propitious come Thou.

4. Whatever has been said by me, Thou the only God, do Thou come to my help, the one true and eternal substance, where is no discord, no confusion, no shifting, no indigence, no death. Where is supreme concord, supreme evidence, supreme steadfastness, supreme fullness, and life supreme. Where nothing is lacking, nothing redundant. Where Begetter and Begotten are one. God, whom all things serve that serve, to whom is compliant every virtuous soul. By whose laws the poles revolve, the stars fulfill their courses, the sun vivifies the day, the moon tempers the night: and all the framework of things, day after day by vicissitude of light and gloom, month after month by waxings and wanings of the moon, year after year by orderly successions of spring and summer and fall and winter, cycle after cycle by accomplished concurrences of the solar course, and through the mighty orbs of time, folding and refolding upon themselves, as the stars still recur to their first conjunctions, maintains, so far as this merely visible matter allows, the mighty constancy of things. God, by whose everduring laws the stable motion of shifting things is suffered to feel no perturbation, the thronging course of circling ages is ever recalled anew to the image of immovable quiet; by whose laws the choice of the soul is free, and to the good rewards and to the evil pains are distributed by necessities settled throughout the nature of everything. God, from whom distil even to us all benefits, by whom all evils are withheld from us. God, above whom is nothing, beyond whom is nothing, without whom is nothing. God, under whom is the whole, in whom is the whole, with whom is the whole. Who hast made man after Thine image and likeness, which he discovers who has come to know himself. Hear me, hear me, graciously hear me, my God, my Lord, my King, my Father, my Cause, my Hope, my Wealth, my Honor, my House, my Country, my Health, my Light, my Life. Hear, hear, hear me graciously, in that way, all Thine own, which though known to few is to those few known so well.

5. Henceforth Thee alone do I love, Thee alone I follow, Thee alone I seek, Thee alone am I prepared to serve, for Thou alone art Lord by a just title, of Thy dominion do I desire to be. Direct, I pray, and command whatever Thou wilt, but heal and open my ears that I may hear Thine utterances. Heal and open my eyes that I may behold Thy significations of command. Drive delusion from me that I may recognize Thee. Tell me whither I must tend, to behold Thee, and I hope that I shall do all things Thou mayest enjoin. O Lord, most merciful Father, receive, I pray, Thy fugitive; enough already, surely, have I been punished, long enough have I served Thine enemies, whom Thou hast under Thy feet, long enough have I been a sport of fallacies. Receive me fleeing from these, Thy house-born servant, for did not these receive me, though another Master's, when I was fleeing from Thee? To Thee I feel I must return: I knock; may Thy door be opened to me; teach me the way to Thee. Nothing else have I than the will: nothing else do I know than that fleeting and falling things are to be spurned, fixed and everlasting things to be sought. This I do, Father, because this alone I know, but from what quarter to approach Thee I do not know. Do Thou instruct me, show me, give me my provision for the way. If it is by faith that those find Thee who take refuge with Thee, then grant faith: if by virtue, virtue: if by knowledge, knowledge. Augment in me faith, hope, and charity. O goodness of Thine, singular and most to be admired!

6.
I beseech Thee and once again I beg of Thee the means to beseech Thee. For if Thou abandon me, I perish: but Thou dost not abandon me because Thou art the Supreme Good whom no one ever sought with justice and could not discover. And all have sought Thee rightly to whom Thou hast given to seek Thee rightly. Grant me, Father, that I may seek Thee; keep me from error. Let me find none but Thee when I seek Thee. I beg Thee, Father. But if I have in me any trace of desire, do Thou make me clean and fit to behold Thee. And with regard to the health of this my mortal body, so long as I do not know what advantage it has for me, or those whom I love, I commit it to Thee, Father, most wise and most good; and I shall pray for it when Thou dost advise me. Only this I beg of Thy exceeding mercy—that Thou turnest me wholly to Thee and grantest that nothing stand in my way when I come to Thee. And do Thou command me, so long as I move and wear this body, that I be pure and high of soul and just and prudent, that I be the perfect lover and perceiver of Thy wisdom and worthy of Thy dwelling place; and grant me to dwell in Thy most blessed kingdom. Amen. Amen.

LATE HAVE I LOVED THEE*

Late have I loved Thee, O Beauty so ancient and so new, late have I loved Thee! And behold, Thou wert within and I was without. I was looking for Thee out there, and I threw myself, deformed as I was, upon those well-formed things which Thou hast made. Thou wert with me, yet I was not with Thee. These things held me far from Thee, things which would not have existed had they not been in Thee. Thou didst call and cry out and burst in upon my deafness; Thou didst shine forth and glow and drive away my blindness; Thou didst send forth Thy fragrance, and I drew in my breath and now I pant for Thee; I have tasted, and now I hunger and thirst; Thou didst touch me, and I was inflamed with desire for Thy peace.

27.38.

When I shall cleave to Thee with all my being, sorrow and toil will no longer exist for me, and my life will be alive, being wholly filled with Thee. At the present time, however, because Thou dost lift up whomever Thou fillest and I am not filled with Thee, I am a burden to myself. My joys, which are to be lamented, struggle against my sorrows, which are cause for joy, and I know not on which side victory may stand.

28.39.

* *Confessions*, X, 27.38-28.39; trans. FOC 5 (1953) 297.

VII. MORAL AND RELIGIOUS LIFE

We remarked at the end of the introduction to the preceding chapter that man's approach to God is not merely cognitive but involves his heart and his very existence. This present chapter deals with some of Augustine's views on this practical life of man. He is not interested in theory or speculation for its own sake; Augustine's wisdom is always eminently practical. He does not separate ethics from religious morality and spiritual life. Aristotle's *Nicomachean Ethics,* with its fundamental naturalism, was quite unknown to Augustine. The return of the soul to its Source is a constant theme in Neoplatonic treatises, which Augustine had read. It never occurred to him to separate ethics from religion, however. Here as elsewhere, his insights are triggered by some innocent-looking text from Scripture. This is illustrated in our first selection, where the basic tenet of moral eudaimonism (that all men desire happiness) is enunciated—not from Plato or Aristotle but from a remark in the Psalms!

The over-all orientation of man's life toward God as the perfect good is treated at great length in Book XIX of the *City of God.* Augustine there examines three types of finite goods (bodily, psychic and social), and argues that none of these could wholly satisfy man's aspirations. It is an argument by exclusion, eventually leading to the conclusion that God is the only goal worthy of man's efforts. The fitting end of human existence is a loving union with God. In various forms, this reasoning is also found in Boethius' *Consolation of Philosophy* (Book III), in Aquinas' *Summa contra Gentiles* (Book III), and in many later ethical treatises.

A famous description of virtue runs through medieval treatises in moral theology and is called the Augustinian definition. Actually it was gathered in the twelfth century by Peter Lombard from several works of Augustine (mostly from *On Free Choice,* II, 19). The famous definition is this: "Virtue is a good quality of the mind, by which we live righteously, of which no one can make bad use, which God works within us, but without us." (For a discussion of it, see St. Thomas Aquinas, *Disputed Questions on Virtues in General,* article 2.) While the final form of this statement is not the work of Augustine, the thought is typically his. This may be verified in the second from last selection of this chapter.

Augustine's approach to morality, and particularly to questions of religious perfection, is not legalistic. He frequently speaks of the eternal law of God and of the moral law that is inscribed in the hearts of man. Moral conscience is an expression of this divinely implanted law of goodness (*Exp. on Psalm 57,* 1; and *On Order,* II, 8, 25). However, he does not especially emphasize duties, obligations, sanctions, and all the judicial trappings of some later moral theology. The selections below, on the precepts of love and on the diversities of local customs, illustrate how foreign to the mind of our author is legal quibbling.

The two passages dealing with telling lies exemplify his judgment on a particular moral problem. Augustine's definition of lying included the intention to deceive another person. (Thomas Aquinas' definition excludes such an intention.) As a result, lying is always treated by Augustine as an interpersonal action, and he has the greatest difficulty in maintaining the view that he feels called upon to support: that all lies are morally evil. There are obviously some cases where a speaker intends to deceive another person for the real good of that person, or for some other important good. It is not evident that all such deceptions are immoral. Later Catholic theology has modified Augustine's definition and treated lying as a form of self-abuse—but has admitted that not all deceptions are lies. Augustine's frank puzzlement on such a problem has aided others in their search for a better solution.

Augustine is also one of the pioneers in the development of religious exercises. The basic pattern of many later methods of advancing in spiritual perfection is forecast in Augustine's description of seven stages of life in the human soul (*On the Magnitude of the Soul,* 33). Essentially, the movement of such exercises is triadic: withdrawal of psychic attention from the things of this world; concentration on what is best within the soul; and a rising above the soul to focus upon God as the transcendent Good. It is possible to see this pattern on a grand scale in many of the great Augustinian treatises, notably in the *Confessions.*

There are even passages in St. Augustine which suggest, at least to some readers, that he knew from his own life the meaning of mystical experience. Dom Cuthbert Butler always maintained that Augustine was a true mystic. Oddly, there has been much difference of opinion on this point. Certain scholars (E. Hendrikx, G. Ellard) bluntly deny that Augustine's experiences were mystical. For those interested, the article of Mandouze gives complete details on the technical controversy. There is little doubt that critics of Augustine's claims as a mystic make a radical differentiation between intellectualism and mysticism. One is inclined to agree with the sharp comment of Father Charles Boyer, in this connection: "If we admit this opposition, even the intuitive vision in Heaven will not be mystical—in which case, one wonders what mysticism really is!" (*Augustinus Magister*, III, 168).

ALL MEN DESIRE HAPPINESS*

But what is this? [V. 12] *Blessed is the nation.*
15. Who would not rouse himself at hearing this? All men love happiness, and therefore men are unreasonable in wanting to be wicked without being unhappy. And whereas unhappiness is the inseparable companion of wickedness, these perverse folk not only want wickedness without unhappiness, which is an impossibility, but they want to be wicked on purpose to avoid being unhappy. What do I mean by saying they want to be wicked on purpose to avoid being unhappy? Consider this point for a moment: in all the wickedness men commit, they always desire happiness. A man steals; you ask: "Why?" For hunger, for need. So he is wicked for fear of being unhappy, and all the more unhappy for being wicked. For the sake of driving away unhappiness and obtaining happiness, all men do whatever they do, good or bad; they invariably, you see, want to be happy. Whether they lead a good life or a bad one, they want to be happy; but not all attain to what all desire. All wish to be happy; none will be so but those who wish to be good. And then, lo and behold, someone or other, although doing wrong, wants to be happy. How? With money, with silver and gold, with estates and farms, with houses and servants, with worldly magnificence, with fleeting and perishable honors. He wish-

* *On Psalm 32,* Serm. 3, 15-16; trans. ACW 30, 130-133.

es to find happiness in possessing something; well then, find out what you want to possess to be happy. When you attain to happiness, of course you will be better off than now that you are unhappy. But it is impossible for anything falling short of yourself to add to your happiness. You are a human being; whatever you covet as a source of happiness is inferior to yourself. Gold and silver and various material things, which you so eagerly long to obtain, to possess, to enjoy, are of less value than yourself. You are more excellent, you are more important; and when you wish to be happy because you are unhappy undoubtedly you wish to be better off than you are. Certainly it is better to be happy than unhappy. You want to be better off than you are now; yet as means to that end you are seeking and searching for things inferior to yourself. Whatever you possess on earth is inferior to yourself. Every man wishes well to his friend thus, charging him in suchlike terms as these: "I hope you fare better," "I hope to see you better off," "I hope to have the joy of knowing you are better off," What he wishes his friend is what he wants for himself. Now take a piece of trustworthy advice. You want to be better off; I know it, we all know it, we all want the same thing. Look for what is better than yourself, so that by that means you may become better off than you are.

16.   Now consider heaven and earth: physical beauty must not so delight you that you want to find your happiness in it. What you are looking for is in the soul. You want to be happy; look for something better than your soul itself. Granted that there are these two things, namely, soul and body, then, since that which is called soul is the nobler of the two, your body can benefit through that which is superior, because the body is subject to the soul. Hence your body can benefit through your soul, so that when your soul is found just, your body also may hereafter become immortal. Through the enlightenment of your soul, your body earns incorruption; thus the nobler restores the integrity of the less noble. Hence if your body's good is your soul because it is superior to your body, when you seek your own good, seek that which is better for your soul.

Now, what is your soul? Pay attention; otherwise perhaps despising your soul and esteeming it some mean and worthless thing, you may be seeking yet more worthless things to make your soul happy. In your soul is the image of God; the human mind contains that image. It received it and by stooping to sin defiled it. He comes to refashion it who had first of all fashioned it; for by the Word all things were made, and by the Word this image was stamped on it. The Word Himself came, so that we might hear from the Apostle: *Be reformed in the newness of your mind.* [Rom. 12:2] It now remains for you, then, to seek out what is of better worth than your soul. What will that be, pray, except your God? You can find nothing of more worth than your own soul; for when your nature is perfected it will be equal to the angels. Higher indeed than this there is nothing save the Creator. Stretch upwards towards Him, do not despair, do not say: "It is beyond me." With greater reason is it beyond you to enjoy the gold which you possibly covet. Gold, even though you desire it, you may perhaps never possess; God you will possess as soon as you desire Him. For He came to you before you desired Him; when your will was turned away from Him He called you, when you had turned to Him He put fear into you, and when full of fear you made confession He consoled you. He who has given you all things, He who has brought you into being, He who gives sunlight to your fellow creatures, even to the wicked, who gives rain, fruits and fountains, life and health, and so many comforts—He holds back something for you which He gives only to yourself. What is it that He holds back for you, if not Himself? Look for anything better if you can find it; God keeps Himself for you. You moneygrubber, why are you gaping after heaven and earth? Better is He who has made heaven and earth; He it is whom you are to behold and possess.

MAN'S GREATEST GOOD*

3.   How then, according to reason, ought man to live? We all certainly desire to live happily; and there is no human being but assents to this statement almost before it is made. But the title happy cannot, in my opinion, belong either to him who has not what he loves, whatever it may be, or to him who has what he loves if it is hurtful, or to him who does not love what he has, although it is good in perfection. For one who seeks what he cannot obtain suffers torture, and one who has got what is not desirable is cheated, and one who does not seek for what is worth seeking for

* *Moral Behavior of the Catholic Church,* 3-8; trans. Dods.

is diseased. Now in all these cases the mind cannot but be unhappy, and happiness and unhappiness cannot reside at the same time in one man; so in none of these cases can the man be happy. I find, then, a fourth case, where the happy life exists—when that which is man's chief good is both loved and possessed. For what do we call enjoyment but having at hand the objects of love? And no one can be happy who does not enjoy what is man's chief good, nor is there any one who enjoys this who is not happy. We must then have at hand our chief good, if we think of living happily.

We must now inquire what is man's chief good, which of course cannot be anything inferior to man himself. For whoever follows after what is inferior to himself, becomes himself inferior. But every man is bound to follow what is best. Wherefore man's chief good is not inferior to man. Is it then something similar to man himself? It must be so, if there is nothing above man which he is capable of enjoying. But if we find something which is both superior to man, and can be possessed by the man who loves it, who can doubt that in seeking for happiness man should endeavor to reach that which is more excellent than the being who makes the endeavor? For if happiness consists in the enjoyment of a good than which there is nothing better, which we call the chief good, how can a man be properly called happy who has not yet attained to his chief good? or how can that be the chief good beyond which something better remains for us to arrive at? Such, then, being the chief good, it must be something which cannot be lost against the will. For no one can feel confident regarding a good which he knows can be taken from him, although he wishes to keep and cherish it. But if a man feels no confidence regarding the good which he enjoys, how can he be happy while in such fear of losing it?

4. Let us then see what is better than man. This must necessarily be hard to find, unless we first ask and examine what man is. I am not now called upon to give a definition of man. The question here seems to me to be—since almost all agree, or at least, which is enough, those I have now to do with are of the same opinion with me, that we are made up of soul and body—What is man? Is he both of these? or is he the body only, or the soul only? For although the things are two, soul and body, and although neither without the other could be called man (for the body would not be man without the soul, nor again would the soul be man if there were not a body animated by it), still it is possible that one of these may be held to be man, and may be called so. What then do we call man? Is he soul and body, as in a double harness, or like a centaur? Or do we mean the body only, as being in the service of the soul which rules it, as the word lamp denotes not the light and the case together, but only the case, yet it is on account of the light that it is so called? Or do we mean only the mind, and that on account of the body which it rules, as horseman means not the man and the horse, but the man only, and that as employed in ruling the horse? This dispute is not easy to settle; or, if the proof is plain, the statement requires time. This is an expenditure of time and strength which we need not incur. For whether the name man belongs to both, or only to the soul, the chief good of man is not the chief good of the body; but what is the chief good either of both soul and body, or of the soul only, that is man's chief good.

5.   Now if we ask what is the chief good of the body, reason obliges us to admit that it is that by means of which the body comes to be in its best state. But of all the things which invigorate the body, there is nothing better or greater than the soul. The chief good of the body, then, is not bodily pleasure, not absence of pain, not strength, not beauty, not swiftness, or whatever else is usually reckoned among the goods of the body, but simply the soul. For all the things mentioned the soul supplies to the body by its presence, and, what is above them all, life. Hence I conclude that the soul is not the chief good of man, whether we give the name of man to soul and body together, or to the soul alone. For as, according to reason, the chief good of the body is that which is better than the body, and from which the body receives vigor and life, so whether the soul itself is man, or soul and body both, we must discover whether there is anything which goes before the soul itself, in following which the soul comes to the perfection of good of which it is capable in its own kind. If such a thing can be found, all uncertainty must be at an end, and we must pronounce this to be really and truly the chief good of man.

If, again, the body is man, it must be admitted that the soul is the chief good of man. But clearly, when we treat of morals—when we inquire what manner of life must be held in order to obtain happiness—it is not the body to which the precepts are addressed, it is not bodily discipline which we discuss. In short, the observance of good *customs* belongs to that part of us which inquires and learns, which are the prerogatives of the soul; so, when we speak of attaining to virtue, the question does not regard the body. But if it follows, as it does, that the body which is ruled over by a soul possessed of virtue is ruled both better and more honorably, and is in its greatest perfection in consequence of the perfection of the soul which rightfully governs it, that which gives perfection to the soul will be man's chief good, though we call the body man. For if my coachman, in obedience to me, feeds and drives the horses he has charge of in the most satisfactory manner, himself enjoying the more of my bounty in proportion to his good conduct, can any one deny that the good condition of the horses, as well as that of the coachman, is due to me? So the question seems to me to be not whether soul and body is man, or the soul only, or the body only, but what gives perfection to the soul; for when this is obtained, a man cannot but be either perfect, or at least much better than in the absence of this one thing.

6.   No one will question that virtue gives perfection to the soul. But it is a very proper subject of inquiry whether this virtue can exist by itself or only in the soul. Here again arises a profound discussion, needing lengthy treatment; but perhaps my summary will serve the purpose. God will, I trust, assist me, so that, notwithstanding our feebleness, we may give instruction on these great matters briefly as well as intelligibly. In either case, whether virtue can exist by itself without the soul, or can exist only in the soul, undoubtedly in the pursuit of virtue the soul follows after something, and this must be either the soul itself, or virtue, or something else. But if the soul follows after itself in the pursuit of virtue, it follows after a foolish thing; for before obtaining virtue it is foolish. Now the height of a follower's desire is to reach that which he follows after. So the soul must either not wish to reach what it follows after, which is utterly absurd and unreasonable, or, in following after itself while foolish, it reaches the folly which it flees from. But if it follows after virtue in the desire to reach it, how can it follow what does not exist? or how can it desire to reach what it already possesses? Either, therefore, virtue exists beyond the soul, or if we are not allowed to give the name of virtue except to the habit and disposition of the wise soul, which can exist only in the soul, we must allow that the soul follows after something else in order that virtue may be produced in itself; for neither by following after nothing, nor by following after folly, can the soul, according to my reasoning, attain to wisdom.

This something else then, by following after which the soul becomes possessed of virtue and wisdom, is either a wise man or God. But we have said already that it must be something that we cannot lose against our will. No one can think it necessary to ask whether a wise man, supposing we are content to follow after him, can be taken from us in spite of our unwillingness or our persistence. God then remains, in following after whom we live well, and in reaching whom we live both well and happily. If any deny God's existence, why should I consider the method of dealing with them, when it is doubtful whether they ought to be dealt with at all? At any rate, it would require a different starting point, a different plan, a different investigation from what we are now engaged in. I am now addressing those who do not deny the existence of God, and who moreover allow that human affairs are not disregarded by Him. For there is no one, I suppose, who makes any profession of religion but will hold that divine Providence cares at least for our souls.

7. But how can we follow after Him whom we do not see? or how can we see Him, we who are not only men, but also men of weak understanding? For though God is seen not with the eyes but with the mind, where can such a mind be found as shall, while obscured by foolishness, succeed or even attempt to drink in that light? We must therefore have recourse to the instructions of those whom we have reason to think wise. Thus far argument brings us. For in human things reasoning is employed, not as of greater certainty, but as easier from use. But when we come to divine things, this faculty turns away; it cannot behold; it pants and gasps and burns with desire; it falls back from the light of truth and turns again to its wonted obscurity, not from choice but from exhaustion. What a dreadful catastrophe is this, that the soul should be reduced to greater helplessness when it is seeking rest from its toil! So, when we are hasting to retire into darkness, it will be well that by the appointment of adorable Wisdom we should be met by the friendly shade of authority, and should be attracted by the wonderful character of its contents, and by the utterance of its pages which, like shadows, typify and attemper the truth.

What more could have been done for our salvation? What can be more gracious and bountiful than divine providence, which, when man had fallen from its laws, and, in just retribution for his coveting mortal things, had brought forth a mortal offspring, still did not wholly abandon him? For in this most righteous government, whose ways are strange and inscrutable, there is, by means of unknown connections established in the creatures subject to it, both a severity of punishment and a mercifulness of salvation. How beautiful this is, how great, how worthy of God, in fine, how true, which is all we are seeking for, we shall never be able to perceive, unless, beginning with things human and at hand, and holding by the faith and the precepts of true religion, we continue without turning from it in the way which God has secured for us by the separation of the patriarchs, by the bond of the law, by the foresight of the prophets, by the witness of the apostles, by the blood of the martyrs, and by the subjugation of the Gentiles. From this point, then, let no one ask me for my opinion, but let us rather hear the oracles, and submit our weak inferences to the announcements of Heaven.

8. Let us see how the Lord Himself in the gospel has taught us to live; how, too, Paul the apostle—for the Manicheans dare not reject these Scriptures. Let us hear, O Christ, what chief end Thou dost prescribe to us; and that is evidently the chief end after which we are told to strive with supreme affection. "Thou shalt love," He says, "the Lord thy God." Tell me also, I pray Thee, what must be the measure of love; for I fear lest the desire enkindled in my heart should either exceed or come short in fervor. "With all thy heart," He says. Nor is that enough. "With all thy soul." Nor is it enough yet. "With all thy mind." What do you wish more? I might perhaps wish more if I could see the possibility of more. What does Paul say on this? "We know," he says, "that all things issue in good to them that love God." Let him, too, say what is the measure of love. "Who then," he says, "shall separate us from the love of Christ? shall tribulation or distress or persecution or famine or nakedness or peril or the sword?" We have heard, then, what and how much we must love; this we must strive after, and to this we must refer all our plans. The perfection of all our good things and our perfect good is God. We must neither come short of this nor go beyond it; the one is dangerous, the other impossible.

GOOD LOVE AND BAD LOVE*

6. The condition of man's will is important. If it is perverse, then these emotions will be perverse; but if the will is right, then they are not only blameless,

* *City of God*, XIV, 6-7; trans. V.J.B.

they will even be praiseworthy. In fact, the will is present in all feelings; indeed, they are all nothing but movements of will. For what are cupidity and joy but the will tending to consent to the objects that we do will? What are fear and sorrow but the will tending to dissent from the objects that we volitionally reject? And when we consent by inclining toward the objects that we will, that is cupidity; when we consent by taking pleasure in the objects that we will, then that is called joy. Similarly, when we dissent from something that has happened against our will, such a will-act is sorrow. In general then, depending on the diversity of things that are desired or rejected, as a man's will is attracted or repelled, so is it changed or diverted into one or the other of these emotions. That is why the man who lives according to God and not according to man should be a lover of the good, and consequently he should hate the evil. Moreover, since no person is evil by nature, but whoever is evil is so because of a fault, he who lives according to God owes a perfect hatred to evil men: not that he should hate the man on account of his fault, nor love the fault because of the man, but he should hate the fault and love the man. For, when the fault is repaired, there will remain something that should be wholly loved and in no way hated.

7.   ... And so, right will is a good love and perverse will is evil love. Love, then, that yearns to possess what is loved is cupidity, and when it takes pleasure in its possession, that is joy; when it tries to avoid what is opposed to it, that is fear, and when it suffers the occurrence of such opposition, that is sorrow. Hence, these feelings are evil if the love is evil; they are good if it is good.

MORAL EVIL STEMS FROM BAD WILL*

6.   If the further question be asked, What was the efficient cause of their evil will? there is none. For what is it which makes the will bad, when it is the will itself which makes the action bad? And consequently the bad will is the cause of the bad action, but nothing is the efficient cause of the bad will. For if anything is the cause,

* *City of God,* XII, 6; trans. Dods.

this thing either has or has not a will. If it has, the will is either good or bad. If good, who is so left to himself as to say that a good will makes a will bad? For in this case a good will would be the cause of sin; a most absurd supposition. On the other hand, if this hypothetical thing has a bad will, I wish to know what made it so; and that we may not go on forever, I ask at once, what made the *first* evil will bad? For that is not the first which was itself corrupted by an evil will, but that is the first which was made evil by no other will. For if it were preceded by that which made it evil, that will was first which made the other evil. But if it is replied, "Nothing made it evil; it always was evil," I ask if it has been existing in some nature. For if not, then it did not exist at all; and if it did exist in some nature, then it vitiated and corrupted it, and injured it, and consequently deprived it of good. And therefore the evil will could not exist in an evil nature, but in a nature at once good and mutable, which this vice could injure. For if it did no injury, it was no vice; and consequently the will in which it was, could not be called evil. But if it did injury, it did it by taking away or diminishing good. And therefore there could not be from eternity, as was suggested, an evil will in that thing in which there had been previously a natural good, which the evil will was able to diminish by corrupting it. If, then, it was not from eternity, who, I ask, made it? The only thing that can be suggested in reply is that something which itself had no will, made the will evil. I ask, then, whether this thing was superior, inferior, or equal to it? If superior, then it is better. How, then, has it no will, and not rather a good will? The same reasoning applies if it was equal; for so long as two things have equally a good will, the one cannot produce in the other an evil will. Then remains the supposition that that which corrupted the will of the angelic nature which first sinned, was itself an inferior thing without a will. But that thing, be it of the lowest and most earthly kind, is certainly itself good, since it is a nature and being, with a form and rank of its own in its own kind and order. How, then, can a good thing be the efficient cause of an evil will? How, I say, can good be the cause of evil? For when the will abandons what is above itself, and turns to what is lower, it becomes evil—not because that is evil to which it turns, but because the turning itself is wicked. Therefore it is not an inferior thing which has made the will evil, but it is itself which has become so by wickedly and inordinately desiring an inferior thing.

TWO PRECEPTS OF LOVE*

14. ... But as this divine Master inculcates two precepts —the love of God and the love of our neighbor—and as in these precepts a man finds three things he has to love—God, himself, and his neighbor—and that he who loves God loves himself thereby, it follows that he must endeavor to get his neighbor to love God, since he is ordered to love his neighbor as himself. He ought to make this endeavor in behalf of his wife, his children, his household, all within his reach, even as he would wish his neighbor to do the same for him if he needed it; and consequently he will be at peace or in well-ordered concord with all men, as far as in him lies. And this is the order of this concord, that a man in the first place injure no one, and in the second do good to every one he can reach. Primarily, therefore, his own household are his care, for the law of nature and of society gives him readier access to them and greater opportunity of serving them. And hence the Apostle says, "Now, if any provide not for his own, and specially for those of his own house, he hath denied the faith, and is worse than an infidel." This is the origin of domestic peace, or the well-ordered concord of those in the family who rule and those who obey. For they who care for the rest rule—the husband the wife, the parents the children, the masters the servants; and they who are cared for obey—the women their husbands, the children their parents, the servants their masters. But in the family of the just man who lives by faith and is as yet a pilgrim journeying on to the celestial city, even those who rule serve those whom they seem to command; for they rule not from a love of power, but from a sense of the duty they owe to others—not because they are proud of authority, but because they love mercy.

ON DIVERSITIES OF LOCAL CUSTOMS†

1. In regard to the questions which you have asked me, I would like to have known what your own answers would have been, for thus I might have made my reply in fewer words, and might most easily confirm

* *City of God*, XIX, 14; trans. Dods.
† *Letter 54*, 1-4 to Januarius; trans. Dods.

or correct your opinions, by approving or amending the answers which you had given. This I would have greatly preferred. But desiring to answer you at once, I think it better to write a long letter than incur loss of time. I desire you therefore, in the first place, to hold fast this as the fundamental principle in the present discussion, that our Lord Jesus Christ has appointed to us a "light yoke" and an "easy burden," as He declares in the Gospel: [Matt. 11:30] in accordance with which He has bound His people under the new dispensation together in fellowship by sacraments, which are in number very few, in observance most easy, and in significance most excellent, as baptism solemnized in the name of the Trinity, the communion of His body and blood, and such other things as are prescribed in the canonical Scriptures, with the exception of those enactments which were a yoke of bondage to God's ancient people, suited to their state of heart and to the times of the prophets, and which are found in the five books of Moses. As to those other things which we hold on the authority, not of Scripture, but of tradition, and which are observed throughout the whole world, it may be understood that they are held as approved and instituted either by the apostles themselves, or by plenary Councils, whose authority in the Church is most useful, *e.g.*, the annual commemoration, by special solemnities, of the Lord's passion, resurrection, and ascension, and of the descent of the Holy Spirit from heaven, and whatever else is in like manner observed by the whole Church wherever it has been established.

2.   There are other things, however, which are different in different places and countries, *e.g.*, some fast on Saturday, others do not; some partake daily of the body and blood of Christ, others receive it on stated days: in some places no day passes without the sacrifice being offered; in others it is only on Saturday and the Lord's day, or it may be only on the Lord's day. In regard to these and all other variable observances which may be met anywhere, one is at liberty to comply with them or not as he chooses; and there is no better rule for the wise and serious Christian in this matter, than to conform to the practice which he finds prevailing in the Church to which it may be his lot to come. For such a custom, if it is clearly not contrary to the faith nor to sound morality, is to be held as a thing indifferent, and ought to be observed for the sake of fellowship with those among whom we live.

3. I think you may have heard me relate before, what I will nevertheless now mention. When my mother followed me to Milan, she found the Church there not fasting on Saturday. She began to be troubled, and to hesitate as to what she should do; upon which I, though not taking a personal interest then in such things, applied on her behalf to Ambrose, of most blessed memory, for his advice. He answered that he could not teach me anything but what he himself practiced, because if he knew any better rule, he would observe it himself. When I supposed that he intended, on the ground of his authority alone, and without supporting it by any argument, to recommend us to give up fasting on Saturday, he followed me, and said: "When I visit Rome, I fast on Saturday; when I am here, I do not fast. On the same principle, do you observe the custom prevailing in whatever Church you come to, if you desire neither to give offense by your conduct, nor to find cause of offense in another's." When I reported this to my mother, she accepted it gladly; and for myself, after frequently reconsidering his decision, I have always esteemed it as if I had received it by an oracle from heaven. For often have I perceived, with extreme sorrow, many disquietudes caused to weak brethren by the contentious pertinacity or superstitious vacillation of some who, in matters of this kind, which do not admit of final decision by the authority of Holy Scripture, or by the tradition of the universal Church, or by their manifest good influence on manners, raise questions, it may be, from some crotchet of their own, or from attachment to the custom followed in one's own country, or from preference for that which one has seen abroad, supposing that wisdom is increased in proportion to the distance to which men travel from home, and agitate these questions with such keenness that they think all is wrong except what they do themselves.

3.4. Some one may say, "The Eucharist ought not to be taken every day." You ask, "On what grounds?" He answers, "Because, in order that a man may approach worthily to so great a sacrament, he ought to choose those days upon which he lives in more special purity and self-restraint; for 'whosoever eateth and drinketh unworthily, eateth and drinketh judgment to himself.'" [1 Cor. 11:29] Another answers, "Certainly; if the wound inflicted by sin and the violence of the soul's distemper be such that the use of these remedies must be put off for a time, every man in this case should be, by the authority of the bishop, forbidden to approach the altar, and appointed to do penance, and should be afterwards restored to privileges by the same authority; for this would be partaking unworthily, if one should partake of it at a time when he ought to be doing penance; and it is not a matter to be left to one's own judgment to withdraw himself from the communion of the Church, or restore himself, as he pleases. If, however, his sins are not so great as to bring him justly under sentence of excommunication, he ought not to withdraw himself from the daily use of the Lord's body for the healing of his soul." Perhaps a third party interposes with a more just decision of the question, reminding them that the principal thing is to remain united in the peace of Christ, and that each should be free to do what, according to his belief, he conscientiously regards as his duty. For neither of them lightly esteems the body and blood of the Lord; on the contrary, both are contending who shall most highly honor the sacrament fraught with blessing. There was no controversy between those two mentioned in the Gospel, Zacchaeus and the Centurion; nor did either of them think himself better than the other, though, whereas the former received the Lord joyfully into his house, [Luke 19:6] the latter said, "I am not worthy that Thou shouldest come under my roof," [Matt. 8:8]—both honoring the Saviour, though in ways diverse and, as it were, mutually opposed; both miserable through sin, and both obtaining the mercy they required.

DOING GOOD TO BODY AND SOUL*

27.   Man, then, as viewed by his fellow man, is a rational soul with a mortal and earthly body in its service. Therefore he who loves his neighbor does good partly to the man's body, and partly to his soul. What benefits the body is called medicine; what benefits the soul, discipline. Medicine here includes everything that either preserves or restores bodily health. It includes, therefore, not only what belongs to the art of medical men, properly so called, but also food and drink, clothing and shelter, and every means of covering and protection to guard our bodies against injuries and mishaps from without as well as from within. For hunger and thirst, and cold and heat, and all violence from

* *Moral Behavior of the Catholic Church,* 27-28; trans. Dods.

without, produce loss of that health which is the point to be considered.

Hence those who seasonably and wisely supply all the things required for warding off these evils and distresses are called compassionate, although they may have been so wise that no painful feeling disturbed their mind in the exercise of compassion. No doubt the word compassionate implies suffering in the heart of the man who feels for the sorrow of another. And it is equally true that a wise man ought to be free from all painful emotion when he assists the needy, when he gives food to the hungry and water to the thirsty, when he clothes the naked, when he takes the stranger into his house, when he sets free the oppressed, when, lastly, he extends his charity to the dead in giving them burial. Still the epithet compassionate is a proper one, although he acts with tranquillity of mind, not from the stimulus of painful feeling, but from motives of benevolence. There is no harm in the word compassionate when there is no passion in the case.

Fools, again, who avoid the exercise of compassion as a vice, because they are not sufficiently moved by a sense of duty without feeling also distressful emotion, are frozen into hard insensibility, which is very different from the calm of a rational serenity. God, on the other hand, is properly called compassionate; and the sense in which He is so will be understood by those whom piety and diligence have made fit to understand. There is a danger lest, in using the words of the learned, we harden the souls of the unlearned by leading them away from compassion instead of softening them with the desire of a charitable disposition. As compassion, then, requires us to ward off these distresses from others, so harmlessness forbids the infliction of them.

28. As regards discipline, by which the health of the mind is restored, without which bodily health avails nothing for security against misery, the subject is one of great difficulty. And as in the body we said it is one thing to cure diseases and wounds, which few can do properly, and another thing to meet the cravings of hunger and thirst, and to give assistance in all the other ways in which any man may at any time help another; so in the mind there are some things in which the high and rare offices of the teacher are not much called for—as, for instance, in advice and exhortation to give to the needy the things already mentioned as required for the body. To give such advice is to aid the mind by discipline, as giving the things themselves is aiding the body by our resources. But there are other cases where diseases of the

mind, many and various in kind, are healed in a way strange and indescribable. Unless His medicine were sent from heaven to men, so heedlessly do they go on in sin, there would be no hope of salvation; and, indeed, even bodily health, if you go to the root of the matter, can have come to men from none but God, who gives to all things their being and their well-being.

This discipline, then, which is the medicine of the mind, as far as we can gather from the sacred Scriptures, includes two things, restraint and instruction. Restraint implies fear, and instruction love, in the person benefited by the discipline; for in the giver of the benefit there is the love without the fear. In both of these God Himself, by whose goodness and mercy it is that we are anything, has given us in the two Testaments a rule of discipline. For though both are found in both Testaments, still fear is prominent in the Old, and love in the New, which the apostle calls bondage in the one, and liberty in the other. Of the marvelous order and divine harmony of these Testaments it would take long to speak, and many pious and learned men have discoursed on it. The theme demands many books to set it forth and explain it as far as is possible for man. He, then, who loves his neighbor endeavors all he can to procure his safety in body and in soul, making the health of the mind the standard in his treatment of the body. And as regards the mind, his endeavors are in this order, that he should first fear and then love God. This is true excellence of conduct, and thus the knowledge of the truth, of which we are ever in pursuit, is acquired.

THE EVIL OF TELLING A LIE*

18.   But here arises a very difficult and very intricate question, about which I once wrote a large book, finding it necessary to give it an answer. The question is this: whether at any time it can become the duty of a good man to tell a lie? For some go so far as to contend that there are occasions on which it is a good and pious work to commit perjury even, and to say what is false about matters that relate to the worship of God, and about the very nature of God Himself. To me, however, it seems certain that every lie

* *Enchiridion,* 18, 19, 22; trans. Dods.

is a sin, though it makes a great difference with what intention and on what subject one lies. For the sin of the man
who tells a lie to help another is not so heinous as that of
the man who tells a lie to injure another; and the man who
by his lying puts a traveler on the wrong road, does not do so
much harm as the man who by false or misleading represen-
tations distorts the whole course of a life. No one, of course,
is to be condemned as a liar who says what is false, believing it to be true, because such a one does not consciously
deceive but rather is himself deceived. And, on the same
principle, a man is not to be accused of lying, though he
may sometimes be open to the charge of rashness, if through
carelessness he takes up what is false and holds it as true;
but, on the other hand, the man who says what is true, believing it to be false, is, so far as his own consciousness is
concerned, a liar. For in saying what he does not believe,
he says what to his own conscience is false, even though it
should in fact be true; nor is the man in any sense free from
lying who with his mouth speaks the truth without knowing it, but in his heart wills to tell a lie. And therefore not
looking at the matter spoken of, but solely at the intention of
the speaker, the man who unwittingly says what is false, thinking all the time that it is true, is a better man than the
one who unwittingly says what is true but in his conscience
intends to deceive. For the former does not think one thing
and say another, but the latter, though his statements may
be true in fact, has one thought in his heart and another on
his lips; and that is the very essence of lying. But when we
come to consider truth and falsehood in respect to the subjects
spoken of, the point on which one deceives or is deceived
becomes a matter of the utmost importance. For although,
as far as a man's own conscience is concerned, it is a greater
evil to deceive than to be deceived, nevertheless it is far
less evil to tell a lie in regard to matters that do not relate
to religion, than to be led into error in regard to matters
the knowledge and belief of which are essential to the
right worship of God. To illustrate this by example: suppose
that one man should say of some one who is dead that
he is still alive, knowing this to be untrue; and that another
man should, being deceived, believe that Christ shall at the
end of some time (make the time as long as you please)
die; would it not be incomparably better to lie like the former, than to be deceived like the latter? and would it not be
a much less evil to lead some man into the former error,
than to be led by any man into the latter?

19.

In some things, then, it is a great evil to be deceived; in some it is a small evil, in some no evil at all, and in some it is an actual advantage. It is to his grievous injury that a man is deceived when he does not believe what leads to eternal life, or believes what leads to eternal death. It is a small evil for a man to be deceived, when, by taking falsehood for truth, he brings upon himself temporal annoyances; for the patience of the believer will turn even these to a good use, as when, for example, taking a bad man for a good, he receives injury from him. But one who believes a bad man to be good, and yet suffers no injury, is nothing the worse for being deceived, nor does he fall under the prophetic denunciation: "Woe to those who call evil good!" [Isa. 5:20] For we are to understand that this is spoken not about evil man, but about the things that make men evil. Hence the man who calls adultery good, falls justly under that prophetic denunciation. But the man who calls the adulterer good, thinking him to be chaste, and not knowing him to be an adulterer, falls into no error in regard to the nature of good and evil, but only makes a mistake as to the secrets of human conduct. He calls the man good on the ground of believing him to be what is undoubtedly good; he calls the adulterer evil, and the pure man good; and he calls this man good, not knowing him to be an adulterer, but believing him to be pure. Further, if by making a mistake one escape death, as I have said above once happened to me, one even derives some advantage from one's mistake. But when I assert that in certain cases a man may be deceived without any injury to himself, or even with some advantage to himself, I do not mean that the mistake in itself is no evil, or is in any sense a good; I refer only to the evil that is avoided, or the advantage that is gained, through making the mistake. For the mistake, considered in itself, is an evil: a great evil if it concern a great matter, a small evil if it concern a small matter, but yet always an evil. For who that is of sound mind can deny that it is an evil to receive what is false as if it were true, and to reject what is true as if it were false, or to hold what is uncertain as certain, and what is certain as uncertain? But it is one thing to think a man good when he is really bad, which is a mistake; it is another thing to suffer no ulterior injury in consequence of the mistake, supposing that the bad man whom we think good inflicts no damage upon us. In the same way, it is one thing to think that we are on the right road when we are not; it is another thing when this mistake of ours, which is an evil, leads to some good, such as saving us from an ambush of wicked men. . . .

22. But every lie must be called a sin, because not only when a man knows the truth but even when, as a man may be, he is mistaken and deceived, it is his duty to say what he thinks in his heart, whether it be true or whether he only think it to be true. But every liar says the opposite of what he thinks in his heart, with purpose to deceive. Now it is evident that speech was given to man, not that men might therewith deceive one another, but that one man might make known his thoughts to another. To use speech, then, for the purpose of deception, and not for its appointed end, is a sin. Nor are we to suppose that there is any lie that is not a sin, because it is sometimes possible, by telling a lie, to do service to another. For it is possible to do this by theft also, as when we steal from a rich man, who never feels the loss, to give to a poor man, who is sensibly benefited by what he gets. And the same can be said of adultery also, when, for instance, some woman appears likely to die of love unless we consent to her wishes, while if she lived she might purify herself by repentance; but yet no one will assert that on this account such an adultery is not a sin. And if we justly place so high a value upon chastity, what offense have we taken at truth, that, while no prospect of advantage to another will lead us to violate the former by adultery, we should be ready to violate the latter by lying? It cannot be denied that they have attained a very high standard of goodness who never lie except to save a man from injury; but in the case of men who have reached this standard, it is not the deceit, but their good intention, that is justly praised, and sometimes even rewarded.

LYING AND CONCEALING THE TRUTH*

7. *Thou hatest all the workers of iniquity.* God's hatred has the same signification as the hatred of every sinner for the truth. It would seem as if Truth in its turn detests them, since it will not permit to dwell in its presence those who cannot endure it. *Thou will destroy all that speak a lie,* for a lie is contrary to truth. No one must

* *On Psalm 5, 7; trans. ACW 29, 52-55.*

imagine, however, that there exists some substance or nature opposed to truth; you must realize, on the contrary, that a lie partakes of nonbeing, not of being. To speak of what is, is to speak the truth; to speak of what is not, is to tell a lie. Therefore, says the Psalmist, *Thou wilt destroy all that speak a lie,* since in turning their backs upon that which has existence, they turn aside to that which has none.

Many lies are apparently told out of kindness, not malice, the object being someone's safety or advantage; such were the lies told by the midwives in Exodus who gave a false report to Pharaoh in order to save the male infants of Israel from death. [Exod. 1:17] But even here what is praiseworthy is not the action but the motive, since those who merely tell lies such as theirs will deserve in time to be set free from all dissimulation, for in the perfect not even these are to be found. *Let your speech be Yea. Yea. No, No,* we are told. *And that which is over and above these is of evil.* [Matt. 5:37] Not without reason does Scripture elsewhere declare: *The mouth that belieth killeth the soul,* [Wisd. 1:11] in order to teach us that no perfect and spiritual man is free to tell a lie to save this transitory life either for himself or another, since its loss does not kill the soul.

On the other hand, it is one thing to tell a lie, another to conceal the truth; one thing to speak falsehood, another to pass the truth over in silence. If, for instance, we would avoid exposing a man to the risk of visible death, we must be prepared to conceal the truth but not to tell an untruth. We must neither expose him nor lie, otherwise we shall kill our own soul for the sake of another man's body. If this is at present beyond us, we must at least admit of lies only in strict necessity. We may then deserve to get rid even of white lies, if we do no worse, and receive strength from the Holy Ghost to make light of any suffering for truth's sake.

To sum up: There are two kinds of lies which are no great crime but not exactly free from sin, the lie spoken in jest, and the lie spoken to render some service. The lie spoken in jest does very little harm, since it deceives nobody. The man to whom it is told knows it is only banter. And the second lie is all the less offensive because it means well. As a matter of fact, where no duplicity is intended, no lie can be imputed. A man, to take an example, has been entrusted with a sword and has promised to return it at the owner's request. What if the latter should demand it in a fit of madness? Obviously he must not be handed it there and then, for fear he may kill himself or other people. It must wait until he is restored to his right mind. Here, then, there is no duplicity, because when the friend entrusted with the sword promised to return it at the owner's request, he never imagined it would be demanded in a fit of madness. Even our Lord therefore concealed the truth when His disciples were unprepared for it. *I have yet many things to say to you,* He told them, *but you cannot bear them now.* [John 16:12] The Apostle Paul has likewise declared: *I, brethren, could not speak to you as unto spiritual, but as unto carnal.* [I Cor. 3:1] Hence it follows that to suppress the truth is not necessarily wrong. But you will never find lying conceded to the perfect.

FAITH, HOPE, AND CHARITY*

8. Again, can anything be hoped for which is not an object of faith? It is true that a thing which is not an object of hope may be believed. What true Christian, for example, does not believe in the punishment of the wicked? And yet such a one does not hope for it. And the man who believes that punishment to be hanging over himself, and who shrinks in horror from the prospect, is more properly said to fear than to hope. And these two states of mind the poet carefully distinguishes, when he says: "Permit the fearful to have hope." [Lucan, *Pharsalia,* 2.15] Another poet, who is usually much superior to this one, makes a wrong use of the word, when he says: "If I have been able to hope for so great a grief as this." [Virgil, *Aeneid,* 4.419] And some grammarians take this case as an example of impropriety of speech, saying, "He said *sperare* [to hope] instead of *timere* [to fear]." Accordingly, faith may have for its object evil as well as good; for both good and evil are believed, and the faith that believes them is not evil, but good. Faith, moreover, is concerned with the past, the present, and the future, all three. We believe, for example, that Christ died—an event in the past; we believe that He is sitting at the right hand of God—a state of things which is present; we believe that He will come to judge the quick and the dead—an event of the future. Again, faith applies both to one's own circumstances and those of others. Everyone, for example, believes that his own existence had a

* *Enchiridion,* 8; trans. Dods.

beginning, and was not eternal, and he believes the same both of other men and other things. Many of our beliefs in regard to religious matters, again, have reference not merely to other men, but to angels also. But hope has for its object only what is good, only what is future, and only what affects the man who entertains the hope. For these reasons, then, faith must be distinguished from hope, not merely as a matter of verbal propriety, but because they are essentially different. The fact that we do not see either what we believe or what we hope for, is all that is common to faith and hope. In the *Epistle to the Hebrews,* for example, faith is defined (and eminent defenders of the Catholic Faith have used the definition as a standard) "the evidence of things not seen." [Heb. 11:1] Although, should any one say that he believes, that is, has grounded his faith, not on words, nor on witnesses, nor on any reasoning whatever, but on the direct evidence of his own senses, he would not be guilty of such an impropriety of speech as to be justly liable to the criticism, "You saw, therefore you did not believe." And hence it does not follow that an object of faith is not an object of sight. But it is better that we should use the word "faith" as the Scriptures have taught us, applying it to those things which are not seen. Concerning hope, again, the apostle says: "Hope that is seen is not hope; for what a man seeth, why doth he yet hope for? But if we hope for that we see not, then do we with patience wait for it." [Rom. 8:24-25] When, then, we believe that good is about to come, this is nothing else but to hope for it. Now what shall I say of love? Without it, faith profits nothing; and in its absence, hope cannot exist. The Apostle James says: "The devils also believe, and tremble" [Jas. 2:19] —that is, they, having neither hope nor love, but believing that what we hope and hope for is about to come, are in terror. And so the Apostle Paul approves and commends the "faith that worketh by love"; [Gal. 5:6] and this certainly cannot exist without hope. Wherefore there is no love without hope, no hope without love, and neither love nor hope without faith.

NO VIRTUES APART FROM GOD*

25.   For though the soul may seem to rule the body admirably, and the reason the vices, if the soul and reason do not themselves obey God, as God has com-

* *City of God,* XIX, 25; trans. Dods.

manded them to serve Him, they have no proper authority over the body and the vices. For what kind of mistress of the body and the vices can that mind be which is ignorant of the true God, and which, instead of being subject to His authority, is prostituted to the corrupting influences of the most vicious demons? It is for this reason that the virtues which it seems to itself to possess, and by which it restrains the body and the vices that it may obtain and keep what it desires, are rather vices than virtues so long as there is no reference to God in the matter. For although some suppose that virtues which have a reference only to themselves, and are desired only on their own account, are yet true and genuine virtues, the fact is that even then they are inflated with pride, and are therefore to be reckoned vices rather than virtues. For as that which gives life to the flesh is not derived from flesh, but is above it, so that which gives blessed life to man is not derived from man, but is something above him; and what I say of man is true of every celestial power and virtue whatsoever.

OUR REWARD IS NOT IN THIS LIFE*

5. ... Perchance thy heart saith, Wretch that I am, I suppose to no purpose I have believed, God doth not regard things human. God therefore doth awaken us: and He saith what? "Fear not, though a man have become rich" (ver. 16). For why didst thou fear, because a man hath become rich? Thou didst fear that thou hadst believed to no purpose, that perchance thou shouldest have lost the labor for thy faith, and the hope of thy conversion: because perchance there hath come in thy way gain with guilt, and thou couldest have been rich, if thou hadst seized upon that same gain with the guilt, and neededst not have labored; and thou, remembering what God hath threatened, hast refrained from guilt, and hast contemned the gain: thou seest another man that hath made gain by guilt, and hath suffered no harm; and thou fearest to be good. "Fear not," saith the Spirit of God to thee, "though a man shall have become rich." Wouldest thou not have eyes but for things present? Things future He hath promised, who hath risen again; peace in this world, and repose in this life, He hath not promised. Every man doth seek repose; a good thing

* On Psalm 48, Serm. 2; trans. Nicene.

he is seeking, but not in the proper region thereof he is seeking it. There is no peace in this life; in Heaven hath been promised that which on earth we are seeking: in the world to come hath been promised that which in this world we are seeking.

6.

"Fear not, though a man be made rich, and though the glory of his house be multiplied." Wherefore "fear not"? "For when he shall die, he shall not receive anything" (ver. 17). Thou seest him living, consider him dying. Thou markest what he hath here, mark what he taketh with him. What doth he take with him? He hath store of gold, he hath store of silver, numerous estates, slaves: he dieth, these remain, he knoweth not for whom. For though he leaveth them for whom he will, he keepeth them not for whom he will.

VIII. DIMENSIONS OF GRACE

It is as the Doctor of Grace that St. Augustine is best known in the history of Christian theology; no anthology would be complete without some examples of his teaching in this important area. Yet the Augustinian view of divine grace has occasioned centuries of controversy and no definitive interpretation can be attempted in this brief forenote.

Augustine took grace to mean a help which God gives to men, over and above their natural endowments, to enable them to will and to accomplish actions that may merit eternal salvation. If we were dealing with a theologian of the sixteenth century, it would be possible to say that divine grace lifts man to the level of "supernatural" life and action. But the distinction between the natural and the supernatural orders is not formally treated by St. Augustine (see T.A Deman, in *Augustinus Magister*, III, 258; and Henri De Lubac, *Surnaturel: Etudes Historiques* [Paris: Aubier, 1946]), and this precision is not available for our use. This is not to say that Augustine is antagonistic to the idea of the supernatural; he simply does not discuss the matter in these terms.

During the latter part of Augustine's lifetime, the Pelagians were teaching that the free choice of man's will is by itself powerful enough to enable a person to perform actions that will merit Heaven. Pelagius did not deny that God may help man through grace—but he claimed that such gratuitous help is not really necessary, that grace is more like an ornament than a necessity in the spiritual life. Augustine (and the whole central tradition in Christian theology) insisted that divine grace is essential to the performance of meritorious action, that such grace cannot be merited by any preceding act of man, and so, that grace is a free gift to men by God. These points are anticipated in our second selection, in which Augustine is reviewing his treatise *On Free Choice* and the attempt of the Pelagians to claim the patronage of this youthful dialogue. It is clear that St. Augustine never thought as a Pelagian.

Important for the understanding of this whole problem of the relation between human action and God's activity is the Augustinian distinction between free choice (*liberum arbitrium*) and a higher freedom (*libertas*). The point is touched on in the selection from the *Enchiridion*: "How Freedom Is Restored by Grace." The former is a part of man's created nature: the soul as will is endowed at birth with the ability to turn toward or away from its supreme good; this ability is *liberum arbitrium*. It implies a freedom of alternatives: to do what is good or what is evil. On the other hand, God may so dispose the human will that it inclines only toward its true good. This divine disposition would *free* the will from its tendency toward evil; such eminent freedom is *libertas*. Obviously, *libertas* is a resultant of the action of God's grace. (Consult: Gilson, *Christian Philosophy of St. Augustine*, Part II, chap. 3.)

In his highly regarded introduction to St. Augustine, Eugène Portalié offered a final summary of the teaching on grace, in terms of the following three propositions: (1) "The absolute sovereignty of God over the will is opposed to the Pelagian principle of the emancipation of liberty." (2) "Freedom of choice, even under the influence of efficacious grace, was always safeguarded by St. Augustine." (3) "The Augustinian theory on the divine influence reconciles both grace and freedom of the will." (*Guide*, pp. 192-198.)

WHAT THE GRACE OF GOD IS*

2.3. The grace of God through Jesus Christ our Lord must be understood as that by which alone men are delivered from evil, and without which they do absolutely no good thing, whether in thought, or will and affection, or in deed; not only in order that they may know by the manifestation of the same what should be done, but moreover in order that by its enabling they may do with love what they know. Indeed, the apostle requested this inspiration to good willing and working for those to whom he said: "But we pray God that you may do no evil at all, not wishing ourselves to appear approved, but that you may do what is good." [2 Cor. 13:7]

* *On Admonition and Grace*, 2.3; trans. Nicene.

AUGUSTINE WAS NEVER A PELAGIAN*

9.2. Because of the nature of the problem faced here, there is no discussion in these books [*On Free Choice*] concerning the grace of God, by which He has predestined His chosen ones in such a manner that He Himself has even made ready the volitions of those whom He has already endowed with free choice. Wherever the occasion arose when this grace might be mentioned, it was noted in passing but not defended by elaborate arguments, as if it were the main topic. Indeed, it is one question to inquire into the source of evil and quite a different one to ask how we may return to our original goodness, or achieve a greater good....

9.3. For this reason, the new heretics, the Pelagians— who make such claims for the free choice of the will that they leave no place for God's grace, because they say that grace is given according to our merits— should not boast that I formerly supported their claims, simply because I said a great deal in favor of free choice, as the nature of my discussion required....

9.4. In these and similar texts of mine, since God's grace is not mentioned because at that time it was not a subject of dispute, the Pelagians thought, or tried to think, that we held their view. But they were quite wrong. The will is, indeed, that whereby we sin and that whereby we live justly; this is the point that we treated in those texts. So, unless the will itself be freed by the grace of God from the servitude whereby it has become the slave of sin, and unless it be helped so that it may overcome defects, it is impossible for mortal men to live righteously and piously. And if this divine assistance, whereby the will is freed, were granted for its merits, it would not be a "grace"—a gratuitous gift—for it would not have preceded the willing. We have treated this sufficiently in our other short works where we refute the enemies of this grace, the new heretics. Nevertheless, in these books *On Free Choice* (which were in no way directed against them, for they were not yet active, but were written against the Manichees), we have not been completely silent concerning this grace of God, which they are attempting to suppress by their harmful impiety.

* *Retractations,* I, 9.2-4; trans. V.J.B.

WHAT TRUE GRACE IS*

26.27. Now even Pelagius should frankly confess that this grace is plainly set forth in the inspired Scriptures; nor should he with shameless effrontery hide the fact that he has too long opposed it, but admit it with salutary regret, so that the holy Church may cease to be harassed by his stubborn persistence, and rather rejoice in his sincere conversion. Let him distinguish between knowledge and love, as they ought to be distinguished; because "knowledge puffeth up, but love edifieth" [I Cor. 8:1]. And then knowledge no longer puffeth up when love builds up. And inasmuch as each is the gift of God (although one is less, and the other greater), he must not extol our righteousness above the praise which is due to Him who justifies us, in such a way as to assign to the lesser of these two gifts the help of divine grace, and to claim the greater one for the human will. And should he consent that we receive love from the grace of God, he must not suppose that any merits of our own preceded our reception of the gift. For what merits could we possibly have had at the time when we loved not God? In order, indeed, that we might receive that love whereby we might love, we were loved while as yet we had no love ourselves. . . . Hence also that grace of God, whereby "His love is shed abroad in our hearts through the Holy Spirit, which is given unto us," [Rom. 5:5] must be so confessed by the man who would make a true confession, as to show his undoubting belief that nothing whatever in the way of goodness pertaining to godliness and real holiness can be accomplished without it.

THE WORK OF GRACE†

15. Nevertheless, in the "heavy yoke that is laid upon the sons of Adam, from the day that they go out of their mother's womb to the day that they return to

---

* On the Grace of Christ, 26.27; trans. Dods.
† City of God, XXI, 15-16; trans. Dods.

the mother of all things," there is found an admirable though painful monitor teaching us to be sober-minded, and convincing us that this life has become penal in consequence of that outrageous wickedness which was perpetrated in Paradise, and that all to which the New Testament invites belongs to that future inheritance which awaits us in the world to come, and is offered for our acceptance, as the earnest that we may, in its own due time, obtain that of which it is the pledge. Now, therefore, let us walk in hope, and let us by the spirit mortify the deeds of the flesh, and so make progress from day to day. For "the Lord knoweth them that are His"; [2 Tim. 2:19] and "as many as are led by the Spirit of God, they are sons of God," [Rom. 8:14] but by grace, not by nature. For there is but one Son of God by nature, who in His compassion became Son of man for our sakes, that we, by nature sons of men, might by grace become through Him sons of God. For He, abiding unchangeable, took upon Him our nature, that thereby He might take us to Himself; and, holding fast His own divinity, He became partaker of our infirmity, that we, being changed into some better thing, might, by participating in His righteousness and immortality, lose our own properties of sin and mortality, and preserve whatever good quality He had implanted in our nature, perfected now by sharing in the goodness of His nature. For as by the sin of one man we have fallen into a misery so deplorable, so by the righteousness of one Man, who also is God, shall we come to a blessedness inconceivably exalted. Nor ought any one to trust that he has passed from the one man to the other until he shall have reached that place where there is no temptation, and have entered into the peace which he seeks in the many and various conflicts of this war, in which "the flesh lusteth against the spirit, and the spirit against the flesh." [Gal. 5:17] Now, such a war as this would have had no existence, if human nature had, in the exercise of free will, continued steadfast in the uprightness in which it was created. But now in its misery it makes war upon itself, because in its blessedness it would not continue at peace with God; and this, though it be a miserable calamity, is better than the earlier stages of this life, which do not recognize that a war is to be maintained. For better is it to contend with vices than without conflict to be subdued by them. Better, I say, is war with the hope of peace everlasting than captivity without any thought of deliverance. We long, indeed, for the cessation of this war, and, kindled by the flame of divine love, we burn for entrance on that well-ordered peace in which whatever is inferior is forever subordinated to what is above it. But if (which God forbid) there had been no hope of so blessed a consummation, we should still have preferred to endure the hardness of this conflict, rather than, by our nonresistance, to yield ourselves to the dominion of vice.

16. But such is God's mercy towards the vessels of mercy which He has prepared for glory, that even the first age of man, that is, infancy, which submits without any resistance to the flesh, and the second age, which is called boyhood, and which has not yet understanding enough to undertake this warfare, and therefore yields to almost every vicious pleasure (because though this age has the power of speech, and may therefore seem to have passed infancy, the mind is still too weak to comprehend the commandment), yet if either of these ages has received the sacraments of the Mediator, then, although the present life be immediately brought to an end, the child, having been translated from the power of darkness to the kingdom of Christ, shall not only be saved from eternal punishments, but shall not even suffer purgatorial torments after death. For spiritual regeneration of itself suffices to prevent any evil consequences resulting after death from the connection with death which carnal generation forms. But when we reach that age which can now comprehend the commandment, and submit to the dominion of law, we must declare war upon vices, and wage this war keenly, lest we be landed in damnable sins. And if vices have not gathered strength, by habitual victory they are more easily overcome and subdued; but if they have been used to conquer and rule, it is only with difficulty and labor they are mastered. And indeed this victory cannot be sincerely and truly gained but by delighting in true righteousness, and it is faith in Christ that gives this. For if the law be present with its command, and the Spirit be absent with His help, the presence of the prohibition serves only to increase the desire to sin, and adds the guilt of transgression. Sometimes, indeed, patent vices are overcome by other and hidden vices, which are reckoned virtues, though pride and a kind of ruinous self-sufficiency are their informing principles. Accordingly vices are then only to be considered overcome when they are conquered by the love of God, which God Himself alone gives, and which He gives only through the Mediator between God and men, the man

Christ Jesus, who became a partaker of our mortality that He might make us partakers of His divinity. But few indeed are they who are so happy as to have passed their youth without committing any damnable sins, either by dissolute or violent conduct, or by following some godless and unlawful opinions, but have subdued by their greatness of soul everything in them which could make them the slaves of carnal pleasures. The greater number having first become transgressors of the law that they have received, and having allowed vice to have the ascendency in them, then flee to grace for help, and so, by a penitence more bitter, and a struggle more violent than it would otherwise have been, they subdue the soul to God, and thus give it its lawful authority over the flesh, and become victors. Whoever, therefore, desires to escape eternal punishment, let him not only be baptized, but also justified in Christ, and so let him in truth pass from the devil to Christ.

HOW FREEDOM IS RESTORED BY GRACE*

30. But this part of the human race to which God has promised pardon and a share in His eternal kingdom, can they be restored through the merit of their own works? God forbid. For what good work can a lost man perform, except so far as he has been delivered from perdition? Can they do anything by the free determination of their own will? Again I say, God forbid. For it was by the evil use of his free will that man destroyed both it and himself. For, as a man who kills himself must, of course, be alive when he kills himself, but after he has killed himself ceases to live, and cannot restore himself to life; so, when man by his own free will sinned, then sin being victorious over him, the freedom of his will was lost. "For of whom a man is overcome, of the same is he brought in bondage." [2 Peter 2:19] This is the judgment of the Apostle Peter. And as it is certainly true, what kind of liberty, I ask, can the bondslave possess, except when it pleases him to sin? For he is freely in bondage who does with pleasure the will of his master. Accordingly, he who is the servant of sin is free to sin. And hence he will not be free to do right, until, being freed from sin, he shall begin to be the servant of righteousness. And this is true liberty, for he has pleasure in the righteous deed;

* *Enchiridion,* 30-32; trans. Dods.

and it is at the same time a holy bondage, for he is obedient to the will of God. But whence comes this liberty to do right to the man who is in bondage and sold under sin, except he be redeemed by Him who has said, "If the Son shall make you free, ye shall be free indeed'? [John 8:36] And before this redemption is wrought in a man, when he is not yet free to do what is right, how can he talk of the freedom of his will and his good works, except he be inflated by that foolish pride of boasting which the apostle restrains when he says, "By grace are ye saved, through faith." [Eph. 2:8]

31. And lest men should arrogate to themselves the merit of their own faith at least, not understanding that this too is the gift of God, this same apostle, who says in another place that he had "obtained mercy of the Lord to be faithful," [1 Cor. 7:25] here also adds: "and that not of yourselves; it is the gift of God, not of works, lest any man should boast." [Eph. 2:8-9] And lest it should be thought that good works will be wanting in those who believe, he adds further: "For we are His workmanship, created in Christ Jesus unto good works, which God hath before ordained that we should walk in them." [Eph. 2:10] We shall be made truly free, then, when God fashions us, that is, forms and creates us anew, not as men—for He has done that already—but as good men, which His grace is now doing, that we may be a new creation in Christ Jesus, according as it is said: "Create in me a clean heart, O God." [Ps. 50:12] For God had already created his heart, so far as the physical structure of the human heart is concerned; but the psalmist prays for the renewal of the life which was still lingering in his heart.

32. And further, should any one be inclined to boast, not indeed of his works, but of the freedom of his will, as if the first merit belonged to him, this very liberty of good action being given to him as a reward he had earned, let him listen to this same preacher of grace, when he says: "For it is God which worketh in you, both to will and to do of His own good pleasure"; [Phil. 2:13] and in another place: "So, then, it is not of him that willeth, nor of him that runneth, but of God that showeth mercy." [Rom. 9:16] Now as, undoubtedly, if a man is of the age to use his reason, he cannot believe, hope, love, unless he will to do so, nor obtain the prize of the high calling of God unless he voluntarily run for it; in what sense is it "not of him that willeth, nor of him that runneth, but of God that showeth mercy," except that, as it is written, "the preparation of the heart is from the Lord"? [Prov. 16:1] Otherwise, if it is said, "It is not of him that willeth, nor of him that runneth, but of God that showeth mercy," because it is of both, that is, both of the will of man and of the mercy of God, so that we are to understand the saying, "It is not of him that willeth, nor of him that runneth, but of God that showeth mercy," as if it meant the will of man alone is not sufficient, if the mercy of God go not with it—then it will follow that the mercy of God alone is not sufficient, if the will of man go not with it; and therefore, if we may rightly say, "It is not of man that willeth, but of God that showeth mercy," because the will of man by itself is not enough, why may we not also rightly put it in the converse way: "It is not of God that showeth mercy, but of man that willeth," because the mercy of God by itself does not suffice? Surely, if no Christian will dare to say this, "It is not of God that showeth mercy, but of man that willeth," lest he should openly contradict the apostle, it follows that the true interpretation of the saying, "It is not of him that willeth, nor of him that runneth, but of God that showeth mercy," is that the whole works belongs to God, who both makes the will of man righteous and thus prepares it for assistance, and assists it when it is prepared. For the man's righteousness of will precedes many of God's gifts, but not all; and it must itself be included among those which it does not precede. We read in Holy Scripture, both that God's mercy "shall meet me," [Ps. 59:10] and that His mercy "shall follow me." [Ps. 23:6] It goes before the unwilling to make him willing; it follows the willing to make his will effectual. Why are we taught to pray for our enemies, [Matt. 5:44] who are plainly unwilling to lead a holy life, unless that God may work willingness in them? And why are we ourselves taught to ask that we may receive, [Matt. 7:7] unless that He who has created in us the wish, may Himself satisfy the wish? We pray, then, for our enemies, that the mercy of God may prevent them, as it has prevented us: we pray for ourselves that His mercy may follow us.

GOD'S FOREKNOWLEDGE AND HUMAN WILLING*

10.   Wherefore, neither is that necessity to be feared, for dread of which the Stoics labored to make such distinctions among the causes of things as should

* *City of God*, V, 10; trans. Dods.

enable them to rescue certain things from the dominion of necessity, and to subject others to it. Among those things which they wished not to be subject to necessity they placed our wills, knowing that they would not be free if subjected to necessity. For if that is to be called *our necessity* which is not in our power, but even though we be unwilling effects what it can effect—as, for instance, the necessity of death—it is manifest that our wills by which we live uprightly or wickedly are not under such a necessity; for we do many things which, if we were not willing, we should certainly not do. This is primarily true of the act of willing itself—for if we will, it *is;* if we will not, it *is* not—for we should not will if it were unwilling. But if we define necessity to be that according to which we say that it is necessary that anything be of such or such a nature, or be done in such and such a manner, I know not why we should have any dread of that necessity taking away the freedom of our will. For we do not put the life of God or the foreknowledge of God under necessity if we should say that it is necessary that God should live forever, and foreknow all things; as neither is His power diminished when we say that He cannot die or fall into error—for this is in such a way impossible to Him, that if it were possible for Him, He would be of less power. But assuredly He is rightly called omnipotent, though He can neither die nor fall into error. For He is called omnipotent on account of His doing what He wills, not on account of His suffering what He wills not; for if that should befall Him, He would by no means be omnipotent. Wherefore, He cannot do some things for the very reason that He is omnipotent. So also, when we say that it is necessary that, when we will, we will by free choice, in so saying we both affirm what is true beyond doubt, and do not still subject our wills thereby to a necessity which destroys liberty. Our wills, therefore, *exist* as *wills,* and do themselves whatever we do by willing, and which would not be done if we were unwilling. But when any one suffers anything, being unwilling, by the will of another, even in that case will retains its essential validity—we do not mean the will of the party who inflicts the suffering, for we resolve it into the power of God. For if a will should simply exist, but not be able to do what it wills, it would be overborne by a more powerful will. Nor would this be the case unless there had existed will, and that not the will of the other party, but the will of him who willed but was not able to accomplish what he willed. Therefore, whatsoever a man suffers contrary to his own will, he ought not to attribute to the will of men or of angels or of any created spirit, but rather to His will who gives power to wills. It is not the case, therefore, that because God foreknew what would be in the power of our wills, there is for that reason nothing in the power of our wills. For he who foreknew this did not foreknow nothing. Moreover, if He who foreknew what would be in the power of our wills did not foreknow nothing, but something, assuredly, even though He did foreknow, there is something in the power of our wills. Therefore we are by no means compelled either, retaining the prescience of God, to take away the freedom of the will or, retaining the freedom of the will, to deny that He is prescient of future things, which is impious. But we embrace both. We faithfully and sincerely confess both. The former, that we may believe well; the latter, that we may live well. For he lives ill who does not believe well concerning God. Wherefore be it far from us, in order to maintain our freedom, to deny the prescience of Him by whose help we are or shall be free. Consequently, it is not in vain that laws are enacted, and that reproaches, exhortations, praises, and vituperations are had recourse to; for these also He foreknew, and they are of great avail, even as great as He foreknew that they would be of. Prayers, also, are of avail to procure those things which He foreknew that He would grant to those who offered them; and with justice have rewards been appointed for good deeds, and punishments for sins. For a man does not therefore sin because God foreknew that he would sin. Nay, it cannot be doubted but that it is the man himself who sins when he does sin, because He, whose foreknowledge is infallible, foreknew not that fate or fortune or something else would sin, but that the man himself would sin who, if he wills not, sins not. But if he shall not will to sin, even this did God foreknow.

GRACE BEFORE AND AFTER THE FALL*

104.
Wherefore, God would have been willing to preserve even the first man in that state of salvation in which he was created, and after he had begotten sons to remove him at a fit time, without the intervention of death, to a better place, where he should have been not only free from sin but free even from the desire of sinning, if He had foreseen that man would have the steadfast will to persist in

* *Enchiridion,* 104-106; trans. Dods.

the state of innocence in which he was created. But as He foresaw that man would make a bad use of his free will, that is, would sin, God arranged His own designs rather with a view to do good to man even in his sinfulness, that thus the good will of the Omnipotent might not be made void by the evil will of man, but might be fulfilled in spite of it.

105. Now it was expedient that man should be at first so created as to have it in his power both to will what was right and to will what was wrong, not without reward if he willed the former, and not without punishment if he willed the latter. But in the future life it shall not be in his power to will evil, and yet this will constitute no restriction on the freedom of his will. On the contrary, his will shall be much freer when it shall be wholly impossible for him to be the slave of sin. We should never think of blaming the will, or saying that it was no will or that it was not to be called free, when we so desire happiness that not only do we shrink from misery but find it utterly impossible to do otherwise. As then the soul even now finds it impossible to desire unhappiness, so in future it shall be wholly impossible for it to desire sin. But God's arrangement was not to be broken, according to which He willed to show how good is a rational being who is able even to refrain from sin, and yet how much better is one who cannot sin at all; just as that was an inferior sort of immortality, and yet it was immortality, when it was possible for man to avoid death, although there is reserved for the future a more perfect immortality, when it shall be impossible for man to die.

106. The former immortality man lost through the exercise of his free will; the latter he shall obtain through grace, whereas, if he had not sinned, he should have obtained it by desert. Even in that case, however, there could have been no merit without grace, because, although the mere exercise of man's free will was sufficient to bring in sin, his free will would not have sufficed for his maintenance in righteousness, unless God had assisted it by imparting a portion of His unchangeable goodness. Just as it is in man's power to die whenever he will (for, not to speak of other means, any one can put an end to himself by simple abstinence from food), but the mere will cannot preserve life in the absence of food and the other means of life; so man in paradise was able of his mere will, simply by abandoning righteousness, to destroy himself; but to have maintained a life of righteousness would have been too much for his will,

unless it had been sustained by the Creator's power. After the fall, however, a more abundant exercise of God's mercy was required, because the will itself had to be freed from the bondage in which it was held by sin and death. And the will owes its freedom in no degree to itself but solely to the grace of God, which comes by faith in Jesus Christ; so that the very will through which we accept all the other gifts of God which lead us on to His eternal gift, is itself prepared of the Lord, as the Scripture says. [Prov. 16:1]

GRACE AND GOOD WORKS*

6. ... Supposing you are hoping for a right reward, I mean eternal life, but not from the Lord God through Jesus Christ, through whom alone eternal life is given, but you think you can attain to eternal life by means of the host of heaven, the sun and moon, the powers of air and sea, of earth and stars? You are godless. Believe in Him who justifies the ungodly, so that your good works may really be good works. For I should not call them good as long as they do not proceed from a right foundation. How does the matter stand? Either you look for temporal life from God the Eternal, or you look for eternal life from the devils; in either case, you are ungodly. Put your faith right, set your faith in order, set your life in order; and now if you have sound feet, go straight ahead without anxiety; run, you are on the right road; the faster you run the sooner you will get there. But possibly you are a little lame. At least do not turn back from the road; you will arrive, even if rather late; do not stand still, do not retrace your steps, do not wander off the track.

7. What then? Who are the blessed? Not those in whom God has not found sin; for He has found it in all men. *For all have sinned and do need the glory of God.* [Rom. 3:23] Therefore if sin is found in all, it follows that none are blessed but those whose sins are forgiven. Now this the apostle pointed out in these words: *Abraham believed God, and it was reputed to him unto justice. Now to him that worketh*—that is, who trusts to works, and affirms that by virtue of them he received the grace of faith—*the reward is not reckoned according to grace, but according to*

* *On Psalm 31, Serm.* 2, 6-8; trans. ACW 30, 72-74.

debt. [Rom. 4:3] What does this mean but that our reward is called grace? If it is grace, it is given gratis. What is the meaning of "it is given gratis"? On every count it is a free gift. You have done nothing to deserve it, and you receive the remission of your sins. Your works are examined and found to be all evil. If God were to give you their due for such works, undoubtedly He would condemn you: *For the wages of sin is death.* [Rom. 6:23] What do wicked deeds deserve, except condemnation? And good deeds? The kingdom of heaven. But you have been found out in wicked deeds; if you receive your deserts you will be punished. Now what is it that happens? God does not mete out the penalty you deserved, but He bestows on you the grace you did not deserve. He should have punished you; instead He pardoned you. So by virtue of His pardon you enter upon a life of faith; and at once that faith, taking to itself hope and love, begins to perform good works. But do not forthwith grow boastful and exalt yourself. Never forget who set you on the right road; never forget that, though sturdy and fleet of foot, you were straying off it; never forget how, sick as you were, and lying half-dead by the roadside, you were placed upon a beast and brought to the inn. [Luke 10:34] *Now to him that worketh,* the apostle continues, *the reward is not reckoned according to grace, but according to debt.* If you want to be cast forth from grace, brag about your merits. God sees what is in you, and He knows what is each one's due. *But to him that worketh not*—what? Take, for instance, some godless sinner; he produces no works. What then? But he *believeth in Him that justifieth the ungodly.* In so far, then, as he does no works to the purpose, he is ungodly; and if he appears to perform good works, yet being performed without faith they are not to be called good. *But to him that believeth in Him that justifieth the ungodly, his faith is reputed to justice; as David also termeth the blessedness of a man to whom God reputeth justice without works.* [Rom. 4:4-6] But what justice? That of faith, which is not preceded, but is followed, by good works.

8.   Now pay attention: otherwise, if you misunderstand, you will fling yourselves into that whirlpool of thinking you may sin with impunity; and I shall be free from blame, just as the apostle himself was free from blame for all those who misinterpreted him. They willfully misunderstood; otherwise they would have had to follow it up with good works. Do not make common cause with such people, brethren. Another Psalm has said of one such man, and it

applies to the class as to the individual: *He would not understand, that he might do well.* [Ps. 35:4] It does not say: "He could not understand." Therefore to act aright you must have the will to understand; then you will arrive at a clear understanding. What do I mean by a clear understanding? Nobody must boast of the good works he did before he had faith; nobody must be sluggish in doing good works now that faith is his. It is God who pardons all the ungodly and makes them just through faith.

PREVENIENT GRACE*

[Verse 1] This *glory the heavens show forth.* The heavens are the saints, poised above the earth, bearing the Lord. Yet the sky, too, after its fashion, has proclaimed the glory of Christ. When? When at the birth of this same Lord there appeared a new star never seen before. However, there are truer and loftier heavens, of which the following verses tell us: *There are no speeches nor languages where their voices are not heard. Their sound hath gone forth into all the earth, and their words unto the ends of the world.* Whose words, but those of the heavens? Whose, then, but those of the apostles? It is they who proclaim to us the glory of God, residing in Christ Jesus and manifested through His grace for the remission of sins. For all have sinned and do need the glory of God, being justified gratuitously by His blood. [Rom. 3:23] Because gratuitously, therefore by grace; for grace is no grace unless it is gratuitous. Because we had done nothing good beforehand to deserve such great gifts and all the more because punishment, by no means undeserved, was to be inflicted, the favor was granted freely. There was nothing in our preceding merits that would earn anything but our condemnation. But He, not because of our own justice, but in accordance with His own mercy, saved us with the cleansing power which gives us new birth. This, I say, is the glory of God; this it is that the heavens have shown forth. This, I repeat, is God's glory, not yours; you have done nothing good, and yet you have received such an immense benefit. If therefore you share in the glory that the heavens proclaim, say to the Lord your God: *My God, His mercy shall prevent me.* [Ps. 58:11] Truly He forestalled you; He had to forestall you, because He found not an atom of virtue in you.

* *On Psalm 18,* Serm. 2; trans. ACW 29, 183-184.

You had forestalled His chastisement by your pride; He has forestalled your punishment by wiping out your sins.

GRACE AND HUMAN MISERIES*

20. Far be it from us to fear that the omnipotence of the Creator cannot, for the resuscitation and reanimation of our bodies, recall all the portions which have been consumed by beasts or fire, or have been dissolved into dust or ashes, or have decomposed into water, or evaporated into the air. Far from us be the thought, that anything which escapes our observation in any most hidden recess of nature either evades the knowledge or transcends the power of the Creator of all things. Cicero, the great authority of our adversaries, wishing to define God as accurately as possible, says, "God is a mind free and independent, without materiality, perceiving and moving all things, and itself endowed with eternal movement." [*Tusc. Disp*. I. 27] This he found in the systems of the greatest philosophers. Let me ask, then, in their own language, how anything can either lie hid from Him who perceives all things, or irrevocably escape Him who moves all things?

This leads me to reply to that question which seems the most difficult of all— To whom, in the resurrection, will belong the flesh of a dead man which has become the flesh of a living man? For if some one, famishing for want and pressed with hunger, use human flesh as food—an extremity not unknown, as both ancient history and the unhappy experience of our own days have taught us—can it be contended, with any show of reason, that all the flesh eaten has been evacuated, and that none of it has been assimilated to the substance of the eater though the very emaciation which existed before, and has now disappeared, sufficiently indicates what large deficiencies have been filled up with this food? But I have already made some remarks which will suffice for the solution of this difficulty also. For all the flesh which hunger has consumed finds its way into the air by evaporation, whence, as we have said, God Almighty can recall it. That flesh, therefore, shall be restored to the man in whom it first became human flesh. For it must be looked upon as borrowed by the other person, and, like a pecuniary loan, must be returned to the lender. His own flesh, however,

* *City of God*, XXII, 20-22; trans. Dods.

which he lost by famine, shall be restored to him by Him who can recover even what has evaporated. And though it had been absolutely annihilated, so that no part of its substance remained in any secret spot of nature, the Almighty could restore it by such means as He saw fit. For this sentence, uttered by the Truth, "Not a hair of your head shall perish," forbids us to suppose that, though no hair of a man's head can perish, yet the large portions of his flesh eaten and consumed by the famishing can perish.

From all that we have thus considered, and discussed with such poor ability as we can command, we gather this conclusion, that in the resurrection of the flesh the body shall be of that size which it either had attained or should have attained in the flower of its youth, and shall enjoy the beauty that arises from preserving symmetry and proportion in all its members. And it is reasonable to suppose that, for the preservation of this beauty, any part of the body's substance, which, if placed in one spot, would produce a deformity, shall be distributed through the whole of it, so that neither any part nor the symmetry of the whole may be lost, but only the general stature of the body somewhat increased by the distribution in all the parts of that which in one place would have been unsightly. Or if it is contended that each will rise with the same stature as that of the body he died in, we shall not obstinately dispute this, provided only there be no deformity, no infirmity, no languor, no corruption—nothing of any kind which would ill become that kingdom in which the children of the resurrection and of the promise shall be equal to the angels of God, if not in body and age, at least in happiness.

21. Whatever therefore has been taken from the body, either during life or after death, shall be restored to it, and, in conjunction with what has remained in the grave, shall rise again, transformed from the oldness of the animal body into the newness of the spiritual body, and clothed in incorruption and immortality. But even though the body has been all quite ground to powder by some severe accident or by the ruthlessness of enemies, and though it has been so diligently scattered to the winds or into the water that there is no trace of it left, yet it shall not be beyond the omnipotence of the Creator—no, not a hair of its head shall perish. The flesh shall then be spiritual and subject to the spirit, but still flesh not spirit, as the spirit itself, when subject to the flesh, was fleshly but still spirit and not flesh. And of this we have experimental proof in the deformity of

our penal condition. For those persons were carnal, not in a fleshly but in a spiritual way, to whom the apostle said, "I could not speak to you as unto spiritual, but as unto carnal." [1 Cor. 3:1] And a man is in this life spiritual in such a way, that he is yet carnal with respect to his body, and sees another law in his members warring against the law of his mind; but even in his body he will be spiritual when the same flesh shall have had that resurrection of which these words speak, "It is sown an animal body, it shall rise a spiritual body." [1 Cor. 15:44] But what this spiritual body shall be and how great its grace, I fear it were but rash to pronounce, seeing that we have as yet no experience of it. Nevertheless, since it is fit that the joyfulness of our hope should utter itself, and so show forth God's praise, and since it was from the profoundest sentiment of ardent and holy love that the Psalmist cried, "O Lord, I have loved the beauty of Thy house," [Ps. 25:8] we may with God's help speak of the gifts He lavishes on men, good and bad alike, in this most wretched life, and may do our best to conjecture the great glory of that state which we cannot worthily speak of, because we have not yet experienced it. For I say nothing of the time when God made man upright; I say nothing of the happy life of "the man and his wife" in the fruitful garden, since it was so short that none of their children experienced it: I speak only of this life which we know and in which we now are, from the temptations of which we cannot escape so long as we are in it, no matter what progress we make, for it is all temptation, and I ask, Who can describe the tokens of God's goodness that are extended to the human race even in this life?

    That the whole human race has been condemned
22. in its first origin, this life itself, if life it is to be
    called, bears witness by the host of cruel ills with

which it is filled. Is not this proved by the profound and dreadful ignorance which produces all the errors that enfold the children of Adam, and from which no man can be delivered without toil, pain, and fear? Is it not proved by his love of so many vain and hurtful things, which produces gnawing cares, disquiet, griefs, fears, wild joys, quarrels, lawsuits, wars, treasons, angers, hatreds, deceit, flattery, fraud, theft, robbery, perfidy, pride, ambition, envy, murders, parricides, cruelty, ferocity, wickedness, luxury, insolence, impudence, shamelessness, fornications, adulteries, incests, and the numberless uncleannesses and unnatural acts of both sexes, which it is shameful so much as to mention; sacrileges, heresies, blasphemies, perjuries, oppression of the innocent, calumnies, plots, falsehoods, false witnessings, unrighteous judgments, violent deeds, plunderings, and whatever similar wickedness has found its way into the lives of men, though it cannot find its way into the conception of pure minds? These are indeed the crimes of wicked men, yet they spring from that root of error and misplaced love which is born with every son of Adam. For who is there that has not observed with what profound ignorance, manifesting itself even in infancy, and with what superfluity of foolish desires, beginning to appear in boyhood, man comes into this life, so that, were he left to live as he pleased, and to do whatever he pleased, he would plunge into all, or certainly into many of those crimes and iniquities which I mentioned and could not mention?

But because God does not wholly desert those whom He condemns, nor shuts up in His anger His tender mercies, the human race is restrained by law and instruction, which keep guard against the ignorance that besets us and oppose the assaults of vice, but are themselves full of labor and sorrow. For what mean those multifarious threats which are used to restrain the folly of children? What mean pedagogues, masters, the birch, the strap, the cane, the schooling which Scripture says must be given a child, "beating him on the sides lest he wax stubborn," [Ecclus. 30:12] and it be hardly possible or not possible at all to subdue him? Why all these punishments, save to overcome ignorance and bridle evil desires—these evils with which we come into the world? For why is it that we remember with difficulty, and without difficulty forget? learn with difficulty, and without difficulty remain ignorant? are diligent with difficulty, and without difficulty are indolent? Does not this show what vitiated nature inclines and tends to by its own weight, and what succor it needs if it is to be delivered? Inactivity, sloth, laziness, negligence, are vices which shun labor, since labor, though useful, is itself a punishment.

But besides the punishments of childhood, without which there would be no learning of what the parents wish—and the parents rarely wish anything useful to be taught—who can describe, who can conceive the number and severity of the punishments which afflict the human race—pains which are not only the accompaniment of the wickedness of godless men, but are a part of the human condition and the common misery—what fear and what grief are caused by bereavement and mourning, by losses and condemnations, by fraud and falsehood, by false suspicions, and all the crimes and wicked deeds of other men? For at their hands we suffer robbery, captivity, chains, imprisonment, exile, torture, mutilation, loss of sight, the violation of chastity to satisfy the lust of the oppressor, and many other dreadful evils. What numberless casualties threaten our bodies from without—extremes of heat and cold, storms, floods, inundations, lightning, thunder, hail, earthquakes, houses falling; or from the stumbling or shying or vice of horses; from countless poisons in fruits, water, air, animals; from the painful or even deadly bites of wild animals; from the madness which a mad dog communicates, so that even the animal which of all others is most gentle and friendly to its own master, becomes an object of intenser fear than a lion or dragon, and the man whom it has by chance infected with this pestilential contagion becomes so rabid, that his parents, wife, children, dread him more than any wild beast! What disasters are suffered by those who travel by land or sea! What man can go out of his own house without being exposed on all hands to unforeseen accidents? Returning home sound in limb, he slips on his own doorstep, breaks his leg, and never recovers. What can seem safer than a man sitting in his chair? Eli the priest fell from his, and broke his neck. How many accidents do farmers, or rather all men, fear that the crops may suffer from the weather or the soil or the ravages of destructive animals? Commonly they feel safe when the crops are gathered and housed. Yet to my certain knowledge sudden floods have driven the laborers away, and swept the barns clean of the finest harvest. Is innocence a sufficient protection against the various assaults of demons? That no man might think so, even baptized infants, who are certainly unsurpassed in innocence, are sometimes so tormented, that God, who permits it, teaches us hereby to bewail the calamities of this life, and to desire the felicity of the life to come. As to bodily diseases, they are so numerous that they cannot all be contained even in medical books. And in very many, or almost all of them, the cures and remedies are themselves tortures, so that men are delivered from a pain that destroys by a cure that pains. Has not the madness of thirst driven men to drink human urine, and even their own? Has not hunger driven men to eat human flesh, and that the flesh not of bodies found dead but of bodies slain for the purpose?

Have not the fierce pangs of famine driven mothers to eat their own children, incredibly savage as it seems? In fine, sleep itself, which is justly called repose, how little of repose there sometimes is in it when disturbed with dreams and visions; and with what terror is the wretched mind overwhelmed by the appearances of things which are so presented, and which, as it were, so stand out before the senses, that we can not distinguish them from realities! How wretchedly do false appearances distract men in certain diseases! With what astonishing variety of appearances are even healthy men sometimes deceived by evil spirits, who produce these delusions for the sake of perplexing the senses of their victims, if they cannot suceed in seducing them to their side!

From this hell upon earth there is no escape, save through the grace of the Saviour Christ, our God and Lord. The very name Jesus shows this, for it means Saviour; and He saves us especially from passing out of this life into a more wretched and eternal state, which is rather a death than a life. For in this life, though holy men and holy pursuits afford us great consolations, yet the blessings which men crave are not invariably bestowed upon them, lest religion should be cultivated for the sake of these temporal advantages, while it ought rather to be cultivated for the sake of that other life from which all evil is excluded. Therefore, also, does grace aid good men in the midst of present calamities, so that they are enabled to endure them with a constancy proportioned to their faith. The world's sages affirm that philosophy contributes something to this—that philosophy which, according to Cicero, the gods have bestowed in its purity only on a few men. They have never given, he says, nor can ever give, a greater gift to men. So that even those against whom we are disputing have been compelled to acknowledge, in some fashion, that the grace of God is necessary for the acquisition, not indeed of any philosophy but of the true philosophy. And if the true philosophy—this sole support against the miseries of this life—has been given by Heaven only to a few, it sufficiently appears from this that the human race has been condemned to pay this penalty of wretchedness. And as, according to their acknowledgment, no greater gift has been bestowed by God, so it must be believed that it could be given only by that God whom they themselves recognize as greater than all the gods they worship.

THE BEATIFIC VISION*

And their inheritance shall be forever. This we take
8. on faith. Does the Lord also take it on faith? The
Lord knows these things with a clarity so distinct that
it is beyond our reach to describe, even when we are made
equal to the angels. For the things to be revealed will not
show forth as plainly to us as they show forth to Him who
is incapable of change. Yet what are we told even of ourselves? *Dearly beloved, we are now the sons of God, and
it hath not yet appeared what we shall be. We know that,
when He shall appear, we shall be like to Him, because
we shall see Him as He is.* [I John 3:2] There is obviously,
then, some kind of blissful vision reserved for us; and if at
present only a partial glimpse may be caught *through a glass
in a dark manner,* [1 Cor. 13:12] yet the radiant beauty of
that beatitude which God stores up for them that fear Him,
which He perfects for them that hope in Him, utterly transcends the power of speech. It is for this that our hearts are
being trained in all the hardships and trials of this life. Do
not feel surprise at being schooled amid toil: you are being
schooled for a wondrous destiny.

This explains the cry of the just man who has been
strengthened: *The sufferings of this time are not worthy to
be compared with the glory to come, that shall be revealed
in us.* [Rom. 8:18] What is that glory of ours to come, unless it be equality with the angels, and the vision of God?
What a gift is bestowed on a blind man by one who restores
his eyesight so that he can see the light of day! When cured,
the man can find nothing sufficiently worthy to repay his
healer; however much he gives, indeed, what gift can equal
that which the other has bestowed? Desiring to give as much
as he can, he will give him gold, yes, even masses of it; but
the other has given him light! If the one would realize that
he is repaying absolutely nothing, he should look at his gift
in pitch darkness. And as to ourselves? What shall we give to
that Physician who heals our inward sight and enables us to
behold that very light eternal which is Himself?

* *On Psalm 36,* Serm. 2, 8; trans. ACW 30, 274-275.

IX. THE TWO CITIES

From Charlemagne onward, the Holy Roman Empire was inspired by a misreading of Augustine's *City of God*. Many people felt that he had planned the establishment of a Kingdom of God on this earth, in the form of a Christian renewal of the Empire of ancient Rome. This was not really his intent; Augustine's was an other-worldly ideal, a distinction of two kinds of men, and two societies which would never be formally institutionalized in the course of time. After the Last Judgment, they were to be separated in Heaven and Hell.

At the time that Augustine began to write the *City of God,* Rome was crumbling before the advances of the hordes from the north. Many of these invaders were Christians, partisans of the Arian heresy. To the old-line, pagan families of patrician Rome, Christianity now loomed as an insidious threat from within, and an open danger from outside the Empire. Various people, including the important Roman official Marcellinus, brought this charge to the attention of the Bishop of Hippo. It was widely rumored that Christianity had become a corroding influence to the Pax Romana. Supporters of the old paganism welcomed the opportunity to attack the spread of Christianity.

In the year 413 Augustine set to work to write a reply to this charge. He took more than thirteen years to complete the twenty-two books of the *City of God.* In a recently discovered *Letter to Firmus* (see the first selection, below), he has himself indicated the structure of this huge work. The first ten books answer the claim that Christianity is a corrosive social and political influence. In effect, Augustine denies the charge and argues that pagan polytheism has brought no good to Rome. In comparing his religion with the neopaganism then witnessing a brief revival in the last days of the Empire, Augustine utilized all the vast resources of his literary and historical scholarship. It is like an encyclopedia of late Roman culture. In the last twelve books, the theme becomes a description of the rise, progress and terminations of the two Cities.

Several of the first selections show how the citizens of these two societies are set apart by the contrast of their loves. In the Heavenly City, the members love God; in the Earthly City, the citizens have chosen another ruler. Sometimes Augustine suggests that the terrestrial chief is the Devil. The distinction of these societies then is a moral and religious one. The two cities are not differentiated by virtue of political organization but by the inner characters of their respective memberships.

Augustine was not entirely original in his theme of the two Cities. A Donatist scholar, Tychonius, had written earlier about these societies and Augustine recognizes his claim to priority. However, the real source of the theme is to be found in the Book of Psalms. Several of our middle selections indicate this biblical origin of the two Cities: the dualism is prefigured in Jerusalem and Babylon.

There has always been a certain understandable confusion concerning the relation of the City of God to the Christian Church. Actually, the selection included from the exposition of Psalm 98 suggests the identity of Church and Heavenly City. The problem is more involved than that. The citizens of God include all men and all angels of good will; the membership of the Church is somewhat different. It is not usual to speak of even the good angels as Christians; and again, there are both good and bad members in the visible Church, while there can be no really bad persons in the City of God. The memberships overlap but are not identical in the Church and the City of God.

Many of the most quoted and influential passages from Augustine are represented, at least in part, in the passages chosen for this present chapter. His definition of a "people" ("an assemblage of reasonable beings bound together by a common agreement as to the objects of their love") has clearly figured in later social and political philosophies. The description of peace as the "tranquillity of order," with the associated essay on various types of order, has been repeated in other times by many other writers.

Secondary literature on the *City of God* and its leading themes is very extensive. Our list of items in the Bibliography is very selective. Many histories of political and social theories in the middle ages devote at least a chapter to it. Gilson's lengthy introduction to the translation of the *City of God* discusses the major problems of interpretation and cites the standard interpretative works.

AUGUSTINE'S ANALYSIS OF THE CITY OF GOD*

The books on the City of God which you most eagerly requested I have sent you as I promised, having also reread them myself. That this, with God's help, should be done has been urged by my son and your brother, Cyprian, who has furnished just that insistence I hoped would be forthcoming.

There are twenty-two sections. To put all these into one whole would be cumbersome. If you wish that two volumes be made of them, they should be so apportioned that one volume contain ten books, the other twelve. For in those ten the empty teachings of the pagans have been refuted, and in the remainder our own religion has been demonstrated and defended—though, to be sure, in the former books the latter subject has been dealt with when it was more suitable to do so, and in the latter, the former.

If, however, you should prefer that there be more than two volumes, you should make as many as five. The first of these would contain the first five books, where argument has been advanced against those who contend that the worship, not indeed of gods, but of demons, is of profit for happiness in this present life. The second volume would contain the next five books, where [a stand has been taken against those] who think that, for the sake of the life which is to come after death, worship should be paid, through rites and sacrifices, whether to these divinities or to any plurality of gods whatever. The next three volumes ought to embrace four books each; for this part of our work has been so divided that four books set forth the origin of that City, a second four its progress—or, as we might choose to say, its development—the final four its appointed ends.

If the diligence you have shown for procuring these books will be matched by diligence in reading them, it is rather from your testing than from my promises that you will learn how far they will help you. As for those books belonging to this work on the City of God which our brothers there in Carthage do not yet have, I ask that you graciously and willingly accede to their requests to have copies made. You will

* *Letter to Firmus*, ed. C. Lambot in *Revue Bénédictine*, 51 (1939) 109-121; trans. FOC 6 (1950) 399-401.

not grant this favor to many, but to one or two at most, and they themselves will grant it to others. Among your friends, some, within the body of Christian folk, may desire instruction; in the case of others, bound by some superstition, it may appear that this labor of ours can through God's grace be used to liberate them. How you are to share it with them you must yourself decide.

For my part I shall take care to make frequent inquiry, God willing, what progress you are making in my writings as you read them. Surely, you cannot fail to know how much a man of education is helped toward understanding the written word by repeated reading. No difficulty in understanding occurs (or, if any, very little) where there is facility in reading, and this gains in scope with successive repetitions. Constant application [brings to fruition] what [through inattention] would have remained immature.

In earlier letters, my distinguished and deservedly honored lord and my son Firmus, you have shown acquaintance with the books on the Academics that I composed when my conversion was yet fresh. Please write in reply how you came to this knowledge.

The range of subject matter comprised in the twenty-two books of my composition is shown in the epitome that I send you.

HOW THE TWO CITIES DIFFER*

1.   We have already stated in the preceding books that God, desiring not only that the human race might be able by their similarity of nature to associate with one another, but also that they might be bound together in harmony and peace by the ties of relationship, was pleased to derive all men from one individual, and created man with such a nature that the members of the race should not have died, had not the two first (of whom the one was created out of nothing, and the other out of him) merited this by their disobedience; for by them so great a sin was committed that by it human nature was altered for the worse, and was transmitted also to their posterity, liable to sin and subject to death. And the kingdom of death so reigned over men, that the deserved penalty of sin would have

* *City of God,* XIV, 1; trans. Dods.

hurled all headlong even into the second death, of which there is no end, had not the undeserved grace of God saved some therefrom. And thus it has come to pass that, though there are very many and great nations all over the earth, whose rites and customs, speech, arms, and dress, are distinguished by marked differences, yet there are no more than two kinds of human society, which we may justly call two cities, according to the language of our Scriptures. The one consists of those who wish to live after the flesh, the other of those who wish to live after the spirit; and when they severally achieve what they wish, they live in peace, each after its kind.

TWO LOVES MAKE TWO CITIES*

15.20. These are the two loves: the first is holy, the second foul; the first is social, the second selfish; the first consults the common welfare for the sake of a celestial society, the second grasps at a selfish control of social affairs for the sake of arrogant domination; the first is submissive to God, the second tries to rival God; the first is quiet, the second restless; the first is peaceful, the second trouble-making; the first prefers truth to the praises of those who are in error, the second is greedy for praise, however it may be obtained; the first is friendly, the second envious; the first desires for its neighbor what it wishes for itself, the second desires to subjugate its neighbor; the first rules its neighbor for the good of its neighbor, the second for its own advantage; and these two loves produce a distinction among the angels: the first love belongs to the good angels, the second to the bad angels; and they also separate the two cities founded among the race of men, under the wonderful and ineffable Providence of God, administering and ordering all things that have been created: the first city is that of the just, the second is that of the wicked. Although they are now, during the course of time, intermingled, they shall be divided at the last judgment; the first, being joined by the good angels under its King, shall attain eternal life; the second, in union with the bad angels under its king, shall be sent into eternal fire. Perhaps, we shall treat, God willing, of these two cities more fully in another place.

* *Literal Commentary on Genesis*, XI, 15.20; trans. V.J.B.

28. Accordingly, two cities have been formed by two loves: the earthly by the love of self, even to the contempt of God; the heavenly by the love of God, even to the contempt of self. The former, in a word, glories in itself, the latter in the Lord. For the one seeks glory from men, but the greatest glory of the other is God, the witness of conscience. The one lifts up its head in its own glory; the other says to its God, "Thou art my glory, and the lifter up of mine head." [Ps. 3:4] In the one, the princes and the nations it subdues are ruled by the love of ruling; in the other, the princes and the subjects serve one another in love, the latter obeying, while the former take thought of all. The one delights in its own strength, represented in the persons of its rulers; the other says to its God, "I will love Thee, O Lord, my strength." [Ps. 17:1] And therefore the wise men of the one city, living according to man, have sought for profit to their own bodies or souls or both, and those who have known God "glorified Him not as God, neither were thankful, but became vain in their imaginations, and their foolish heart was darkened; professing themselves to be wise"—that is, glorying in their own wisdom, and being possessed by pride—"they became fools, and changed the glory of the incorruptible God into an image made like to corruptible man, and to birds, and four-footed beasts, and creeping things." For they were either leaders or followers of the people in adoring images, "and worshipped and served the creature more than the Creator, who is blessed forever." [Rom. 1:21-25] But in the other city there is no human wisdom, but only godliness, which offers due worship to the true God, and looks for its reward in the society of the saints, of holy angels as well as holy men, "that God may be all in all." [1 Cor. 15:28]

THE UNIMPORTANCE OF EXTERNALS†

19. It is a matter of no moment in the city of God whether he who adopts the faith that brings men to God adopts it in one dress and manner of life or

* *City of God*, XIV, 28; trans. Dods.
† *City of God*, XIX, 19; trans. Dods.

another, so long only as he lives in conformity with the commandments of God. And hence, when philosophers themselves become Christians, they are compelled, indeed, to abandon their erroneous doctrines, but not their dress and mode of living, which are no obstacle to religion. So that we make no account of the distinction of sects which Varro adduced in connection with the Cynic school, provided always nothing indecent or self-indulgent is retained.

RELATION OF THE HEAVENLY
AND EARTHLY CITIES*

17. But the families which do not live by faith seek their peace in the earthly advantages of this life; while the families which live by faith look for those eternal blessings which are promised, and use as pilgrims such advantages of time and of earth as do not fascinate and divert them from God, but rather aid them to endure with greater ease, and to keep down the number of those burdens of the corruptible body which weigh upon the soul. Thus the things necessary for this mortal life are used by both kinds of men and families alike, but each has its own peculiar and widely different aim in using them. The earthly city, which does not live by faith, seeks an earthly peace, and the end it proposes, in the well-ordered concord of civic obedience and rule, is the combination of men's wills to attain the things which are helpful to this life. The heavenly city, or rather the part of it which sojourns on earth and lives by faith, makes use of this peace only because it must, until this mortal condition which necessitates it shall pass away. Consequently, so long as it lives like a captive and a stranger in the earthly city, though it has already received the promise of redemption, and the gift of the Spirit as the earnest of it, it makes no scruple to obey the laws of the earthly city, whereby the things necessary for the maintenance of this mortal life are administered; and thus, as this life is common to both cities, so there is a harmony between them in regard to what belongs to it. But, as the earthly city has had some philosophers whose doctrine is condemned by the divine teaching, and who, being deceived either by their own conjectures or by demons,

* *City of God*, XIX, 17; trans. Dods.

supposed that many gods must be invited to take an interest in human affairs, and assigned to each a separate function and a separate department—to one the body, to another the soul; and in the body itself, to one the head, to another the neck, and each of the other members to one of the gods; and in like manner, in the soul, to one god the natural capacity was assigned, to another education, to another anger, to another lust; and so the various affairs of life were assigned—cattle to one, corn to another, wine to another, oil to another, the woods to another, money to another, navigation to another, wars and victories to another, marriages to another, births and fecundity to another, and other things to other gods: and as the celestial city, on the other hand, knew that one God only was to be worshipped, and that to Him alone was due that service which the Greeks call *latreia,* and which can be given only to a god, it has come to pass that the two cities could not have common laws of religion, and that the heavenly city has been compelled in this matter to dissent and to become obnoxious to those who think differently, and to stand the brunt of their anger and hatred and persecutions, except in so far as the minds of their enemies have been alarmed by the multitude of the Christians and quelled by the manifest protection of God accorded to them. This heavenly city, then, while it sojourns on earth, calls citizens out of all nations, and gathers together a society of pilgrims of all languages, not scrupling about diversities in the manners, laws, and institutions whereby earthly peace is secured and maintained, but recognizing that, however various these are, they all tend to one and the same end of earthly peace. It therefore is so far from rescinding and abolishing these diversities, that it even preserves and adopts them, so long only as no hindrance to the worship of the one supreme and true God is thus introduced. Even the heavenly city, therefore, while in its state of pilgrimage, avails itself of the peace of earth, and, so far as it can without injuring faith and godliness, desires and maintains a common agreement among men regarding the acquisition of the necessaries of life, and makes this earthly peace bear upon the peace of heaven; for this alone can be truly called and esteemed the peace of the reasonable creatures, consisting as it does in the perfectly ordered and harmonious enjoyment of God and of one another in God. When we shall have reached that peace, this mortal life shall give place to one that is eternal, and our body shall be no more this animal body which by its corruption weighs down the soul, but a spiritual body feeling no want and in all its members subjected to the will. In its pilgrim state the heavenly city possesses this peace by faith; and by this faith it lives righteously when it refers to the attainment of that peace every good action towards God and man; for the life of the city is a social life.

JERUSALEM AND BABYLON*

2. And see ye the names of those two cities, Babylon and Jerusalem. Babylon is interpreted confusion, Jerusalem vision of peace. Observe now the city of confusion, in order that ye may perceive the vision of peace, that ye may endure that, sigh for this. Whereby can those two cities be distinguished? Can we anywise now separate them from each other? They are mingled, and from the very beginning of mankind mingled they run on unto the end of the world. Jerusalem received beginning through Abel, Babylon through Cain: for the buildings of the cities were afterwards erected. That Jerusalem in the land of the Jebusites was built: for at first it used to be called Jebus; from thence the nation of the Jebusites was expelled, when the people of God was delivered from Egypt and led into the land of promise. But Babylon was built in the most interior regions of Persia, which for a long time raised its head above the rest of nations. These two cities then at particular times were built, so that there might be shown a figure of two cities begun of old, and to remain even unto the end in this world, but at the end to be severed. Whereby then can we now show them that are mingled? At that time the Lord shall show, when some He shall set on the right hand, others on the left. Jerusalem on the right hand shall be, Babylon on the left. . . . Two loves make up these cities: love of God maketh Jerusalem, love of the world maketh Babylon. Therefore let each one question himself as to what he loveth, and he shall find of which he is a citizen; and if he shall have found himself to be a citizen of Babylon, let him root out cupidity, implant charity, but if he shall have found himself a citizen of Jerusalem, let him endure captivity, hope for liberty. . . .

* On Psalm 64, 2; trans. Nicene.

SUMMARY ON THE TWO CITIES*

1.   I promised to write of the rise, progress, and appointed end of the two cities, one of which is God's, the other this world's, in which, so far as mankind is concerned, the former is now a stranger. But first of all I undertook, so far as His grace should enable me, to refute the enemies of the city of God, who prefer their gods to Christ its founder, and fiercely hate Christians with the most deadly malice. And this I have done in the first ten books. Then, as regards my three-fold promise which I have just mentioned, I have treated distinctly, in the four books which follow the tenth, of the rise of both cities. After that I have proceeded from the first man down to the flood in one book, which is the fifteenth of this work, and from that again down to Abraham our work has followed both in chronological order. From the patriarch Abraham down to the time of the Israelite kings, at which we close our sixteenth book, and thence down to the advent of Christ Himself in the flesh, to which period the seventeenth book reaches, the city of God appears from my way of writing to have run its course alone; whereas it did not run its course alone in this age, for both cities, in their course amid mankind, certainly experienced chequered times together just as from the beginning. But I did this in order that, first of all, from the time when the promises of God began to be more clear, down to the virgin birth of Him in whom those things promised from the first were to be fulfilled, the course of that city which is God's might be made more distinctly apparent, without interpolation of foreign matter from the history of the other city, although down to the revelation of the new covenant it ran its course, not in light, but in shadow. Now, therefore, I think fit to do what I passed by, and show, so far as seems necessary, how that other city ran its course from the times of Abraham, so that attentive readers may compare the two.

City of God, XVIII, 1; trans. Dods.

ALL NATIONS ARE IN THE CITY OF GOD*

5. "Very excellent things are said of thee, thou city of God" (ver. 3). He was as it were contemplating that city of Jerusalem on earth; for consider what city he alludes to, of which certain very excellent things are spoken. Now the earthly city has been destroyed: after suffering the enemy's rage, it fell to the earth; it is no longer what it was: it exhibited the emblem, and the shadow hath passed away. Whence then are "very excellent things spoken of thee, thou city of God"? Listen whence: "I will think upon Rahab and Babylon, with them that know Me" (ver. 4). In that city, the Prophet, in the person of God, says, "I will think upon Rahab and Babylon." Rahab belongs not to the Jewish people, Babylon belongs not to the Jewish people, as is clear from the next verse: "For the Philistines also, and Tyre with the Ethiopians, were there." Deservedly then, "very excellent things are spoken of thee, thou city of God"; for not only is the Jewish nation, born of the flesh of Abraham, included therein, but all nations also, some of which are named that all may be understood. "I will think," he says, "upon Rahab"; who is that harlot? That harlot in Jericho, who received the spies and conducted them out of the city by a different road; who trusted beforehand in the promise, who feared God, who was told to hang out of the window a line of scarlet thread, that is, to bear upon her forehead the sign of the blood of Christ. She was saved there, and thus represented the Church of the Gentiles; whence our Lord said to the haughty Pharisees, "Verily I say unto you, that the publicans and the harlots go into the kingdom of God before you." They go before because they do violence; they push their way by faith, and to faith a way is made nor can any resist, since they who are violent take it by force. For it is written, "The kingdom of Heaven suffereth violence, and the violent take it by force." Such was the conduct of the robber, more courageous on the cross than in the place of ambush. "I will think upon Rahab and Babylon." By Babylon is meant

* On Psalm 86, 5; trans. Nicene.

the city of this world: as there is one holy city, Jerusalem, one unholy, Babylon; all the unholy belong to Babylon, even as all the holy to Jerusalem. But he slideth from Babylon to Jerusalem. How but by Him who justifieth the ungodly: Jerusalem is the city of the saints, Babylon of the wicked: but He cometh who justifieth the ungodly, since it is said, "I will think" not only "upon Rahab," but "upon Babylon," but with whom? "With them that know Me." ...

THE CHURCH AND THE CITY OF GOD*

4.
"The Lord is great in Sion, and high above all people" (ver. 2)....He whom I spoke to thee of as above the Cherubim, is great in Sion. Ask thou now, what is Sion? We know Sion to be the city of God. The city of Jerusalem is called Sion, and is so called according to a certain interpretation, for that Sion signifieth watching, that is, sight and contemplation, for to watch is to look forward to or gaze upon or strain the eyes to see. Now every soul is a Sion if it trieth to see that light which is to be seen. For if it shall have gazed upon a light of its own, it is darkened; if upon His, it is enlightened. But, now that it is clear that Sion is the city of God; what is the city of God, but the Holy Church? For men who love one another, and who love their God who dwelleth in them, constitute a city unto God. Because a city is held together by some law; their very law is Love, and that very Love is God; for openly it is written, "God is Love." He therefore who is full of Love is full of God; and many full of love constitute a city full of God. That city of God is called Sion; the Church therefore is Sion. In it God is great....

THE FOUNDATION OF THE HOLY CITY†

4.
...This city is therefore now in building; stones are cut down from the hills by the hands of those who preach truth, they are squared that they may enter into an everlasting structure. There are still many stones in the hands of the Builder: let them not fall from His hands,

* On Psalm 98, 4; trans. Nicene.
† On Psalm 121, 4; trans. Nicene.

that they may be built perfect into the structure of the temple. This, then, is the "Jerusalem that is being built as a city": Christ is its foundation. The Apostle Paul saith, "Other foundation can no man lay than that is laid, which is Christ Jesus." [I Cor. 3:11] When a foundation is laid on earth, the walls are built above, and the weight of the walls tends towards the lowest parts, because the foundation is laid at the bottom. But if our foundation be in heaven, let us be built towards heaven. Bodies have built the edifice of this basilica, the ample size of which ye see, and since bodies have built it, they placed the foundation lowest, but since we are spiritually built, our foundation is placed at the highest point. Let us therefore run thither, where we may be built.... But what Jerusalem do I speak of? Is it that, he asketh, which ye see standing, raised on the structure of its walls? No, but the "Jerusalem which is being built as a city." Why not, "a city" instead of "as a city"; save because those walls, so built in Jerusalem, were a visible city, as it is by all called a city, literally, but this is being built "as a city," for they who enter it are like living stones; for they are not literally stones? Just as they are called stones, and yet are not so, so the city styled "as a city" is not a city; for he said, "is being built." For by the word building, he meant to be understood the structure, and cohesion of bodies and walls. For a city (*civitas*) is properly understood of the men that inhabit there. But in saying "is building," he showed us that he meant a town. And since a spiritual building hath some resemblance to a bodily building, therefore it "is building as a city."

RELIGION AND HUMAN DESTINY*

7.13. The starting point for following this religion is the record and the foretelling of the temporal dispensation of divine providence in its work of reforming and restoring the human race to fit it for its eternal destiny. After belief in this revelation, a mode of life in accordance with the divine commands will purify the mind and make it able to perceive spiritual things. These are neither past nor future, but remain the same in every way forever, subject to no

* *The True Religion*, 7.13-8.14; trans. C.A. Hangartner, S.J., *De vera religione* (*chapters* 1-17) (St. Louis University Master's Thesis, 1945), pp. 37-41. Used with permission.

change: as, for example, the one God the Father Himself, the Son, and the Holy Spirit. With a knowledge of this Trinity proportioned to this life, we can see beyond the shadow of a doubt that every intellectual, animate, and corporeal creature has its existence, in so far as it exists, its proper nature, and its perfectly ordered career, from the creative power of this same Trinity. Not that the Father is thought to have produced one part of the whole creature, the Son another part, and the Holy Spirit still another; but rather that at one and the same time each and every nature has been made by the Father through the Son and in the gift of the Holy Spirit. For every thing or substance or essence or nature, or whatever else it may be more properly termed, has these three perfections at once: it exists as a single something; its own nature sets it off from other beings; and it does not deviate from the universal order of things.

8.14. What necessary, unalterable, and just laws bind all things to their God and Lord will appear clearly enough from this knowledge, as far as man can grasp the matter. Some of the things which we first believed merely on the basis of authority are now so well understood that, regarding them, we see by reason that they are altogether certain. Others we see to be both possible and fitting, and we are sorry for those who do not believe them, and who prefer to laugh at us for our belief rather than to share it. For the sacred assumption of human nature, the Virgin birth, the death of the Son of God for us, His resurrection from the dead, His ascension into heaven, His seat at the right hand of the Father, the removal of sins, the day of judgment, and the resurrection of the body, are no longer merely matters of faith believed in the light of the knowledge of the eternal immutability of the Trinity and the changeable nature of creatures, but are recognized as fitting in with the mercy which the supreme God shows to men.

15. But since it has been said most truly, "There should be many heresies, that the faithful among you may become known," [I Cor. 11:19] let us also use this help of divine providence. For heretics spring from among those who, even though they are members of the Church, fall into error. When they have been expelled, they are very helpful, not by teaching the truth, for they do not know it, but by awakening material-minded Catholics to seek the truth, and wise Catholics to unfold it. There are innumerable faithful souls in Holy Church, but we do not recognize them as such, as long as we prefer to sleep comfortably in the darkness of our lack of understanding and not to look on the light of truth. Thus many are awakened from sleep by the heretics to look on the daylight of God and to rejoice in it.

THE MEANING OF A PEOPLE*

23. ... And therefore, where there is not this righteousness whereby the one supreme God rules the obedient city according to His grace, so that it sacrifices to none but Him, and whereby, in all the citizens of this obedient city, the soul consequently rules the body and reason the vices in the rightful order, so that, as the individual just man, so also the community and people (*populus*) of the just, live by faith, which works by love, that love whereby man loves God as He ought to be loved, and his neighbor as himself—there, I say, there is not an assemblage associated by a common acknowledgment of right, and by a community of interests. But if there is not this, there is not a people, if our definition be true, and therefore there is no republic; for where there is no people there can be no republic.

24. But if we discard this definition of a people, and assuming another say that a people is an assemblage of reasonable beings bound together by a common agreement as to the objects of their love, then, in order to discover the character of any people, we have only to observe what they love. Yet whatever it loves, if only it is an assemblage of reasonable beings and not of beasts, and is bound together by an agreement as to the objects of love, it is reasonably called a people; and it will be a superior people in proportion as it is bound together by higher interests, inferior in proportion as it is bound together by lower. According to this definition of ours, the Roman people is a people, and its weal is without doubt a commonwealth or republic. But what its tastes were in its early and subsequent days, and how it declined into sanguinary seditions and then to social and civil wars, and so burst asunder or rotted off the bond of concord in which the health of a people consists, history shows, and in the preceding books I have related at

* *City of God*, XIX, 23-24: trans. Dods.

large. And yet I would not on this account say either that it was not a people, or that its administration was not a republic, so long as there remains an assemblage of reasonable beings bound together by a common agreement as to the objects of love. But what I say of this people and of this republic I must be understood to think and say of the Athenians or any Greek state, of the Egyptians, of the early Assyrian Babylon, and of every other nation, great or small, which had a public government. For, in general, the city of the ungodly, which did not obey the command of God that it should offer no sacrifice save to Him alone, and which, therefore, could not give to the soul its proper command over the body, nor to the reason its just authority over the vices, is void of true justice.

PEACE: THE TRANQUILLITY OF ORDER*

11. And thus we may say of peace, as we have said of eternal life, that it is the end of our good; and the rather because the Psalmist says of the city of God, the subject of this laborious work, "Praise the Lord, O Jerusalem, praise thy God, O Zion; for He hath strengthened the bars of thy gates, He hath blessed thy children within thee, who hath made thy borders peace." [Ps. 147:12-14] For when the bars of her gates shall be strengthened, none shall go in or come out from her; consequently we ought to understand the peace of her borders as that final peace we are wishing to declare. For even the mystical name of the city itself, that is, *Jerusalem*, means, as I have already said, "Vision of Peace." But as the word peace is employed in connection with things in this world in which certainly life eternal has no place, we have preferred to call the end or supreme good of this city life eternal rather than peace. Of this end the apostle says, "But now, being freed from sin, and become servants to God, ye have your fruit unto holiness, and the end life eternal." [Rom. 6:22] But on the other hand, as those who are not familiar with Scripture may suppose that the life of the wicked is eternal life, either because of the immortality of the soul, which some of the philosophers even have recognized, or because of the endless punishment of the wicked, which forms a part of our faith, and which seems impossible unless the wicked live for ever, it

* *City of God*, XIX, 11-13; trans. Dods.

may therefore be advisable, in order that every one may readily understand what we mean, to say that the end or supreme good of this city is either peace in eternal life, or eternal life in peace. For peace is a good so great, that even in this earthly and mortal life there is no word we hear with such pleasure, nothing we desire with such zest or find to be more thoroughly gratifying. So that if we dwell for a little longer on this subject, we shall not in my opinion be wearisome to our readers, who will attend both for the sake of understanding what is the end of this city of which we speak, and for the sake of the sweetness of peace which is dear to all.

12. Whoever gives even moderate attention to human affairs and to our common nature, will recognize that if there is no man who does not wish to be joyful, neither is there any one who does not wish to have peace. For even they who make war desire nothing but victory—desire, that is to say, to attain to peace with glory. For what else is victory than the conquest of those who resist us? and when this is done there is peace. It is therefore with the desire for peace that wars are waged, even by those who take pleasure in exercising their warlike nature in command and battle. And hence it is obvious that peace is the end sought for by war. For every man seeks peace by waging war, but no man seeks war by making peace. For even they who intentionally interrupt the peace in which they are living have no hatred of peace, but only wish it changed into a peace that suits them better. They do not, therefore, wish to have no peace, but only one more to their mind. And in the case of sedition, when men have separated themselves from the community, they yet do not effect what they wish, unless they maintain some kind of peace with their fellow-conspirators. And therefore even robbers take care to maintain peace with their comrades, that they may with greater effect and greater safety invade the peace of other men. And if an individual happen to be of such unrivaled strength, and to be so jealous of partnership that he trusts himself with no comrades but makes his own plots and commits depredations and murders on his own account, yet he maintains some shadow of peace with such persons as he is unable to kill and from whom he wishes to conceal his deeds. In his own home too he makes it his aim to be at peace with his wife and children and any other members of his household; for unquestionably their prompt obedience to his every look is a source of pleasure to him. And if this be not rendered, he is angry, he chides and punishes; and even by this storm he secures the calm peace of his own home as occasion demands. For he sees that peace cannot be maintained unless all the members of the same domestic circle be subject to one head, such as he himself is in his own house. And therefore if a city or nation offered to submit itself to him, to serve him in the same style as he had made his household serve him, he would no longer lurk in a brigand's hiding places, but lift his head in open day as a king, though the same coveteousness and wickedness should remain in him. And thus all men desire to have peace with their own circle whom they wish to govern as suits themselves. For even those whom they make war against they wish to make their own, and impose on them the laws of their own peace.

But let us suppose a man such as poetry and mythology speak of—a man so insociable and savage as to be called rather a semiman than a man. Although, then, his kingdom was the solitude of a dreary cave, and he himself was so singularly bad-hearted that he was named *Kakos,* which is the Greek word for *bad;* though he had no wife to soothe him with endearing talk, no children to play with, no sons to do his bidding, no friend to enliven him with intercourse, not even his father Vulcan (though in one respect he was happier than his father, not having begotten a monster like himself); although he gave to no man, but took as he wished whatever he could, from whomsoever he could, when he could; yet in that solitary den, the floor of which, as Virgil [*Aeneid,* 8.195] says, was always reeking with recent slaughter, there was nothing else than peace sought, a peace in which no one should molest him, or disquiet him with any assault or alarm. With his own body he desired to be at peace, and he was satisfied only in proportion as he had this peace. For he ruled his members, and they obeyed him; and for the sake of pacifying his mortal nature, which rebelled when it needed anything, and of allaying the sedition of hunger which threatened to banish the soul from the body, he made forays, slew, and devoured, but used the ferocity and savageness he displayed in these actions only for the preservation of his own life's peace. So that, had he been willing to make with other men the same peace which he made with himself in his own cave, he would neither have been called bad, nor a monster, nor a semiman. Or if the appearance of his body and his vomiting smoky fires frightened men from having any dealings with him, perhaps his fierce ways arose not from a desire to do mischief, but from the necessity of finding a living. But he may have had no existence, or, at least, he was not such as the poets fancifully describe him, for they had to exalt Hercules, and did so at the expense of Cacus. It is better, then, to believe that such a man or semiman never existed, and that this, in common with many other fancies of the poets, is mere fiction. For the most savage animals (and he is said to have been almost a wild beast) encompass their own species with a ring of protecting peace. They cohabit, beget, produce, suckle, and bring up their young, though very many of them are not gregarious, but solitary —not like sheep, deer, pigeons, starlings, bees, but such as lions, foxes, eagles, bats. For what tigress does not gently purr over her cubs, and lay aside her ferocity to fondle them? What kite, solitary as he is when circling over his prey, does not seek a mate, build a nest, hatch the eggs, bring up the young birds, and maintain with the mother of his family as peaceful a domestic alliance as he can? How much more powerfully do the laws of man's nature move him to hold fellowship and maintain peace with all men so far as in him lies, since even wicked men wage war to maintain the peace of their own circle, and wish that, if possible, all men belonged to them, that all men and things might serve but one head, and might, either through love or fear, yield themselves to peace with him! It is thus that pride in its perversity apes God. It abhors equality with other men under Him, but, instead of His rule, it seeks to impose a rule of its own upon its equals. It abhors, that is to say, the just peace of God, and loves its own unjust peace, but it cannot help loving peace of one kind or other. For there is no vice so clean contrary to nature that it obliterates even the faintest traces of nature.

He, then, who prefers what is right to what is wrong, and what is well-ordered to what is perverted, sees that the peace of unjust men is not worthy to be called peace in comparison with the peace of the just. And yet even what is perverted must of necessity be in harmony with, and in dependence on, and in some part of the order of things, for otherwise it would have no existence at all. Suppose a man hangs with his head downwards, this is certainly a perverted attitude of body and arrangement of its members; for that which nature requires to be above is beneath, and *vice versâ*. This perversity disturbs the peace of the body, and is therefore painful. Nevertheless the spirit is at peace with its body and labors for its preservation, and hence the suffering; but if it is banished from the body by its pains, then, so long as the bodily framework holds together, there is in the remains a kind of peace among the members and hence the body remains suspended. And inasmuch as the earthly body tends towards the earth and rests on the bond by which it is suspended, it tends thus to its natural peace, and the voice of its own weight demands a place for it to rest; and though now lifeless and without feeling, it does not fall from the peace that is natural to its place in creation, whether it already has it or is tending towards it. For if you apply embalming preparations to prevent the bodily frame from mouldering and dissolving, a kind of peace still unites part to part and keeps the whole body in a suitable place on the earth—in other words, in a place that is at peace with the body. If, on the other hand, the body receive no such care but be left to the natural course, it is disturbed by exhalations that do not harmonize with one another and that offend our senses; for it is this which is perceived in putrefaction until it is assimilated to the elements of the world, and particle by particle enters into peace with them. Yet throughout this process the laws of the most high Creator and Governor are strictly observed, for it is by Him the peace of the universe is administered. For although minute animals are produced from the carcass of a larger animal, all these little atoms, by the law of the same Creator, serve the animals they belong to in peace. And although the flesh of dead animals be eaten by others, no matter where it be carried nor what it be brought into contact with nor what it be converted and changed into, it still is ruled by the same laws which pervade all things for the conservation of every mortal race and which bring things that fit one another into harmony.

13. The peace of the body then consists in the duly proportioned arrangement of its parts. The peace of the irrational soul is the harmonious repose of the appetites, and that of the rational soul the harmony of knowledge and action. The peace of body and soul is the well-ordered and harmonious life and health of the living creature. Peace between man and God is the well-ordered obedience of faith to eternal law. Peace between man and man is well-ordered concord. Domestic peace is the well-ordered concord between those of the family who rule and those who obey. Civil peace is a similar concord among the citizens. The peace of the celestial city is the perfectly ordered and harmonious enjoyment of God, and of one another in God. The peace of all things is the tranquillity of order. Order is the distribution which allots things equal and unequal, each to its own place. And hence, though the miserable, in so far as they are such, do certainly not enjoy peace, but are severed from that tranquillity of order in which there is no disturbance, nevertheless, inasmuch as they are deservedly and justly miserable, they are by their very misery connected with order. They are not, indeed, conjoined with the blessed, but they are disjoined from them by the law of order. And though they are disquieted, their circumstances are notwithstanding adjusted to them, and consequently they have some tranquillity of order, and therefore some peace. But they are wretched because, although not wholly miserable, they are not in that place where any mixture of misery is impossible. They would, however, be more wretched if they had not had that peace which arises from being in harmony with the natural order of things. When they suffer, their peace is in so far disturbed; but their peace continues in so far as they do not suffer, and in so far as their nature continues to exist. As, then, there may be life without pain, while there cannot be pain without some kind of life, so there may be peace without war, but there cannot be war without some kind of peace, because war supposes the existence of some natures to wage it, and these natures cannot exist without peace of one kind or other.

And therefore there is a nature in which evil does not or even cannot exist; but there cannot be a nature in which there is no good. Hence not even the nature of the devil himself is evil, in so far as it is nature, but it was made evil by being perverted. Thus he did not abide in the truth, but could not escape the judgment of the Truth; he did not abide in the tranquillity of order, but did not therefore escape the power of the Ordainer. The good imparted by God to his nature did not screen him from the justice of God by which order was preserved in his punishment; neither did God punish the good which He had created, but the evil which the devil had committed. God did not take back all He had imparted to his nature, but something He took and something He left, that there might remain enough to be sensible of the loss of what was taken. And this very sensibility to pain is evidence of the good which has been taken away and the good which has been left. For, were nothing good left, there could be no pain on account of the good which had been lost. For he who sins is still worse if he rejoices in his loss of righteousness. But he who is in pain, if he derives no benefit from it, mourns at least the loss of health. And as righteousness and health are both good things, and as the loss of any good thing is matter of grief, not of joy—if, at least, there is no compensation, as spiritual righteousness may compensate for the loss of bodily health—certainly it is more suitable for a wicked man to grieve in punishment than to rejoice in his fault. As, then, the joy of a sinner who has abandoned what is good is evidence of a bad will, so his grief for the good he has lost when he is punished is evidence of a good nature. For he who laments the peace his nature has lost is stirred to do so by some relics of peace which make his nature friendly to itself. And it is very just that in the final punishment the wicked and godless should in anguish bewail the loss of the natural advantages they enjoyed, and should perceive that they were most justly taken from them by that God whose benign liberality they had despised. God, then, the most wise Creator and most just Ordainer of all natures, who placed the human race upon earth as its greatest ornament, imparted to men some good things adapted to this life, to wit, temporal peace, such as we can enjoy in this life from health and safety and human fellowship, and all things needful for the preservation and recovery of this peace, such as the objects which are accommodated to our outward senses, light, night, the air, and waters suitable for us, and everything the body requires to sustain, shelter, heal, or beautify it; and all under this most equitable condition, that every man who made a good use of these advantages suited to the peace of this mortal condition, should receive ampler and better blessings, namely, the peace of immortality, accompanied by glory and honor in an endless life made fit for the enjoyment of God and of one another in God, but that he who used the present blessings badly should both lose them and should not receive the others.

TWO KINGDOMS AFTER THE RESURRECTION*

111.   After the resurrection, however, when the final, universal judgment has been completed, there shall be two kingdoms, each with its own distinct boundaries: the one Christ's, the other the devil's; the one consisting of the good, the other of the bad—both, however, consisting of angels and men. The former shall have no will, the latter no power, to sin, and neither shall have any power to choose

* *Enchiridion,* 111; trans. Dods.

death; but the former shall live truly and happily in eternal life, the latter shall drag out a miserable existence in eternal death without the power of dying; for the life and the death shall both be without end. But among the former there shall be degrees of happiness, one being more preeminently happy than another, and among the latter there shall be degrees of misery, one being more endurably miserable than another.

X. PHILOSOPHY OF HISTORY

Augustine was a pioneer in the study of the meaning of history. Before his time, historians were chiefly storytellers, little concerned with anything more than a surface record of human events. His thinking in this area may be called either a philosophy or a theology of history; the name is not important but his accomplishment is.

Implicit in the Augustinian view of history are the essential beliefs of Christianity: there is but one God; all men are creatures with a single ancestor in Adam; all things and events come under the care of divine Providence; mankind has fallen from a more privileged original condition and is now subject to suffering and other evils; man has been redeemed through the Incarnation of Christ; all men should try to attain final happiness with God in a future life. Seen from the point of view of this Christian setting, the events of temporal history become actions in the drama of redemption and eternal salvation.

If there was a prevailing theory of history before Augustine, it could be summed up in one word: fatalism. In ancient literature man was regarded as a puppet bound to the wheel of fate. Time was thought to revolve in giant cycles. Men were doomed to a perpetual recurrence of the same trials and petty joys. No linear progress was possible: man lived on a huge merry-go-round from which escape was utterly impossible. As Toynbee has said of this cyclicism: "We can hardly escape the conclusion that we are the perpetual victims of an everlasting cosmic practical joke, which condemns us to endure our sufferings and to overcome our difficulties and to purify ourselves of our sins—only to know in advance that the automatic and inevitable lapse of a certain meaningless measure of time cannot fail to stultify all our human exertions." (Cited from *A Study of History*, IV 30, in Shinn, p. 141.)

Augustine broke this wheel of fate by appealing to one

great event that cannot be repeated: "Christ died but once for our sins; now that He is risen from the dead, He will die no more." (*City of God*, XII, 13, 2.) This Christian teaching on the uniqueness of the redemption freed men's minds and wills from Greek determinism and fatalism. It also gave mankind a positive goal beyond time and temporal events. It expanded human horizons beyond limitations of race, cultural differences, and diversities of political institutions.

Human events become significant when viewed in the light of divine Providence. God is the focal point of explanation here, as elsewhere in Augustine's thought. Even within Augustinianism there are at least two different interpretations of the climax of history. Some scholars (*see* Paul Henry) think that the high point is the Incarnation; all later events are, then, anticlimactic. The drama has reached its peak; now we have but to finish the last act. Other writers shift the emphasis to the end of time; they see human history as a gradual progress toward a not yet attained but ultimate condition of mankind. This view is eschatological. It has become popular through the writings of Teilhard de Chardin. (*See* Tresmontant, C., *Père Teilhard de Chardin, His Thought* [Baltimore: Helicon Press, 1959].) Both interpretations find some support in Augustine.

The selections in this last chapter could all have been taken from the *City of God*, for it contains most of the elements of this remarkable approach to history. Instead, the texts below represent a variety of writings in which time and eternity are treated. The long quotation from the *Confessions*, on the nature of time, is one of the most famous passages in all patristic literature.

BELIEF AND HISTORICAL EVENTS*

48. There are three kinds of objects of belief. One kind consists of those that are always believed and never understood: such is history in every case, running through the course of temporal and human events. Second, there are those objects which, as soon as they are believed, are understood: such are all human uses of reason, in the field of numbers or in any of the academic studies. Third are those objects that are first believed and later on understood: such are those items that cannot be understood about divine matters except by the clean of heart, a condition

* *Eighty-three Different Questions*, q. 48; trans. V.J.B.

achieved by obeying the commandments which have to do with proper living.

THE UNIVERSALITY OF PROVIDENCE*

11. Therefore God supreme and true, with His Word and Holy Spirit (which three are one), one God omnipotent, creator and maker of every soul and of every body; by whose gift all are happy who are happy through verity and not through vanity; who made man a rational animal consisting of soul and body; who, when he sinned, neither permitted him to go unpunished, nor left him without mercy; who has given to the good and to the evil, being in common with stones, vegetable life in common with trees, sensuous life in common with brutes, intellectual life in common with angels alone; from whom is every mode, every species, every order; from whom are measure, number, weight; from whom is everything which has an existence in nature, of whatever kind it be, and of whatever value; from whom are the seeds of forms and the forms of seeds, and the motion of seeds and of forms; who gave also to flesh its origin, beauty, health, reproductive fecundity, disposition of members, and the salutary concord of its parts; who also to the irrational soul has given memory, sense, appetite, but to the rational soul, in addition to these, has given intelligence and will; who has not left, not to speak of heaven and earth, angels and men, but not even the entrails of the smallest and most contemptible animal, or the feather of a bird or the little flower of a plant or the leaf of a tree without a harmony and as it were a mutual peace among all its parts —that God can never be believed to have left the kingdoms of men, their dominations and servitudes, outside of the laws of His providence.

MEANING IN HISTORY †

50.98. If as yet we cannot bring ourselves to cling to the things of eternity, at least let us reprove our phantasms and remove from the looking glass of our

* *City of God,* V, 11; trans. Dods.
† *The True Religion,* 50.98-99; trans. W. G. Renn, S.J., *De vera religione (chapters* 39-55) (St. Louis University Master's Thesis, 1947), pp. 79-83. Used with permission.

minds such worthless and deceptive diversions. Let us use the
steps which Divine Providence has deigned to fashion for us.
For if we should take too great delight in empty imaginings,
we would then be lost in our thoughts and would turn
our whole life into empty dreams. In the case of a rational
creature keeping its laws revealed by words and letters, fire,
smoke, by a cloud, and by a column, all visible words, as it
were, the ineffable mercy of God did not disdain, so to say,
to sport with our childish mentality by speaking in parables
and similes and to cure with clay of this kind the interior
eyes of our souls.

99. Let us distinguish, therefore, what credence we
should put in history, what in understanding, and
what in memory, not knowing what the truth is but
believing. Let us find where that truth is which neither comes
nor goes but always remains the same. What is the manner
of interpreting allegory, which, spoken in wisdom, is believed
in the Holy Spirit? Is it sufficient to follow it from the
visible things of old to more recent manifestations; or should
it be followed to the affections and nature of the soul; or to
immutable eternity? Or do some allegories signify deeds
which were done and seen; others, the workings of minds;
others, the eternal law? Can some be found in which
traces of all the above may be discovered? Further, what is
that firm faith, be it based on history and material things,
or on things spiritual and eternal, toward which every interpretation carrying authority must be directed? What
help does faith in temporal things lend to the understanding
and grasping of eternal things, the end of all good actions?
What is the difference between historical allegory, allegory of
the thing done, allegory of word, and allegory of the sacrament? Further, how should the wording itself of Divine Scripture be rendered according to the idiom of each language?
For each tongue has its own peculiar way of expression,
which seems absurd when translated into another language.
Of what profit is such lowliness of speech in which the
Sacred Books tell not only of the wrath of God, of sorrow,
of arousing from sleep, of memory, of forgetfulness, and of
not a few other incidents which can befall all men, but also
they speak of penance, of zeal, of the names of surfeits, and
of other things of a like nature? Again, are the eyes of God,
His hands and feet, and other like members which are named
in Scripture, to be considered as standing for powers both
intellectual and spiritual, as does a helmet, shield, sword, a

belt, and other such things? Lastly, the most pressing question concerns what profit the human race has gained by having Divine Providence speak to us through a rational, begetting, corporeal creature serving it. The solution of this question given, all childish petulance is excluded from the mind and sacred religion makes its entrance.

SIX AGES IN BIBLICAL HISTORY*

As therefore God made man in His own image on the sixth day: thus we find that our Lord Jesus Christ came into the sixth age, that man might be formed anew after the image of God. For the first period, as the first day, was from Adam until Noah; the second, as the second day, from Noah unto Abraham; the third, as the third day, from Abraham unto David; the fourth, as the fourth day, from David unto the removal to Babylon; the fifth period, as the fifth day, from the removal to Babylon unto the preaching of John. The sixth day beginneth from the preaching of John, and lasteth unto the end; and after the end of the sixth day, we reach our rest. The sixth day, therefore, is even now passing.

THE SYMBOLIC MEANING OF JEWISH HISTORY†

1.   . . . It came to pass, when the seventy years had been completed the temple was restored which had been thrown down: and there returned from captivity a great part of that people. But whereas the apostle saith, "These things in figure happened unto them, but they have been written for our sakes, upon whom the end of the world hath come"; we also ought to know first our captivity, then our deliverance: we ought to know the Babylon wherein we are captives, and the Jerusalem for a return to which we are sighing. For these two cities, according to the letter, in reality are two cities. And the former Jerusalem indeed by the Jews is not now inhabited. For after the crucifixion of the Lord vengeance was taken upon them with a great scourge,

* *On Psalm 92,* 1; trans. Nicene.
† *On Psalm 64,* 1; trans. Nicene.

and being rooted up from that place where, with impious licentiousness being infuriated, they had madly raged against their Physician, they have been dispersed throughout all nations, and that land hath been given to Christians; and there is fulfilled what the Lord had said to them, "Therefore the kingdom shall be taken away from you, and it shall be given to a nation doing justice." But when they saw great multitudes then following the Lord, preaching the kingdom of Heaven, and doing wonderful things, the rulers of that city said, "If we shall have let Him go, all men will go after Him, and there shall come the Romans, and shall take from us both place and nation." That they might not lose their place, they killed the Lord; and they lost it, even because they killed. Therefore that city, being one earthly, did bear the figure of a certain city everlasting in the Heavens; but when that which was signified began more evidently to be preached, the shadow whereby it was being signified was thrown down; for this reason in that place now the temple is no more, which had been constructed for the image of the future Body of the Lord. We have the light, the shadow hath passed away; nevertheless, still in a kind of captivity we are: "So long as we are," he saith, "in the body, we are sojourning afar from the Lord."

CHRIST IN HISTORY*

Who would not be moved to faith by so remarkable an order of events from the beginning and by this concatenation of the ages, which makes the past credible by means of the present and in which the earlier things are confirmed by the later, the recent by the ancient? A man was chosen from the nation of the Chaldaeans, one endowed with great piety and faith, that to him might be given divine promises to be fulfilled after long centuries in the last days, and it is foretold to him that in his seed all nations shall be blessed [Gen. 12:2]. This man, worshipping the one true God, the Creator of the universe, begets in his old age a son of a wife who, through sterility and old age, had wholly given up hope of bringing forth a child. From him there proceeded a very numerous people which multiplied in Egypt whither it had been led from out of the East by divine dis-

4.15.

---

* *Letter to Marcellinus*, 137, 4.15-16; trans. Nicene.

position, continuing to increase according to the promises made and fulfilled.

It was as a powerful nation that it was led out of Egypt with terrible signs and wonders, and the wicked peoples being driven out before them, it was brought to the land of promise and established there and exalted to be a kingdom. Thereafter frequently offending the true God Who had bestowed upon them so many benefits, by sin which had become rife among them and by sacrilegious enterprises, they were scourged by various disasters and consoled by restored prosperity, and their history is brought down to the incarnation and manifestation of Christ. And all the promise of this nation, its prophecies, its priesthood, its sacrifices, its temple, all its sacraments announced that this Christ, the Word of God, the Son of God, God Himself, was to come in the flesh, was to die and to rise again and to ascend into heaven, that by the power of His name He would have the multitudes in every nation consecrate to Him, and that those who believed in Him would have in Him remission of their sins and eternal salvation.

16. And Christ comes. All that the prophets had foretold is fulfilled in His birth, life, words, actions, sufferings, death, resurrection, and ascension. He sends the Holy Spirit and fills the faithful gathered together in one house [Acts 2:2] and waiting with prayers and ardent desire for this promised gift. Filled with the Holy Spirit, they immediately speak with the tongues of all nations, they boldly refute errors, they preach the truths of salvation, they exhort men to penance for their past sinful lives, they promise indulgence by the divine grace. Apt signs and miracles follow their preaching of piety and of the true religion. Cruel unbelief is stirred up against them; they suffer the trials foretold to them: they look in trust for the blessings promised them; they teach what was appointed them to teach. Few in number, they are scattered as seed throughout the world; they convert the peoples with marvelous ease; in the midst of enemies they grow in number; by persecution they increase in strength; faced with hardships and distress they spread their influence to the ends of the earth. . . .

And throughout all this the unbelief of the heathen nations continues to rage against the Church of Christ, but she gains the victory by patient endurance and by the maintenance of unshaken faith in the face of the cruelty of His adversaries. The sacrifice of Him Who is revealed Truth, which long had been veiled under mystic promises, having taken place, those sacrifices by which it was prefigured are finally abolished by the destruction of the temple itself. The Jewish nation, condemned for unbelief, is rooted out of its own land and dispersed through every region of the world that it might carry everywhere the Sacred Scriptures, and that the testimony of the prophecies by which Christ and the Church were foretold might be furnished by our adversaries, so that it could not be thought that these predictions had been forged by us to suit the time, in which prophecies too the unbelief of these very Jews is foretold. The temples, idols, and impious rites of the heathen are gradually and in succession overthrown, as had been foretold by the prophets. Heresies bud forth against the name of Christ though under the veil of His name, as had also been foretold, by which the doctrine of our holy religion is disturbed. All these things are now seen to be fulfilled in accordance with the predictions which we read; and these fulfillments are now so many and so great that they lead us to await with confidence fulfillment of the rest. What mind, then, thirsting for eternity, and troubled by the shortness of this present life, can resist the crowning light of this divine corroboration of our faith?

THE TWO CITIES IN HISTORY*

21.37.   Now as Jerusalem signifies the city and fellowship of the saints, so Babylon signifies the city and fellowship of the wicked, since it is said to be interpreted "confusion." We have already spoken a little before of these two cities running on indistinguishably from the beginning of the human race to the end of the world, through the changing ages and destined to be separated at the last judgment. So the captive city of Jerusalem, and the people led forth into Babylon, are bidden to go into bondage by the Lord, through Jeremias, a prophet of that time. And there arose kings of Babylon under whom they were in bondage, who, having been stirred by certain wonders occasioned by their presence, came to know and worship and ordered to be worshipped the one true God, the author of all creation. Moreover, they were bidden both to pray for those by whom they were held captive, and in the peace of these to hope for peace, for the begetting of children and the building of houses

* On Catechizing the Uninstructed, 21, 37; trans. ACW 2 (1946) 67-68.

and the planting of gardens and vineyards. But deliverance from that captivity after seventy years was promised them.

Now, all this signified in a figure that the Church of Christ, in all His saints, who are citizens of the heavenly Jerusalem, was to be in bondage under the kings of this world. For the teaching of the apostle also enjoins that every soul should be subject to higher powers [Rom. 13:1], and that to all men should be rendered all things: tribute to whom tribute is due, custom to whom custom; [Rom. 13:7] and so with other things which, saving the worship of our God, we render to the rulers of the human order, since the Lord Himself, that He might afford us an example of this sound teaching, did not disdain to pay poll tax on the humanity with which He was invested. Moreover, Christian servants and the good faithful are also bidden to serve their temporal masters with patience and fidelity, whom they are to judge if they find them doing wrong to the last; or with whom they are to reign as equals if they likewise turn to the true God. Still, all are directed to be subject to human and earthly powers, until, at the end of the foreordained time, which the seventy years signify, the Church is delivered from the confusion of this world, as was Jerusalem from the captivity of Babylon. And by occasion of this captivity even earthly kings, forsaking the idols for the sake of which they were wont to persecute the Christians, have come to know and worship the one true God and Christ the Lord, and it is on their behalf, even when they were persecuting the Church, that the Apostle Paul bids prayer be made. For these are his words: I desire therefore in the first place that supplications, prayers, intercessions, and thanksgivings be made for kings, for all men, and for all that are in high station; that we may lead a quiet and peaceable life in all piety and charity. [I Tim. 2:1-3] And so through these very kings peace was given to the Church, albeit temporal peace, temporal quietude for the spiritual building of houses and planting of gardens and vineyards.

WHAT IS TIME?*

17. So, at no time hadst Thou not made anything, for Thou hadst made time itself. And no periods of time are coeternal with Thee, for Thou dost abide, but they, if they abided, would not be periods of time.

* *Confessions,* XI, 14.17-30.40; trans. FOC 5 (1953), 343-365.

For, what is time? Who can explain it easily and briefly? Who can grasp this, even in cogitation, so as to offer a verbal explanation of it? Yet, what do we mention, in speaking, more familiarly and knowingly than time? And we certainly understand it when we talk about it; we even understand it when we hear another person speaking about it.

What, then, is time? If no one asks me, I know; but, if I want to explain it to a questioner, I do not know. Yet, I say with confidence that I know that, if nothing passed away, there would be no past time; if nothing were coming, there would be no future time; and if nothing were existing, there would be no present time.

Then, how do those two periods of time, the past and the future, exist, when the past is already not existing, and the future does not yet exist? And again, the present would not pass away into the past, if it were always present; indeed, it would not be time but eternity. So, if the present, in order to be time, must be such that it passes over into the past, then how can we say that it *is;* for the sole reason for its existence is the fact that it will stop being; that is to say, can we not truly say that time *is* only because it inclines not to be?

18.   Still, we speak of a long time and a short time, and we only say this of the past or future. For instance, we call a hundred years ago a long past time, and, likewise, a hundred years ahead a long future time. But we say, for example, that ten days ago is a short past time, and ten days hence is a short future. But how is something long or short which does not exist? For, the past does not now exist and the future does not yet exist. So, let us not say: it *is* long; rather, let us say of past time: it *was* long; and of the future: it *will be* long.

My Lord, my Light, will not Thy Truth here also make sport of man? For was that past time long in the sense that it was long when already past, or when it was still present? Of course, it could have been long only at the time when that existed which was capable of being long, but as past it was already not existing; hence, it could not be long, for it was wholly nonexistent.

So let us not say past time was long; for we will discover nothing which could have been long, since, from the fact that it is past, it does not exist. Rather let us say: "That present time was long," for, when it was present, it was long. For it had not yet passed away into nonexistence, and so there was something which could be long. But once it passed away, it also ceased immediately to be long, for it ceased to be.

19. Let us see then, O human soul, whether present time can be long; for the ability to perceive periods of time, and to measure them, has been given thee. What wilt thou answer me?

Is a hundred present years a long time? First of all, see whether there can be a hundred present years. If the first of these years is going on, it is present, but ninety-nine are still in the future and so they do not yet exist. But, if the second year is going on, one is already past, another is present, and the rest are in the future. And this is so, no matter which of the intervening years of this century we take to be present: the preceding years will be past, the succeeding ones future. For that reason, there cannot be a hundred present years.

Now, see whether even the one which is going on may itself be present. If, now, the first month in it is going on, the rest are future; if the second is, then the first is now past and the rest do not yet exist. Therefore, the year which is now going on is not present as a whole and, if it is not present as a whole, then the year is not present. For a year is twelve months, and whatever one of these months is now going on, that one is present; the rest are either past or future. Yet neither is the month which is now going on present, but one day: if the first, the rest are future; if the last, the rest are past; if any intermediate one, it is between the past and future ones.

20. See how the present time, which we found the only one worthy of being called long, has been contracted to scarcely the extent of one day. But let us look at this carefully, for not even one day is present as a whole. It is made up of all twenty-four hours of night and day. The first of these regards the rest as future, the last one regards them as past; and the intermediate ones are to those preceding, as to the past; to those coming after, as to the future. And this one hour itself goes on by means of fleeting little parts: whatever part of it has flown by is the past; whatever remains to it is the future. If one can conceive any part of time which could not be divided into even the most minute moments, then that alone is what may be called the present, and this flies over from the future into the past so quickly that it does not extend over the slightest instant. For if it has any extension, it is divided into past and future. But the present has no length.

Where then is the time which we may call long? Is it the future? In fact, we do not say: it is long, for it does not yet exist so as to be long; rather, we say: it will be long. When will it be so? For if at a certain instant when it will be still the future, then it will not be long, because that which is capable of being long does not yet exist. But if it will be long at the instant when it will just start to exist, as something from the nonexistent future, and will have become the present in order that it be something that could be long—then, in our remarks above, present time cries out that it cannot be long!

21.   Nevertheless, O Lord, we do perceive intervals of time; we compare them among themselves and we say that some are longer and others shorter. We even measure how much longer or shorter one period of time is than another; we can answer that this period is double or triple, while that is single, that is, just as long as another. But we measure periods of time as they are passing by; we do this measuring at the time of sense perception. So who can measure the past periods which are already out of existence, or the future ones which do not yet exist—unless, perhaps, someone is going to dare to say that the nonexistent can be measured? Therefore, while time is passing into the past it can be perceived and measured; but when it has passed away it cannot, for it does not exist.

22.   I am looking for information, O Father, not making an affirmation: O my God, counsel me and rule me. Who is there who will tell me that there are not three periods of time (just as we learned when children and as we have taught the children): past, present and future, but that there is only the present because the other two do not exist? Or do they also exist but, when the present comes out of the future, does it proceed from something secret and, when the past comes about from the present, does it recede into something hidden? Indeed, where have the people who have foretold the future seen those things, if they are not yet in existence? For what does not exist cannot be seen. And those who tell about past events would certainly not tell the truth, if they did not see these things with their mind. And if there were not in existence, they could not be seen at all. Therefore, both future things and past things do exist.

23.   Permit me, O Lord, to seek further information; "O my Hope," let not my effort be confounded. If future and past things exist, I would like to know

where they are. And if that is impossible for me, at least I do know that, wherever they are, they are not there as future or past things, but as present. For if they are there also as future things, they are not yet there, and if they are there as past things, they are already not there. So, wherever they are, whatever they are, they do not exist unless as present things. Yet when past things are recounted as true, they are brought forth from memory, not as the actual things which went on in the past but as words formed from images of these things; and these things have left their traces as it were in the mind while passing through sense perception. In fact my boyhood, which is not now in existence, is in past time, which does not now exist; but when I recall and tell about it, I see its image in present time, for it is still in my memory.

Whether the same explanation also may be given for the prediction of things, so that presently existing images of things which do not yet exist are perceived beforehand, I confess, O my God, that I do not know. This I know clearly: we often think ahead about our future actions and this premeditation is present, while the action which we think over beforehand is not yet in existence, for it is in the future. When we shall have reached it and have begun to do what we were thinking of before, then that action will be in existence, since it will then be not in the future but present.

24. So in whatever way this mysterious preperception of future things goes on, it is not possible for a thing to be seen unless it is something existing. What exists now is not a future thing but present. Therefore, when future things are said to be seen, the things themselves which do not yet exist, that is, the future things, are not seen, but rather their causes or signs perhaps which now exist. And so they are not future things, but things now present to those who are seeing, from which they foretell future things as conceived by their mind. Again, these conceptions exist now, and those who predict such things see them as present within themselves.

Now, let the abundance of such cases suggest some example to me.

I see the dawn: I foretell that the sun will rise. What I see is present, what I foretell is future; not that the sun is future—it exists now—but rather its rising which is not yet occurring. Yet unless I form an image in my mind of this rising, as I do at this instant when I speak about it, I could not predict it. But the dawn which I see in the sky is not the rising of the sun, though it precedes it, nor is the act of forming the image in my mind that rising; these two present things are discerned so that that future thing may be foretold.

Therefore future things do not yet exist and, if they do not yet exist, they are not existing; if they are not existing, they cannot possibly be seen. But they can be predicted from present things which already exist and are seen.

25. And so what is the mode by which Thou, the Ruler of thy creation, dost teach souls about things which are to be in the future? For Thou hast taught Thy prophets. What then is this mode by which Thou teachest the things of the future—Thou to whom nothing is to come? Or is it rather that Thou teachest present things about future events? For that which does not exist cannot of course be taught. This mode is too far away from my mental gaze; it has become too great for me, I cannot reach it; but with Thy help I can, when Thou wilt grant it, O sweet Light of my hidden eyes.

26. What is now plain and clear is that neither future nor past things are in existence, and that it is not correct to say there are three periods of time: past, present and future. Perhaps it would be proper to say there are three periods of time: the present of things past, the present of things present, the present of things future. For these three are in the soul and I do not see them elsewhere: the present of things past is memory; the present of things present is immediate vision; the present of future things is expectation. If we are permitted to say this, I see three periods of time and I admit there are three.

Still it may be said three periods of time do exist—past, present and future—just as custom falsely put it; it may be so expressed. See, I do not care or make any opposition or criticism—provided the statement be understood: that there is no existing now either of what is to be in the future or that which is past. There are few things which we express properly; more frequent are those that we express improperly, though making out intentions understood.

27. So I said, a little while ago, that, as periods of time are passing by, we measure them, being thus able to say that this period of time is double that single one, or this is just as long as that, and whatever else we can express by measuring concerning the relationship of the parts of time.

For this reason, as I was saying, we do measure periods of time as they are passing by. If anyone say to me: "How do you know this?" I may reply: "I know, because we do measure them, and we cannot measure things which do not exist, yet past and future things do not exist." But how do we measure present time when it has no length? Therefore, it is measured as it is passing by, when it has passed away it is not measured, for what might be measured will not then exist.

But whence, by what way, and whither does it pass, when it is measured? Whence but from the future? By what means but through the present? Whither if not into the past? From that then which does not yet exist, through that which is without length, into that which is already out of existence.

But what do we measure, if not time in some length? For we cannot talk about single, double, triple, and equal periods—and whatever else we say about time in this way —except in terms of lengths of time. In what length then do we measure time as it is passing away? Is it in the future, from which it is passing? But we do not measure a thing of no length. Is it in the past, to which it is passing? But we do not measure what is already out of existence.

28. My mind burns with eagerness to gain knowledge of this complicated problem. Do not hide—O Lord my God, O good Father, I beseech Thee through Christ —do not hide these familiar yet mysterious things from my desire, so that it cannot enter deeply into them; rather may they be illumined by Thy enlightening mercy, O Lord. Whom shall I ask about these things? To whom shall I more fruitfully confess my lack of skill than to Thee, before whom my strongly burning interest in Thy Scriptures is not offensive? Grant what I love; for I do love it. And this love also Thou hast given. Grant it, O Father, who truly knoweth how to give good gifts to Thy children; grant it, for I have taken on the task of knowing it, and it is labor in my sight, until Thou dost reveal it. I beseech Thee through Christ, in the Name of Him who is most holy, let no one interrupt me. "I have believed, therefore do I speak." This is my hope, for this do I live, "that I may see the delight of the Lord." Behold, Thou hast made my days grow old and they pass away—how, I know not.

We speak of this time and that time, of these times and those times: "How long ago did he say this? How long is it since he did this?" and: "What a long time since I have seen it," and: "This syllable takes twice as long a time as that short one." We both say and hear these things, and we understand and make ourselves understood by others. They are very obvious and most familiar, but on the other hand they are deeply hidden and their discovery is a present problem.

29. I have heard from a certain learned man that the movements of the sun, moon, and stars are times, yet I did not agree. For why are not times rather the movements of all bodies? As a matter of fact, if the heavenly bodies stopped moving and a potter's wheel were moving, would there be no time by which we might measure these turnings and say that they go on in equal intervals; or if it were moved sometimes more slowly and sometimes more quickly, that some intervals are longer and some shorter? Or when we should say this, would we not be speaking in time, and would there be in our words some long syllables and others short, except that some sounded for a longer time and others for a shorter?

O God, vouchsafe unto men the ability to see in a small thing the common conceptions of things both small and great. There are stars and shining bodies in the heavens, "for signs and for seasons, and for days and years." There are, indeed. But while I should not say that the revolution of that little wooden wheel is a day, on the other hand that scholar of ours would not say then that time does not exist.

30. I desire to know the meaning and nature of time, by which we measure the movements of bodies and say, for example, that this movement is twice as long as that one. My question is: since a day is spoken of, not only as the period when the sun is above the earth, in the sense that day is distinguished from night, but also in terms of its complete circuit from the east back to the east—as when we say: "so many days went by" (for we speak of a certain number of days as including the nights, not as excluding the length of the nights)—and since a day is made up of the movement of the sun in a circuit from the east back to the east, my question is: whether this movement is itself the day, or is the duration in which it goes on, or both.

For if the first [the movement of the sun] were the day, then it would be a day, even if the sun completed its course in just an hour. If the second [the duration], then it would not be a day if the duration from the rising of the sun to its next rising were so brief as to take but one hour—rather, the sun would have to go around twenty-four times to make a day.

If both, then it could be called a day either if the sun went through its complete circuit in the space of an hour or if, the sun having stopped its movement, just enough time were to go by for the sun to have completed its customary circuit from morning to morning.

So I shall not ask what this thing is which is called a day, but what is time, by means of which we, measuring the course of the sun, might say that it took only half its customary time to go through it, if the amount of time it took were equivalent to the passage of twelve hours and, comparing both, we should say that the one was to the other as one to two—even though sometimes the sun might complete its circuit from east to east in the single period and sometimes in the double of this period.

Therefore let no one tell me that periods of time are equivalent to the movements of the heavenly bodies. For when the sun stood still at the wish of a certain person, in order that he might complete a victorious battle, the sun was standing still but time was going on. Indeed, the fight was waged and finished in its own space of time which was enough for it.

I see then that time is some sort of extension. But do I see it? Do I just seem to myself to see it? Thou wilt point it out, O Light, O Truth!

31. Dost Thou command me to assent when someone says that time is the movement of a body? Thou dost not. I hear that no body can be moved unless in time; Thou sayest it. But I do not hear that the very motion of a body is time; Thou dost not say it. For when a body is moved in time, I can measure it as long as it is moved, from the instant that it began to be moved until it ceases. And if I did not see the point at which it began, and it continued to move so that I cannot see when it stops, I cannot measure it, except perhaps from the point when I begin to see it until I stop. And if I see it for a long time, I can express the fact that it is a long time but not exactly how long; for when we say how much, we say it by means of a comparison—for instance: "This is just as much as that," or "This is twice that," or anything else in the same way. But if we could note the places in space whence and whither the body comes as it is moving, or its parts if it is turning, as though on a lathe, we could say how great the time is in which the movement of a body or its part from one place to another is accomplished.

So since the movement of a body is one thing and that whereby we measure its duration is another, who could not judge which of these should preferably be called time? Indeed, if a body moves sometimes at different speeds and sometimes stands still, we measure not only its movement but also its condition of rest by means of time. We say: "It stood still just as long as it moved," or: "It stood still twice or thrice as long as it moved," and whatever else our act of measuring grasped accurately or, as the common saying is, roughly estimated.

Therefore, time is not the motion of a body.

32. And I confess to Thee, O Lord, that I still do not know what time is; again, I confess to Thee, O Lord, that I know that I am saying these things in time, and that I have spoken at length now about time, and that this length cannot be long without the extent of time. How then do I know this when I do not know what time is? Perhaps I do not know how to say what I do know? Alas, I do not even know what I do not know! Behold, O my God, it is evident to Thee that I do not lie; I speak just as I feel in my heart. Thou wilt light up my lamp, O Lord my God, thou wilt enlighten my darkness.

33. Surely my soul is confessing truthfully to Thee that I do measure periods of time? Yes, O Lord my God, I do measure, but I do not know what I am measuring. I measure the movement of a body in time. But time itself, do I not measure it? Could I really measure the movement of a body, how long it is, and how long it takes to go from here to there, unless I also measure the time in which it is moved?

On what basis, then, do I measure time itself? Do we measure a longer time by means of a shorter time, as the length of a beam is measured by the length of a cubit? Thus we see that the length of a long syllable is measured by the length of a short syllable, and say that it is twice the other. In this way we measure the length of poems by the lengths of the verses, and the lengths of the verses by the lengths of the feet, and the lengths of the feet by the lengths of the syllables, and the lengths of the longs by the lengths of the shorts—not as written on tablets (for in that way we measure space, not time), but while the spoken words are going on. Thus we say: "This poem is long, for it is made up of so many verses; the verses are long, for they consist of so many feet; the feet are long, for they stretch over so many syllables; the syllable is long, for it is double a short one."

But a definite measure of time is not grasped in that way, since it is possible for a short verse to sound over a greater length of time if it be pronounced slowly, than a longer verse spoken hurriedly. The same is true of a poem, of a foot, of a syllable.

From this it appeared to me that time is nothing but extension, but I do not know of what. It is amazing if it is not of the mind itself. I beseech Thee, O my God, what do I measure when I either say, indefinitely: "This time is longer than that," or, definitely: "This is twice that"? I measure time I know. But I do not measure the future, because it does not exist yet; I do not measure the present, for it does not extend over any length; I do not measure the past, for it does not now exist. What then do I measure? Is it periods of time as they go by, but not in the past? So in fact have I said.

34. Keep on, O mind of mine, and firmly direct thy attention. "God is our Helper," "He made us, and not we ourselves." Mark where truth brightens to the dawn.

See, for instance, how a bodily voice begins to sound, and it sounds and still sounds, and then stops; now there is silence: that voice is past, and voice there is no more. It was in the future before it sounded, and could not be measured for it was not yet existing—and now it cannot be because it is already out of existence. The time, then, when it could be measured was when it was sounding, for then there existed something that could be measured. But even then, it did not stand still, it went on and passed by. Was it for this reason more capable of measurement? For while passing by, it extended itself into some space of time by which it could be measured, since the present possesses no extent.

And so, if it was capable of it then, consider another example of a second voice beginning to sound and still sounding in continuous duration without any interruption. Let us measure it while it is sounding for, when it will have ceased its sounding, it will then be past and will not be anything that can be measured. Let us measure it then and say how long it is. But it is still sounding and cannot be measured, except from its start when it began to sound, until its end when it ceases. For what we measure is the very interval from some starting point up to some ending. For this reason, the voice which has not yet ended cannot be measured, so that a statement may be made as to how long or short it is; nor can it be called equal to another, or single or double in relation to some unit, or anything else. But when it will have ended, then it will not exist. How then can it be measured? Yet, we do measure periods of time, and not those which do not yet exist, or those which are no longer in existence, or those which extend over no duration, or those which have no endings. So then we do not measure future ones or present or past or those which are going into the past, yet we do measure periods of time.

35.   "O God, who hast created all"—this verse is of eight syllables, alternately short and long. Thus the four short ones, first, third, fifth, seventh, are simple in relation to the four longs, the second, fourth, sixth, eighth. Each of these latter, in relation to each of the former, has twice as much time. This I proclaim and report, and it is so, in so far as it is perceived by evident perception. To the extent that sense perception is evident, I measure a long syllable by a short one and I perceive that it is just twice as much. But when one sounds after another, the first being short, the following one long, how can I hold on to the short one and how can I apply it to the long as I am making the measurement, so as to find out that the latter is just twice—since the long one does not begin to sound unless the short one stops sounding? And can I even measure the long one while it is present since, unless it has ended, I cannot measure it? But its ending is its passing out of existence.

What then is it that I measure? Where is the short one by which I do the measuring? Where is the long one which I measure? Both have sounded, flown away, passed by; they exist no longer. Yet I do measure and I answer with confidence, in so far as confidence can be placed in any exercise of sense perception, that this one is single, that double —in the extent of time, that is. Nor can I do this except because they have passed away and are ended. Therefore I do not measure these syllables which no longer exist, but something in my memory which remains as a fixed impression.

36.   In thee, O mind of mine, do I measure periods of time. Do not interrupt me by clamoring: "But it does exist," do not interrupt thyself with the noisy disturbances of thy previous mental habits. In thee, I say, do I measure periods of time. I measure the present mental disposition which things passing by produce in thee and which

remains after they have passed away, not the things which have passed away in order to produce it. This I measure when I measure periods of time. Therefore, either these [mental dispositions] are periods of time, or what I measure is not time.

But how is it when we measure periods of silence and say that this silence took as much time as that spoken sound did—do we not direct the attention of our cogitation to the measure of the voice, as if it were sounding, so that we can report something about the intervals of silence in the whole space of time? For even when the voice and lips of the speaker have stopped, we continue to go over, in the act of cogitation, poems, verses, any form of speech, and any means whatever of measuring out motions, and this is the way we report on temporal intervals, how one stands in relation to another, for it is as if we spoke and they were actually sounding. If a person wanted to utter a rather long spoken tone, and decided by thinking it over in advance how long it would be, he has obviously gone through this space of time in silence and then, committing it to his memory, he begins to utter the note which sounds until it reaches the terminus that has been previously determined. Nay, rather, it has sounded and it will sound. For that part of it which is already over certainly has sounded, but the part which remains will sound; and that is how it is completed, while present mental awareness [*intentio*] pushes the future over into the past by decreasing the future and increasing the past, until through the eating up of the future it all becomes past.

37. But how is the future which does not yet exist decreased or eaten up, or how does the past which is no longer existing increase, unless because of the fact that three functions occur in the mind which is doing this? It looks ahead, it attends, and it remembers—in such a way that what it looks forward to passes through what it is attending to into what it is remembering. Who denies that future things are not yet existing? Yet there is now in the mind an expectation of future things. Who denies that past things are already nonexistent? Yet there is still in mind the memory of things past. Who denies that present time lacks extent, for it passes away in an instant, like a point? Yet attention lasts on and, through it, what will be continues to go on into that which is no longer here. So the nonexistent future is not a long time, but a long future period is a long expectation of the future; nor is past time long for it is nonexistent, but a long past is a long memory of that which is past.

I am about to sing a song that I know. Before I be-
38. gin, my expectation is directed to the whole thing
but, when I have begun, in regard to that part
which I have plucked off and committed to the past, my
memory also directs its attention to it, and the life of this
action of mine is spread out both in memory, by virtue of
what I have sung, and in expectation, by virtue of what I
am yet to sing. Yet my attention remains in the present for,
through it, that which is to come is passed over so that it
becomes past. And the more this is done, on and on, the
more is memory lengthened out by a shortening of the
function of expectation—until the whole of expectation is
used up, when the completely finished act has passed over
into memory. What goes on for the whole song occurs also
for each of its parts and for each of its individual syllables;
the same again for a longer action, of which this song is
perhaps but a part; the same for the whole life of a man,
the parts of which are all the actions of men; and the
same for the whole era of the "sons of men," the parts of
which are all the lives of men.

But since "Thy mercy is better than lives," behold
39. my life is but a distraction, and Thy right hand has
held me up, in my Lord the Son of man, the Mediator between Thee as One and us as many, in many ways and
by many means, so that through Him I may lay hold of that
for which He has laid hold of me, and that I may be gathered
in from the days of old and follow the One. Forgetting what
is behind, not straining outward to things which will come
and pass away but straining forward to what is before, not according to distraction but with mental concentration, I press
on toward the prize of my heavenly calling, where I shall
hear the voice of praise and I shall see Thy delight, which
neither comes nor passes away.

Now, indeed, "my years [are spent] in sighs," and Thou
my Consolation, O Lord, Thou art my Eternal Father. But
I have disintegrated into periods of time, of whose order I
am ignorant, and my thoughts, which are the innermost vital
parts of my soul, are rent asunder by tumultuous diversities
—until such time as I shall flow together into Thee, purged
and melted into clear liquid form, by the fire of Thy love.

And I shall become firm and solidify in Thee, in the
40. form made for me in Thy Truth; nor shall I suffer the
questions of men who, as a result of their penal sick-

ness, are thirsty for more than they can take in. They say: "What did God do before He made heaven and earth?" or "How did the thought occur to Him to make something, when He never made anything before?"

Grant to them, O Lord, the ability to think well on what they say and to discover that one should not say "never" in reference to a situation where time does not exist. Thus, when a man says that one "never" made anything, what else is said but that one made it at no time? May they see, then, that time cannot be at all without creation, and may they stop talking this foolishness. May they be inclined forward also to those things which are before, and understand that Thou art before all periods of time, the Eternal Creator of all times, and that no periods of time and no creature, even one which may be above time, are coeternal with Thee.

CRITIQUE OF CYCLICISM*

13. This controversy some philosophers have seen no other approved means of solving than by introducing cycles of time, in which there should be a constant renewal and repetition of the order of nature; and they have therefore asserted that these cycles will ceaselessly recur, one passing away and another coming, though they are not agreed as to whether one permanent world shall pass through all these cycles, or whether the world shall at fixed intervals die out, and be renewed so as to exhibit a recurrence of the same phenomena—the things which have been, and those which are to be, coinciding. And from this fantastic vicissitude they exempt not even the immortal soul that has attained wisdom, consigning it to a ceaseless transmigration between delusive blessedness and real misery. For how can that be truly called blessed which has no assurance of being so eternally, and is either in ignorance of the truth and blind to the misery that is approaching, or, knowing it, is in misery and fear? Or if it passes to bliss and leaves miseries forever, then there happens in time a new thing which time shall not end. Why not then the world also? Why may not man too be a similar thing? So that, by following the straight path of sound doctrine, we escape I know not what circuitous paths, discovered by deceiving and deceived sages.

* *City of God*, XII, 13-15; trans. Dods.

Some, too, in advocating these recurring cycles that restore all things to their original cite in favor of their supposition what Solomon says in the book of Ecclesiastes: "What is that which hath been? It is that which shall be. And what is that which is done? It is that which shall be done; and there is no new thing under the sun. Who can speak and say, See, this is new? It hath been already of old time, which was before us." [Eccles. 1:9-10] This he said either of those things of which he had just been speaking—the succession of generations, the orbit of the sun, the course of rivers—or else of all kinds of creatures that are born and die. For men were before us, are with us, and shall be after us, and so all living things and all plants. Even monstrous and irregular productions, though differing from one another and though some are reported as solitary instances, yet resemble one another generally in so far as they are miraculous and monstrous and, in this sense, have been, and shall be, and are, no new and recent things under the sun. However, some would understand these words as meaning that in the predestination of God all things have already existed, and that thus there is no new thing under the sun. At all events, far be it from any true believer to suppose that by these words of Solomon those cycles are meant in which, according to those philosophers, the same periods and events of time are repeated; as if, for example, the philosopher Plato having taught in the school at Athens which is called the Academy, so, numberless ages before, at long but certain intervals, this same Plato and the same school and the same disciples existed, and so also are to be repeated during the countless cycles that are yet to be—far be it, I say, from us to believe this. For once Christ died for our sins and, rising from the dead, He dieth no more. "Death hath no more dominion over Him"; [Rom. 6:9] and we ourselves after the resurrection shall be "ever with the Lord," [I Thess. 4:16] to whom we now say, as the sacred Psalmist dictates, "Thou shalt keep us, O Lord, Thou shalt preserve us from this generation." [Ps. 11:8] And that too which follows, is, I think, appropriate enough: "The wicked walk *in a circle";* not because their life is to recur by means of these circles, which these philosophers imagine, but because the path in which their false doctrine now runs is circuitous.

14. What wonder is it if, entangled in these circles, they find neither entrance nor egress? For they know not how the human race and this mortal condition of

ours took its origin, nor how it will be brought to an end, since they cannot penetrate the inscrutable wisdom of God. For, though Himself eternal and without beginning, yet He caused time to have a beginning; and man whom He had not previously made He made in time, not from a new and sudden resolution but by His unchangeable and eternal design. Who can search out the unsearchable depth of this purpose, who can scrutinize the inscrutable wisdom wherewith God, without change of will, created man who had never before been, and gave him an existence in time, and increased the human race from one individual? For the Psalmist himself, when he had first said, "Thou shalt keep us, O Lord, Thou shalt preserve us from this generation forever," and had then rebuked those whose foolish and impious doctrine preserves for the soul no eternal deliverance and blessedness, adds immediately, "The wicked walk in a circle." Then, as if it were said to him, "What then do you believe, feel, know? Are we to believe that it suddenly occurred to God to create man, whom He had never before made in a past eternity— God, to whom nothing new can occur and in whom is no changeableness?" The Psalmist goes on to reply, as if addressing God Himself, "According to the depth of Thy wisdom Thou hast multiplied the children of men." Let men, he seems to say, fancy what they please, let them conjecture and dispute as seems good to them, but Thou hast multiplied the children of men according to the depth of thy wisdom, which no man can comprehend. For this is a depth, indeed, that God always has been, and that man, whom He had never made before He willed to make in time, and this without changing His design and will.

15. For my own part, indeed, as I dare not say that there ever was a time when the Lord God was not Lord, so I ought not to doubt that man had no existence before time, and was first created in time. But when I consider what God could be the Lord of, if there was not always some creature, I shrink from making any assertion, remembering my own insignificance, and that it is written, "What man is he that can know the counsel of God? or who can think what the will of the Lord is? For the thoughts of mortal men are timid, and our devices are but uncertain. For the corruptible body presseth down the soul, and the earthly tabernacle weigheth down the mind that museth upon many things." [Wisd. 9:13-15] Many things certainly do I muse upon in this earthly tabernacle, because the one thing which is true among the many, or beyond the many, I cannot find. If then among these many thoughts I say that there have always been creatures for Him to be Lord of, who is always and ever has been Lord, but that these creatures have not always been the same but succeeded one another (for we would not seem to say that any is coeternal with the Creator, an assertion condemned equally by faith and sound reason), I must take care lest I fall into the absurd and ignorant error of maintaining that by these successions and changes mortal creatures have always existed, whereas the immortal creatures had not begun to exist until the date of our own world, when the angels were created; if at least the angels are intended by that light which was first made, or rather by that heaven of which it is said, "In the beginning God created the heavens and the earth." [Gen. 1:1] The angels at least did not exist before they were created; for if we say that they have always existed, we shall seem to make them coeternal with the Creator. Again, if I say that the angels were not created in time but existed before all times, as those over whom God, who has ever been Sovereign, exercised His sovereignty, then I shall be asked whether, if they were created before all time, they, being creatures, could possibly always exist. It may perhaps be replied, Why not *always,* since that which is in all time may very properly be said to be "always"? Now so true is it that these angels have existed in all time that, even before time was, they were created; if, at least, time began with the heavens, and the angels existed before the heavens. And if time was even before the heavenly bodies, not indeed marked by hours, days, months, and years—for these measures of time's periods which are commonly and properly called times, did manifestly begin with the motion of the heavenly bodies, and so God said, when He appointed them, "Let them be for signs, and for seasons, and for days, and for years" [Gen. 1:14] —if, I say, time was before these heavenly bodies by some changing movement, whose parts succeeded one another and could not exist simultaneously, and if there was some such movement among the angels which necessitated the existence of time, and that they from their very creation should be subject to those temporal changes, then they have existed in all time, for time came into being along with them.

APPENDIX I

SELECTED ANNOTATED BIBLIOGRAPHY

Battenhouse, R. (ed.), *Companion to the Study of St. Augustine.* New York: Oxford University Press, 1955.
  A collection of studies illustrating the importance of Augustine in contemporary Protestant scholarship.

Bavel, T. van, *Répertoire Bibliographique de saint Augustin, 1950-1960.* The Hague: Nijhoff, 1963.
  The best bibliography; evaluates thousands of works in all languages.

Berliner, R., *Augustins dialogische Metaphysik.* Frankfurt am Main: Klostermann, 1962.
  Suggestive comparison of Augustine's thought with contemporary German phenomenology, especially that of Heidegger.

Bourke, V. J., *Augustine's Quest of Wisdom.* Milwaukee: Bruce Publishing Company, 1945.
  A standard introduction to the reading of St. Augustine.

————, *Augustine's View of Reality.* Villanova, Pa.: Villanova University Press, 1964.
  Brief study of the general metaphysics of Augustine.

Capanaga, V., *La teologia agustiniana de la gracia.* Madrid: Difusora de Libro, 1933.
  A thorough survey of Augustine's theology of grace.

Cayré, F., *La contemplation Augustinienne.* Paris: Blot, 1927.
  A key exposition of the religious views of Augustine.

Clark, Mary T., *Augustine: Philosopher of Freedom.* New York: Desclée Co., Inc., 1959.
  Studies the notion of free choice and its applications in the historical, social, and cultural spheres.

D'Arcy, M., *et al., A Monument to St. Augustine.* New York: Sheed & Ward, 1930; reprinted as *St. Augustine,* New York: Meridian Books, 1957.
  A collection of essays by outstanding Catholic scholars: Gilson, Dawson, Roland-Gosselin, Watkin, and others.

Gilson, E., *The Christian Philosophy of St. Augustine,* trans. by L. Lynch. New York: Random House, Inc., 1960.
  Generally regarded as the best exposition of Augustine's philosophy.

Grabowski, S. J., *The All-Present God.* St. Louis: B. Herder Book Company, 1954.
  God's presence throughout creation is studied as the central theme of Augustinianism; annotations cite extensive literature on the subject.

Green, W. M., *Augustine on the Teaching of History.* Berkeley-Los Angeles: University of California Press, 1944.
  Useful introduction to Augustine's philosophy of history.

Marrou, H. I., *St. Augustine and His Influence Through the Ages.* New York: Harper & Brothers, 1957.
  Standard interpretation of the educational, cultural, and historical aspects of Augustinianism.

Mausbach, J., *Die Ethik des hl. Augustinus.* Freiburg i. B.: Herder, 1909; reprinted 1929.
  The outstanding account of Augustine's moral views.

Meer, F. G. L. van der, *Augustine the Bishop.* London–New York: Sheed & Ward, 1960.
  Remarkable among recent biographies for its wealth of information on Augustine's later life and on the archaeological remains in North Africa.

O'Meara, J. J., *The Young Augustine.* Paris: Etudes Augustiniennes, 1954.
  A good study of the conversion and early philosophical interests of St. Augustine.

O'Toole, C. J., *The Philosophy of Creation in the Writings of St. Augustine.* Washington: Catholic University Press, 1944.
  Treats the "seminal reasons" and the problem of evolution.

Pope, H., *The Teaching of St. Augustine on Prayer and the Contemplative Life.* London: Burns, Oates & Washbourne, 1935.
  Basic for Augustine's spiritual views.

Portalié, E., *A Guide to the Thought of St. Augustine,* trans. by R. J. Bastian. Chicago: Henry Regnery Company, 1960.
  An excellent general introduction to St. Augustine.

Schmaus, M., *Die psychologische Trinitätslehre de hl. Augustinus.* Münster: Aschendorff, 1927.
  The best account of Augustine's trinitarian psychology.

APPENDIX II

1. Academics, Against the, III (*Contra Academicos*) A.D. 386; PL 32, 905-958; CSEL 63, 3-81; trans. FOC 1 (1948); ACW 12 (1950); Sr. M. Patricia Garvey, Milwaukee: Marquette U. Press, 1948.

2. Adimantus the Disciple of Mani, Against (*Contra Adimantum Manichaei Discipulum*) A.D. 393–396; PL 42, 129-172; CSEL 25, 115-190.

3. Admonition and Grace (*De correptione et gratia*) A.D. 426–427; PL 44, 915-946; trans. FOC 4 (1947).

4. Adversary of the Law and the Prophets, Against the, II (*Contra adversarium Legis et Prophetarum*) A.D. 420; PL 42, 603-666.

5. Arians, Against a Sermon of the (*Contra sermonem quemdam Arianorum*) A.D. 419; PL 42, 683-708.

6. Baptism, Against the Donatists on (*De baptismo contra Donatistas*) A.D. 400; PL 43, 107-244; CSEL 51, 145-375.

7. Baptism Against Petilian, On One (*De unico baptismo contra Petilianum*) A.D. 410; PL 43, 595-614; CSEL 53, 3-34; trans. W. Bright, *Select Anti-Pelagian Treatises*, Edinburgh, 1880.

8. Believing, On the Value of (*De utilitate credendi*) A.D. 391–392; PL 42, 63-92; CSEL 25, 3-48; trans. Nicene, reprinted in Oates, I, 399-427; FOC 2 (1947); LCC 6 (1953).

9. Catechizing the Uninstructed, On (*De catechizandis rudibus*) A.D. 400; PL 40, 309-348; trans. J. P. Christopher, Washington: Catholic U. Press, 1926; reprinted in ACW 2 (1946).

10. Choice, On Free, III (*De libero arbitrio*) A.D. 388–395; PL 32, 1221-1310; CSEL 74, 1-164; trans. R. McKeon, *Selections from Medieval Philosophers*, N.Y.: Scribner's, 1929 (Book II only); F. E. Tourscher, Philadelphia: P. Reilly Co., 1937; LCC 6 (1953); C. M. Sparrow, Charlottesville: U. of Virginia Press, 1947.

11. Christian Combat (*De agone Christiano*) A.D. 397; PL 40, 289-310; CSEL 41, 101-138; trans. FOC 4 (1947).

12. Christian Doctrine, IV (*De doctrina Christiana*) A.D. 397 and (Bk. IV) 426; PL 34, 15-122; CC 32 (1962); trans. Dods; FOC 4 (1947).

13. Church, Letter to Catholics on the Unity of the (*Ad Catholicos epistola de unitate ecclesiae*) A.D. 402; PL 43, 391-446; CSEL 52, 231-322.

14. City of God, XXII (*De civitate Dei*) A.D. 413–426; PL 41, 13-804; CSEL 40, I, 3-660, II, 1-670; crit. ed. B. Dombart & A. Kalb, Leipzig: Teubner, 1928-1929; ed. revised in CC 47-48 (1955); trans. Dods; J. Healey (1610); FOC 6, 7, 8 (1950, 1952, 1954), reprinted partially N. Y.: Doubleday Image Books, 1958.

15. Confessions, XIII (*Confessiones*) A.D. 397–401; PL 32, 659-868; CSEL 33, 1-388; crit. ed. M. Skutella, Leipzig: Teubner, 1934; trans. Sir Tobie Matthew, London 1620; W. Watts, London 1631; E. B. Pusey, London 1838; J. G. Pilkington, London 1876; F. J. Sheed, N. Y.: Sheed and Ward, 1943; FOC 5 (1953).

16. Continence, On (*De continentia*) A.D. 394–395; PL 40, 348-372; CSEL 41, 141-183; trans. FOC 14 (1952).

17. Cresconius the Donatist, Against, IV (*Contra Cresconium grammaticum partis Donati*) A.D. 406; PL 45, 445-594; CSEL 52, 325-582.

18. Dead, Care for the (*De cura pro mortuis gerenda*) A.D. 421; PL 40, 591-610; CSEL 41, 621-660; trans. FOC 15 (1955).

19. Divination of Demons, The (*De divinatione daemonum*) A.D. 406–411; PL 40, 581-592; CSEL 41, 597-618; trans. FOC 15 (1955).

20. Donatists after the Conference, Against the (*Liber contra Donatistas post Collationem*) A.D. 412; PL 43, 651-690; CSEL 53, 97-162.

21. Donatists, Psalm against the (*Psalmus contra partem Donati*) A.D. 393–396; PL 43, 23-32; CSEL 51, 3-15.

22. Donatists, Summary of the Conference with the (*Breviculus Collationis cum Donatistis*) A.D. 411; PL 43, 613-650; CSEL 53, 39-92.

23. Dulcitius, Eight Questions of (*De octo Dulcitii quaestionibus*) A.D. 423; PL 40, 147-170; CC 33 (1958); trans. FOC 14 (1952).

24. Emeritus, Proceedings with (*De gestis cum Emerito Donatistarum episcopo Caesareae*) A.D. 418; PL 43, 697-706; CSEL 53, 181-196.

25. Enchiridion on Faith, Hope and Charity (*Enchiridion ad Laurentium de fide, spe, caritate*) A.D. 421; PL 40, 231-290; trans. Dods, reprinted in Oates I, 658-730; FOC 4 (1947); ACW 3 (1947); LCC 8 (1955).

26. Epistle of John to the Parthians (*In Epistolam Joannis ad Parthos*) A.D. 416; PL 35, 1977-2062.

27. Epistle to the Galatians, Exposition of the (*Expositio Epistolae ad Galatas*) A.D. 394; PL 35, 2105-2148.

28. Epistle to the Romans, Exposition of Certain Propositions from the (*Expositio quarumdam propositionum ex Epistola ad Romanos*) A.D. 393–396; PL 35, 2063-2088; trans. Dods, vol. VIII.

29. Epistle to the Romans, Unfinished Exposition (*Epistolae ad Romanos inchoata expositio*) A.D. 394; PL 35, 2087-2106.

30. Faith and the Creed, On (*De fide et symbolo*) A.D. 393; PL 40, 181-196; CSEL 41, 3-32; trans. FOC 15 (1955); LCC 5 (1953).

31. Faith and Works (*De fide et operibus*) A.D. 413; PL 40, 197-230; CSEL 41, 35-97.

32. Faith in Things Unseen (*De fide rerum quae non videntur*) A.D. 400; PL 40, 171-180; trans. FOC 2 (1947).

33. Fasting, on the Value of (*De utilitate jejunii*) *ca*. A.D. 418; PL 40, 707-716 (incorrect text); crit. ed. D. de Bruyne, in *Miscellanea Agostiniana* (Roma 1931) II, 321-340.

34. Faustus the Manichee, Against, XXII (*Contra Faustum Manichaeum*) A.D. 400; PL 42, 207-518; CSEL 25, 251-797.

35. Felix the Manichee, Proceedings with, II (*De actis cum Felice Manichaeo*) A.D. 404; PL 42, 519-552; CSEL 25, 801-852.

36. Fortunatus, Disputation Against (*Disputatio contra Fortunatum*) A.D. 392; PL 42, 111-130; CSEL 25, 83-112.

37. Gaudentius the Donatist, Against (*Contra Gaudentium Thamugadensem episcopum Donatistarum*) A.D. 420; PL 43, 707-752; CSEL 53, 201-274.

38. Genesis against the Manichees, On, II (*De Genesi contra Manichaeos*) A.D. 388–390; PL 34, 173-220.

39. Genesis, Literal Commentary on, XII (*De Genesi ad litteram*) A.D. 401–415; PL 34, 245-486; CSEL 28, I, 3-435; trans. (Bk. XII only) J. H. Taylor, S. J., St. Louis U. Dissert., 1948.

40. Genesis, Incomplete Literal Commentary on (*De Genesi ad litteram, liber imperfectus*) A.D. 393–394; PL 35, 219-246; CSEL 28, I, 459-503.

41. Gospel of John, On the (*In Joannis Evangelium*) A.D. 416–417; PL 35, 1379-1976; CC 36 (1954); trans. *Homilies on St. John,* Oxford, 1878.

42. Gospels of Matthew and Luke, Questions on the, II (*Quaestiones Evangeliorum ex Mathaeo et Luca*) A.D. 397–400; PL 35, 1321-1364.

43. Gospels, On the Harmony of the (*De consensu Evangelistarum*) A.D. 400; PL 34, 1041-1230; CSEL 43, 1-418; trans. Dods, vol. VIII.

44. Grace and Free Choice to Valentine (*De gratia et libero arbitrio ad Valentinum*) A.D. 426–427; PL 44, 881-912; trans. Dods, reprinted in Oates, I, 733-774.

45. Grace of Christ and Original Sin, II (*De gratia Christi et peccato originali*) A.D. 418; PL 44, 359-410; CSEL 42, 125-206; trans. Dods, reprinted in Oates, I, 583-654.

46. Happy Life, The (*De beata vita*) A.D. 386; PL 32, 959-976; CSEL 63, 89-116; crit. ed. M. Schmaus, Bonn: Florilegium Patristicum, 37; trans. F. E. Tourscher, Philadelphia: P. Reilly, 1933; L. Schopp, St. Louis: Herder, 1939; Ruth Brown, Washington: Catholic U. Press, 1944; FOC 1 (1948).

47. Heptateuch, Explanations of the, VII (*Locutiones in Heptateuchum*) A.D. 419; PL 34, 485-546; CSEL 28, 507-629; CC 33 (1958).

48. Heptateuch, Questions on the, VII (*Quaestiones in Heptateuchum*) A.D. 419; PL 34, 547-824; CSEL 28, 3-506; CC 33 (1958).

49. Heresies for Quodvultdeus, On (*De haeresibus ad Quodvultdeum*) A.D. 428; PL 42, 21-50.

50. Jews, Treatise in Answer to the (*Tractatus contra Judaeos*) A.D. 428; PL 42, 51-64; trans. FOC 15 (1955).

51. Job, Notes on (*Annotationes in Job*) A.D. 397–400; PL 34, 825-886; CSEL 28, II, 509-628.

52. Julian the Heretic, Against, VI (*Contra Julianum haeresis Pelagianae defensorem*) A.D. 421; PL 44, 641-874.

53. Julian, Incomplete Work against, VI (*Opus imperfectum contra Julianum*) A.D. 429-430; PL 45, 1049-1608.

54. Justice, The Perfection of (*De perfectione Justitiae*) A.D. 415; PL 44, 291-318; CSEL 42, 3-48.

55. Letters, about 270 (*Epistolae*) A.D. 386–430 (for detailed chronology see: PL 33, 13-48; Goldbacher in CSEL 58; and

D. de Bruyne, *Revue Bénédictine,* 1931, 284-295); PL 33, 61-1162; CSEL 34, 44, 57 and 58; trans. Nicene, vol. I; Dods, vols. VI and XIII; FOC 9 (1951), 10 (1953), 11 (1953), 12 (1955), 13 (1956); J. H. Baxter, *Select Letters,* (Loeb Series) London: Heinemann, 1930.

56. Lying, On (*De mendacio*) A.D. 394–395; PL 40, 487-518; CSEL 41, 413-466; trans. FOC 14 (1952).

57. Lying, for Consentius, Against (*Contra mendacium ad Consentium*) A.D. 420; PL 40, 517-548; CSEL 41, 469-528; trans. FOC 14 (1952).

58. Mani, Against the so-called Fundamental Letter of (*Contra Epistolam quam vocant fundamenti*) A.D. 397; PL 42, 173-206; CSEL 25, 193-248.

59. Marriage and Concupiscence, II (*De nuptiis et concupiscentia*) A.D. 419–420; PL 44, 413-474; CSEL 42, 209-319.

60. Marriage, The Good of (*De bono conjugali*) A.D. 400–401; PL 40, 373-396; CSEL 41, 187-231; trans. FOC 15 (1955).

61. Marriages, Adulterous, II (*De conjugiis adulterinis*) A.D. 419; PL 40, 451-486; CSEL 41, 347-410; trans. FOC 15 (1955).

62. Maximinus the Arian, Conference with (*Collatio cum Maximino Arianorum episcopo*) A.D. 427–428; PL 42, 709-742.

63. Maximinus the Arian, Against (*Contra Maximinum Arianorum episcopum*) A.D. 428; PL 42, 743-814.

64. Merits and Remission of Sins and Infant Baptism, On the, III (*De peccatorum meritis et remissione et de baptismo parvulorum*) A.D. 412; PL 44, 109-200; CSEL 60, 3-151.

65. Monks, The Work of (*De opere monachorum*) A.D. 400; PL 40, 547-582; CSEL 41, 531-596; trans. FOC 14 (1952).

66. Moral Behavior of the Catholic Church and of the Manichees, II (*De moribus Ecclesiae Catholicae et de moribus Manichaeorum*) A.D. 388; PL 32, 1309-1378; trans. Dods; reprinted in Oates, I, 319-357.

67. Music, On, VI (*De musica*) A.D. 387–391; PL 32, 1081-1194; trans. FOC 2 (1947); Bk. VI only, T. P. Maher, S. J., St. Louis U. Thesis, 1939.

68. Nature and Grace against Pelagius (*De natura et gratia contra Pelagium*) A.D. 415; PL 44, 247-290; CSEL 60, 233-299; trans. Dods; reprinted in Oates, I, 521-579.

69. Nature of the Good against the Manichees (*De natura boni contra Manichaeos*) A.D. 405; PL 42, 551-572; CSEL 25, 855-889; trans. Dods; reprinted in Oates, I, 431-457; LCC 6 (1953).

70. Order, On, II (*De ordine*) A.D. 386; PL 32, 977-1020; CSEL 63, 121-185; trans. FOC 1 (1948).

71. Parmenianus, Against the Letter of, III (*Contra epistolam Parmeniani*) A.D. 400; PL 43, 33-108; CSEL 51, 19-141.

72. Patience, On (*De patientia*) A.D. 418; PL 40, 611-626; CSEL 41, 663-691; trans. FOC 14 (1952).

73. Pelagians to Pope Boniface, Against Two Letters of the, IV (*Contra duas epistolas Pelagianorum ad Bonifacium Papam*) A.D. 420; PL 44, 549-638; CSEL 60, 423-570.

74. Pelagius, The Activities of (*De gestis Pelagii*) A.D. 417; PL 44, 319-360; CSEL 42, 51-122.

75. Perseverance, The Gift of (*De dono perseveratiae*) A.D. 428–429; PL 45, 993-1034; trans. Mary A. Lesousky, Washington: Catholic U. Press, 1956.

76. Petilian the Donatist, Against the Writings of, III (*Contra litteras Petiliani Donatistae*) A.D. 400–402; PL 43, 245-388; CSEL 52, 3-227; trans. Dods., vol. III.

77. Predestination of the Saints (*De praedestinatione Sanctorum*) A.D. 428–429; PL 44, 959-992; trans. Dods; reprinted in Oates, I, 777-817.

78. Priscillianists and Origenists for Orosius, Against the (*Contra Priscillianistas et Origenistas ad Orosium*) A.D. 415; PL 42, 669-678.

79. Psalms, Expositions of the (*Enarrationes in Psalmos*) A.D. 391–430; PL 36, 67-1028, 37, 1033-1968; CC 38-40 (1956); trans. *Library of the Fathers,* Oxford, 1847; partial reprint, Nicene, vol. VIII; On Ps. 1-37, in ACW 29-30 (1960–1961).

80. *Questions,* Answers to Eighty-three Different (*De diversis Quaestionibus LXXXIII*) A.D. 389–396; PL 40, 11-100.

81. Questions for Simplicianus, Answers to Seven (*De diversis quaestionibus VII ad Simplicianum*) A.D. 396–397; PL 40, 101-148.

82. Religion, On the True (*De vera religione*) A.D. 389–391; PL 34, 121-172; CC 32 (1962); trans. LCC 6 (1953); J. H. S. Burleigh, Chicago: Regnery, 1959.

83. Retractations, II (*Retractationes*) A.D. 426–427; PL 32, 583-656; CSEL 36, 7-205.

84. Scripture, Mirror of (*Speculum de Scriptura Sacra*) A.D. 427; PL 34, 887-1040; CSEL 12, 3-285.

85. Secundinus the Manichee, Against (*Contra Secundinum Manichaeum*) A.D. 405–406; PL 42, 577-602; CSEL 25, 905-947.

86. Sermon on the Mount, The Lord's, II (*De Sermone Domini in monte*) A.D. 393–396; PL 34, 1229-1308; trans. ACW 5 (1948); FOC 3 (1951).

87. Sermons (*Sermones*) A.D. 393–430; PL 38, 23-1484, 39, 1493-1736, 46, 817-1004, 47, 1189-1248 (cf. A. Kunzelmann, "Die Chronologie der Sermones des hl. Augustinus," *Miscellanea Agostiniana*, Roma 1931, II, 417-520, for details of authenticity and dates); *Sermones post Maurinos Reperti*, ed. G. Morin, O.S.B., in *Miscellanea Agostiniana*, Roma 1930, vol. I, *in toto; Sermones Selecti Duodeviginti*, ed. D. C. Lambot, O.S.B., Utrecht-Brussels: Spectrum, 1950; *Sermones de vetere testamento*, in CC, 41 (1961); trans. E. B. Pusey, *Sermons on Selected Lessons from the N. T.*, 2 vols., Oxford 1854; *Selected Sermons* in FOC 3 (1951); *Sermons for Christmas and the Epiphany* in ACW (1952).

88. Soliloquies, II (*Soliloquia*) A.D. 387; PL 32, 869-904; trans. Nicene, vol. VII (1888); Dods, reprinted in Oates, I, 259-297; FOC 1 (1948); LCC 6 (1953).

89. Soul and Its Origin, IV (*De anima et ejus origine*) A.D. 419–420; PL 44, 475-548; CSEL 60, 303-419.

90. Soul, Immortality of the (*De immortalitate animae*) A.D. 387; PL 32, 1021-1034; trans. G. C. Leckie, N.Y.: Appleton-Century, 1938; reprinted in Oates, I, 301-316; FOC 2 (1947).

91. Soul, Magnitude of the (*De quantitate animae*) A.D. 387–388; PL 32, 1035-1080; trans. FOC 2 (1947); ACW 9 (1950).

92. Souls against the Manichees, On Two (*De duabus animabus contra Manichaeos*) A.D. 391–392; PL 42, 93-112; CSEL 25, 51-80.

93. Spirit and the Letter, On the (*De spiritu et littera*) A.D. 412; PL 44, 201-246; CSEL 60, 155-229; trans. Dods, reprinted in Oates, I, 461-518; W. J. S. Simpson, London, 1925.

94. Teacher, The (*De Magistro*) A.D. 389; PL 32, 1193-1220; trans. G. C. Leckie (as above in no. 90), reprinted in Oates, I, 361-395; ACW 9 (1950); LCC 6 (1953).

95. Trinity, The, XV (*De Trinitate*) A.D. 400–416; PL 42, 819-1098; trans. Dods, vol. VII, partial reprint in Oates, II, 667-878; Bks. VIII-XV by J. Burnaby in LCC 8 (1955); FOC 45 (1963).

96. Virginity, On Holy (*De sancta virginitate*) A.D. 400–401; PL 40, 397-428; CSEL 41, 235-302; trans. FOC 15 (1955).

97. Widowhood for Juliana, The Good of (*De bono viduitatis ad Julianam*) A.D. 414; PL 40, 429–450; CSEL 41, 303–343; trans. FOC 14 (1952).

SYMBOLS USED IN LIST OF WRITINGS

PL: *Patrologia Latina,* Paris: J. P. Migne, 1844–1864. (Works of St. Augustine reprinted from the seventeenth-century Maurist edition, in PL volumes 32–47.)

CSEL: *Corpus Scriptorum Ecclesiasticorum,* Vienna: Tempsky, 1866–. (Works of St. Augustine are scattered in random numbered volumes.)

CC: *Corpus Christianorum,* Series Latina, under direction of the Monks of the Abbey of St. Pierre de Steenbrugge, Turnholti: Brepols; The Hague: Nijhoff, 1853–. Augustine volumes are: 32, 1962; 33, 1958; 36 (1954); 41, 1961; 38-40 (1956); 47-48 (1955).

ACW: *Ancient Christian Writers,* a series of English translations ed. by J. Quasten et al., Westminster, Md.: Newman Press, 1946–. (Augustine volumes are: 2, 3, 5, 9, 12, 13, 29, 30.)

FOC: *Fathers of the Church,* a series of English translations ed. by R. Deferrari et al., New York: Fathers of the Church, Inc., 1948ff.; since 1960, Washington: Catholic U. Press. (Sixteen volumes of St. Augustine's writings are separately numbered, 1-16.)

Dods: *The Works of Aurelius Augustinus,* ed. by Marcus Dods, 15 vols., Edinburgh: T. & T. Clark Co., 1871–1876.

Nicene: *A Select Library of the Nicene and Post-Nicene Fathers,* ed. by Philip Schaff, New York: The Christian Literature Co. and Scribner's Sons, 1892. (Eight volumes devoted to Augustine.)

Oates: *Basic Writings of St. Augustine,* 2 vols., New York: Random House, 1948. (Reprints portions of Dods, except for two translations by G. C. Leckie.)

LCC: *Library of Christian Classics,* Philadelphia: Westminster Press; vol. 6: Augustine, *Earlier Writings,* ed. J. H. S. Burleigh, 1953; vol. 7: Augustine, *Confessions and Enchiridion,* ed. A. C. Outler, 1955; vol. 8: Augustine, *Later Works,* ed. J. Burnaby, 1955.

APPENDIX III

GLOSSARY OF TERMS

The language of St. Augustine is the resultant of his training in Latin rhetoric (Virgil and Cicero are great influences here), his reading of Neoplatonic treatises in philosophy (parts of Plotinus' *Enneads* and Porphyry's short works), and above all his long study of the Latin Bible. Augustinian terminology is relatively simple and, indeed, familiar to those who have some acquaintance with biblical language. It is possible to read Augustine with understanding and enjoyment even though one does not have technical training in Patristic Latin. What some readers must avoid is attributing the complications of later theology or philosophy to the pioneer simplicity of Augustine's works. The following are key terms that have distinctive meanings. Abundant references to these terms in context will be found in the Index.

Reason: This constantly recurring term (*ratio*) has two basic meanings. Psychologically, reason is the "gaze of the mind" (*aspectus mentis*), which may be turned toward various objects by willing. When reason *sees* such an object, the result is vision (*visio*). Directed upward to God and eternal truths, this gaze is called superior reason (*ratio superior*); turned downward to creatures and temporal activities, it is called inferior reason (*ratio inferior*). Secondly, reason designates an ontological principle or cause of being and action. Thus, eternal reasons (*rationes aeternae*) are the divine archetypes or patterns of all created species and individuals: they are much like Plato's Ideal Forms, placed in the Mind of God. Seminal reasons (*rationes seminales*) are principles of living growth, reproduction, and activity, created by God in the very texture of the material elements. They are the invisible seeds from which all creatures grow during the course of time.

Soul: Each man is a soul using a body (*anima utens corpore*); the human soul is an incorporeal creature that is the immediate

257

source of all man's activities and distinguishing features. Souls are incorruptible. Bodies are not the efficient causes of any actions: souls are. As conscious soul (*animus, mens*), the term is usually limited to men; *anima* is extended to include the life principles of other living beings.

Mind: The human soul as cognitive and feeling is called mind (*mens*); mind is the whole soul as the seat of awareness; it is not an accident, or distinct faculty, of the soul.

Memory: The human soul as container of many thoughts and things is memory (*memoria*). Augustinian memory is not restricted to recall of the past; it applies to consciousness of past, present, and future items. Memory is the whole soul, not a mere faculty or function.

Will: This term completes the psychological trinity (*mens, memoria, voluntas*). Viewed as initiating and causing any and all of man's actions, whether incorporeal or corporeal, the whole soul is called will. Basically, mind, memory, and will are one substance.

Sensation: An active function of the soul, sensation (*sensus*) occurs when some physical change in one's body does not escape the attention of one's soul. The soul is not moved, or impressed, by bodily events. When I cut my finger, my soul "notices" this bodily change: the psychic action of noting the change is the sensation.

Knowledge: In the very general sense of any cognitive activity, knowledge is called *notitia*. More precisely, knowledge (*scientia*) designates that particular type of cognition which is associated with the *inferior reason:* its objects are mutable things and activities.

Wisdom: The use, or habitual condition (*affectio*), of the *superior reason* is called wisdom (*sapientia*). The direct objects of wise contemplation are God and eternal truths: the laws of numbering and logical thinking, and the virtues as moral principles, are known through wisdom.

Belief: In some translations, *fides* is rendered as faith; it means the psychological act of assenting to that which is not seen (or directly understood by the believer). By natural faith Augustine believed that Patricius was his father; by religious faith he believed that there are three Persons in the divine Trinity. Belief rests on the testimony and authority of others.

Cogitation: Sometimes translated as conception, or thinking, *cogitatio* has a very special meaning. It is thinking by means of the collation of images of bodily things. There is, for Augustine, a higher kind of thinking: intuitive understanding (*intellectus*) is imageless thought.

Conversion: A voluntary turning (*versio*) of the soul's attention toward a selected object is the basic meaning of conversion. Religious conversion is the will turning to God. Man's will may turn away (*aversio*) from God and divine truths—this is a perversion, or misuse, (*perversio*) of his attention and is the essence of all sin.

Liberty or *freedom:* In the highest personal sense, eminent liberty (*libertas*) means that special freeing of the soul, under the influence of divine grace, in which condition the soul is able to choose only what is good and is unable to incline toward evil, to sin. A lower type of liberty is the natural endowment of each human soul in this life: this is freedom of choice (*liberum arbitrium*), the ability to choose good or evil. Some versions translate this latter as free will.

Immutability: God transcends temporal changes by virtue of His immutability. This unchangeability (*immutabilitas*) is, for Augustine, one of the greatest attributes of divinity. In contrast, every created thing is mutable; some (bodies) are mutable in both time and space; higher creatures (spirits) are changeable in time but not in space.

Eternity: The duration (*manentia*) proper to God is without beginning or termination; it is also changeless. Such duration is called eternity; it contrasts with temporal duration, or time (*tempus*). Time has a beginning, a terminus, and implies change.

Measure, number and weight: Wisdom 11:21 ("Thou hast ordered all things in measure, and number, and weight") is the source of a theory of the formal determinants of all creatures. Measure (*modus, mensura*) regulates mental functions and is the principle of specific limitations in creatures. Number (*numerus*) is the basis of formal differences and regulates many creaturely functions. Weight (*pondus*) is a principle of inclination, of willing, and of teleological ordering.

Evil: Since all natures have been created good, evil (*malum*) cannot be, for Augustine, a nature or a positive being. Rather, evil is an absence, or better, privation, of goodness in an existing nature, or of due order in an activity. This privation theory does not mean that evil is unreal or unimportant: evil is a wound in being.

People: This is the basic term in Augustine's discussion of human society. A *populus* is a group of rational beings bound together by a common agreement as to the objects of their loves. The will to unite and work together is what constitutes a people.

City: In the ancient classical and patristic sense, city (*civitas*) names the usual type of organized state. Thus, Rome is "The City" to Augustine. Rome means not only the municipality on the Tiber but also the whole empire or nation of the Romans. The *City of God* extends this usage to the point at which "city" designates any duly organized society.

APPENDIX IV

TABLE OF AUGUSTINE TEXTS

between and between the gift [illegible]
or just change but of change [illegible] here are no
future things, they are not [illegible] out the [illegible]
is not there, but are [illegible] that [illegible]
are [illegible] they are, [illegible] the present is [illegible]
them. Yet when the things are [illegible] brought the
through the [illegible] lies in the [illegible]

INDEX